Table of Contents

Dorsey

Essays and Stories
from Black Catholics of Baltimore

By Office of African American Ministries, Archdiocese of Baltimore

Cathedral Press • **Baltimore, Maryland**

Library of Congress Cataloging-in-Publication Data

Office of African American Ministries, Archdiocese of Baltimore
  What we have seen and heard: essays and stories from Black Catholics of Baltimore
          p.   cm.
    ISBN 1-885938-33-0 (pbk. :alk. paper)
      1. African American Catholics -- History. I. Catholic Church. Archdiocese of
    Baltimore (Md.). Office of African American Ministries. II. Title.
  BX1407N4W43 2005
  282'.275271'08996073--dc22   2004030405
                                                          CIP

Published in 2005 by

    Cathedral Press
    P.O. Box 777
    Baltimore, Maryland 21203

Publisher: Daniel L. Medinger
Project Manager: Patti Medinger
Book & Cover Design: Gabriella Ferraro
Printed by: Victor Graphics, Inc.

Dedication

To African American Catholics,

who throughout the centuries "kept the faith" and held on until that "change came";

who in this present age continue the march of faith, pressing forward to tell the story, speak the truth and give glory to God; and

to those who will come in the future so that they may see and hear this story of "what we have seen and heard." May they gain strength and inspiration to march into their future with faith.

Foreword

Peter and John said, "It is impossible for us not to speak about what we have seen and heard." (Acts of the Apostles 4:20)

Our world today is in need of the testimony of African American Catholics who walk by faith and not by sight. Their testimonies bring hope into our world. Their faith story, often rising out of struggle and oppression towards victory and liberation, testifies to the good news of the gospel and to the awesome love of Christ. With great self-determination, steadfast activism and daunting dedication, Black Catholics fashioned a place for themselves within the Catholic Church of Baltimore and throughout the United States. This story needs to be told, so that others may come to know Jesus for themselves through the Catholic Church.

In an archdiocese such as ours, where there is a plurality of cultures and sub-cultures, it is necessary that the message of evangelization be woven into the cultural environment of each people.

Pope Paul VI writes in his apostolic exhortation, "Evangelii Nuntiandi,"

> *"...the Kingdom which the Gospel proclaims is lived by men who are profoundly linked to a culture, and the building up of the Kingdom cannot avoid borrowing elements of human culture or cultures.* (EMW #20)

Evangelization loses much of its force and effectiveness if it does not take into consideration the actual people to whom it is addressed, if it does not use their language, their signs and symbols, if it does not answer the questions they ask and if it does not have an impact on their concrete life.(EMW, #63)

Within these pages, the message of evangelization of the African American Catholic is presented and celebrated in their cultural context. I am delighted to present such faith stirring messages from African American Catholics as they testify to "what they have seen and heard."

His Eminence William Cardinal Keeler
ARCHBISHOP OF BALTIMORE

Introduction

Within these pages are articles written by African American Catholics for "The Catholic Review," the Baltimore archdiocesan newspaper. This partnership with "The Catholic Review" was launched in September, 2000 – The Jubilee Year. The first article written is featured below and serves as the Introduction of this book.

The Journey

Sometimes in life you have to take a walk between the known and the unknown. Oftentimes in faith you have to take a walk where others have not walked before. This is the fact that underlines the nature of these writings entitled "What We Have Seen and Heard." Today, we are establishing a new walk. Today, a new talk is articulated, and it arises from what has been seen and heard in the African American Catholic Community.

Realizing the power of the printed word, Bishop John H. Ricard, S.S.J., along with a number of elders from the African American Catholic Community, approached The Catholic Review editor, Daniel Medinger, with the suggestion to expand its coverage to include issues, events and stories of interest to the African American Community. A committee was formed, and some steps taken. Bishop Gordon D. Bennett, S.J., also championed the cause by re-visiting the idea of establishing a regular column in The Catholic Review, authored by African American Catholics. Today, we are making history, a new journey begins, as this weekly book is launched. "What We Have Seen and Heard" promises to inform, inspire, challenge and, perhaps, help readers to "walk where they have not walked before."

Susan Taylor, editor in chief of Essence magazine, once wrote, "Thoughts have power; thoughts have energy." It is our hope that this weekly column will feature and explore thoughts and the "line of the mind" of African American Catholics so that the faith may be "energized, move and flourish."

These writings will follow a map of various topics and issues, directing its readership to take a "new walk, a new talk, a new attitude" along the journey. It will examine pastoral letters and provide history lessons. It will discuss issues and challenges that impede and enhance evangelization in the African American community. It will display successful models of catechesis, education and evangelization within the African American community. It will navigate through issues and concerns that impact Black Catholic life. It will explore and share the lives and hopes of a people, striving to "take a closer walk with Jesus." With inspired faith, we strive to share "who we are and whose we are" – made in "God's Black image and likeness" – with the mission to transform the world and to make it better than the way we found it. Because our eyes are wide open, what we have seen is without limit, and what we have heard has inspired each of us "to go tell it on the mountain."

Some may be asking the question, "Why is this particular forum needed?" Throughout the Catholic Church, there has been a developing consciousness of the cultural diversity that exists in the universal church as well as the impact that culture plays on proclaiming, teaching and sharing the faith. In this forum, we hope to provide a mini-African American cultural center to discuss theological, spiritual, catechetical, pastoral and evangelization insights and understandings. In "Pontificium Consilium De Cultura" (Catholic Cultural Centre, Vatican City, 1995) the Council writes, "wherever it has been possible to create them, Catholic Cultural centers are an enormous pastoral help ... They can tackle urgent and complex problems encountered in evangelizing culture and inculturating the faith." We see this particular forum as a "cultural center" to inform and to exchange ideas from an Africentric perspective. We see this particular forum as a needed and desired segment of The Catholic Review, as a marvelous contribution to the common good, and as the gift of Blackness we bring to the Body of Christ.

Founded in a belief that "what a people have passion for" provides a critical understanding of that people, we offer these writings. Founded in the belief that the relationship between history and present-day realities can provide direction for constructing and discovering future strategies "to build the Body of Christ", we offer these writings.

Bring your own eyes and ears and join us as African American Catholics reveal "What We Have Seen and Heard."

On Being Black & Catholic

Who do they say that I am?

The story of Black Catholics in the United States is a long and interesting one and it answers the question, "Who do they say I am?" It is punctuated with sacred moments of history, biographies of the faithful as well as a discussion on racism and appropriate actions while confronting the challenge and impact of racism. With a unique spirituality, pride, resiliency and self-determination, this record is set forth leading the way to an authentic experience of faith and freedom.

We are Black and Catholic, a powerful people with a devout respect for life and an affirmation that this Church is our Church. We tell these stories to remember and to teach others that "God's power is at work in and through us." Therefore, the first section of this book explores Black Catholic identity as it relates to history and culture. In doing so, a discussion on racism concludes this section.

Sacred Moments

H am, the second son of Noah, steps onto the biblical scene in
Genesis 5:32 when it is reported that Noah, his wife and their
three sons, Shem, Ham and Japheth (and their wives) went into the boat
to escape the 40 days and nights of rain.

The name "Ham" (Cham) means "hot," and by application, "black."
This is supported by the Hebrew and Arabic, in which the word
"chamam" means to be hot or black.

There is agreement among most scholars that Ham was the father of
indigenous African peoples. A historical, cultural and anthropological
review of the descendants of Ham reveals that they possess the kind
of evident degree of blackness that overshadows any evident black
ethnicity of Noah's other sons' descendants.

Ham was the only son of Noah after whom a nation was named. In
references in Psalms, Ham is synonymous with Egypt. (Psalm 78:51,
Psalm 105:23 and 27, and Psalm 106:21).

Chapter 10 of the book of Genesis is an African family tree. This
chapter, called the Table of Nations, provides basic information about
the origin and classification of peoples and nations in the ancient
world. In respect to Ham, Genesis 10 is an African family tree. The
descendants of Ham influenced the Hebrew-Israelite-Judahite people
more than any other nation in the Old Testament. These descendants
include the Egyptians, Canaanites, Babylonians and others. Their
impact on the covenant people of God was tremendous.

The sons of Ham were: 1. Cush or Ethiopia. 2. Mizraim or Egypt.
3. Put or Libya. 4. Canaan. The descendants of Cush were the people

of Seba, Havilah, Sabtah, Raamah and Sabteca (Gen. 10:7). The descendants of Eygpt were the people of Lydia, Anam, Lehab, Naphtuh, Patrus, Casluh and Crete from whom the Philistines are descended (Genesis 10:13). Canaan's sons, Sidon and Heth were the ancestors of the peoples who bear their names (Gen. 10:15).

The first half of the 19th century brought a popular belief that the descendants of Ham were cursed. (Gen. 20-29). In fact, the descendants of Ham were not cursed. Neither Noah nor God cursed the descendants of Ham to be servants to their brothers. Canaan, the son of Ham, was cursed. Since Ham received the curse, it was popularly applied to all of his descendants as well. This information was used to justify the enslavement of human beings. This is a gross and unfortunate misinterpretation of the passage.

Genesis 49:8-12 reveals to us that the Jewish Messiah was to come through the line of Judah. Judah married Canaanite wives Batshua (Gen. 38:6) and Tamar (1 Chron. 2:3,4). Tamar the Canaanite gave birth to Perez whose descendant of the ninth generation gave birth to King David.

The family tree of David back to Judah was affected by Tamar, who was unambiguously black. From this point on the lineage of David by way of Solomon can be traced through direct descendants (Mt. 1:6-11). Matthew 1:12-16 presents the lineage of David through Joseph, the husband of Mary, from the time of the Babylonian exile.

Zephaniah 1:1 reveals that Hezekiah was the great-great grandfather of the prophet Zephaniah. Hezekiah was the 14th king of the kingdom of Judah (through which the Messianic line continued). Zephaniah says that his father was Cushi. Thus, the Messianic line proceeding from Hezekiah was of Cushite ethnicity.

Joseph was the foster father of Jesus, yet it is important to note that Mary, the biological mother of Jesus was also of the lineage of David. This is referenced in Luke 1:27:cf and Luke 2:4. Mary's relationship to her forefather King David is related in Luke 1:32,69; Matthew 9:27; 15: 22;20:30,31; as well as Mark 10:47,48.

The genealogical line of Jesus was ethnologically Black. This is demonstrable implicitly as well as through specific Hamitic descendants who appear in the line of Judah. Tamar, Rahab and Bathsheba, each of Hamitic descent, are lineal ancestors of Jesus Christ. Ontologically and genealogically speaking Jesus the Christ is a prodigy of the lineage of Ham.

In Colonial America

The Ark and the Dove had 120 settlers aboard when they sailed up the Chesapeake Bay into the Potomac River.

Within the group were three indentured Blacks: Mathias deSousa and Francisco, identified as "mulatto," and John Price, a Negro. The settlers disembarked on St. Clement Island where Father Andrew White, a Jesuit, celebrated Mass on Annunciation Day in 1634. This was the first Roman Catholic Mass celebrated in English-speaking North America.

Soon after their arrival the Jesuits used a wigwam as a chapel in St. Mary's City. It was given to them by the Indians. Father White visited villagers and cleansed them in the sacred water of baptism.

In 1664 an Act was passed that stipulated that Negroes were made slaves forever, and those in the colony and those imported into the colony suffered the same fate. This Act forbade slaves from claiming freedom or manumission because of baptism.

By 1637 the Jesuits had acquired 2,000 acres of land that they named St. Inigoes in honor of Ignatius Loyola, their founder. St. Inigoes was worked by freemen and indentured servants. It is not known exactly when the first slave was brought into the colony, but in 1642 Governor Calvert bargained with a shipmaster for the delivery of 20 slaves.

In that same year the indentured servant deSousa voted in the Provincial Assembly. Evidently, he had served his indenture because only a freeman could participate. It was about this time that the "roots" of Black Catholicism were established and nurtured.

Father White acquired another larger tract of land named Mattapany in 1639. It was given to the Jesuits by an Indian chief. The Jesuits cleared a portion of the land and planted a crop when Lord Baltimore refused to recognize the title that was given them. This was only one of the controversies that the Jesuits endured. The Jesuits missions expanded gradually. The need for more hands to work the fields was apparent. They acquired more slaves to solve this endeavor.

Nevertheless, the Black Catholics continued to serve the Jesuits on their several plantations. At St. Inigoes, Father Walton built St. Ignatius church with the aid of Blacks. Blacks were always welcome to attend Mass at St. Ignatius. The gallery was set aside for their exclusive use.

Children were baptized, made their first Communion and were confirmed. Some were married in a religious ceremony since civil marriage was forbidden between slaves. The slaves were never denied sacraments, in fact, they were encouraged to attend to their religious duties and to keep on the right path.

In a report to the Board of Trade in London, Governor Nicholson in 1698 reported that some 600 Negroes had been imported recently and 400-500 were expected during the summer. The Black population was increasing through natural enhancement.

In spite of its growth, the Jesuits suffered several set backs. In 1704 the Protestant authorities closed the chapel in St Mary's City. The Manor House was attacked in the Revolutionary War and again in the War of 1812 by the British.

In the meantime, the capital of Maryland moved from St. Mary's City in 1694 to Annapolis. St. Mary's County had a total population of 15,544 at the time of the first Census in1790. There were 343 free Blacks and 6,986 slaves.

Francisco, deSousa and Price came to St. Mary's with the original emigrants and assisted in the pious rites of the Catholic Church. Black Catholicism has its beginning in 1634 and became an entrenched institution in spite of slavery. Maryland has the distinction of having the largest Black Catholic community in the colonial era.

Two Peter Claver churches

Maryland was settled by Catholics seeking religious toleration. The Calverts were given land by King James I of England. The king named the colony Mary-land in honor of his wife, Henrietta Maria. Maryland had the distinction of having St. Mary's as the name of both its first capital and its first county.

The first free Blacks to enter Maryland came aboard the Ark and the Dove. They were Mathaise deSousa and John Price. The first Mass was celebrated in the new colony at St. Clement Island, St. Mary's County, on March 25, 1634, the feast of the Annunciation by Father Andrew White, a Jesuit priest. The State of Maryland celebrates the same date as Maryland Day.

St. Peter Claver Church of the Ridge in St. Mary's County was named for the patron saint of Negro missions, St. Peter Claver. He was born in Versu, Spain, in 1580. He earned his first degree in Barcelona and entered the Jesuit novitiate and was ordained in 1615 in Cartagena, in what is now Colombia, South America, where he served for 45 years administering to the physical and religious needs of the slaves.

Thousands of slaves arrived in Cartagena from Africa and the dreadful middle passage in a horrible physical condition. Peter Claver dedicated himself to easing their suffering. He worked diligently to being a slave to the slaves. He cleaned their wounds and begged bread to feed them. His kindness earned him the title of "Apostle of the Negro Slave."

St. Peter Claver Church of the Ridge was not in existence when the Black Catholics attended Mass at various churches in the county. Colored Catholics attended Mass at St. Michael of the Ridge, because they lived in the vicinity. Father Tynan, a Jesuit, founded the Sodality of the Blessed Virgin for colored parishioners of St. Michael. Initially, they met at the home of a colored family on Smith Creek. The rapid growth of the sodality required a larger meeting place. A colored farmer named Benjamin Biscoe and his wife, Sarah, donated an acre of land in 1902 to build a church. Cardinal James Gibbons signed the deed. A meeting hall was built and Mass was celebrated there in 1903. This place was used until 1934 when it burned to the ground.

Philip Huber Frohan, a convert to Catholicism and the foremost architect in the United States, heard of the plight of the Black Catholics of the Ridge. He gained permission from Archbishop Michael Curley to design St. Peter Claver church.

As the colored folks migrated from St. Mary seeking a better life for their families, they never forgot their roots. Many of them knew about St. Peter Claver church in Baltimore. A number of them commuted between the two churches because of the seasonal work. In the winter some of them traveled to Baltimore to work and in the summer they went back to the farm.

On arriving in Baltimore City, they attended services at the Chapel of the Oblate Sisters of Providence, others at St. Francis Xavier in East Baltimore. In the meantime, St. Peter Claver church was built in 1888 for the convenience of Black Catholics living west of Charles Street.

From the moment the immigrants stepped off the boat on Pratt Street, they found their way to St. Peter. In some instances, they could not find their relatives, so the church acted as a clearing house.

It was well known that the priests and nuns would help to find a friend or relative, a place to sleep, food to eat or a job regardless of how menial the task. Such action created a formidable bond between the two churches. The two Peter Claver churches, though miles apart, were linked in name, kinship, parishioners, aid of family, remembrance of ancestors and the love of God and Catholicism.

Most importantly, the two churches are appropriately named; they are a mirror image of the deeds of St. Peter Claver.

Loyalty and Faith

Maryland, one of the 13 original colonies, was the sanctuary for the origin of Black Catholicism. By the latter part of the 1700s there were established Catholic parishes in Southern Maryland counties, the Eastern Shore and Baltimore.

With the gradual expansion of Catholicism, the growth of the slave population gained in number. The Black presence was evident in the handiwork and devotion to Catholicism with the establishment of each new chapel or church. Blacks were seldom mentioned, rarely documented, and records of their labor and achievement are almost non-existent.

St. Mary Church in Bryantown, Charles County, was one of the early Catholic churches built there. Its origin can be traced to a chapel on land owned by a lay Catholic named Boarman. The Jesuits conducted the services. The Protestants complained to the governor that the papists were going up and down the county persuading the populace to join the Catholic religion.

The Jesuits through Bishop John Carroll invited Carmelite nuns from Holland, (who originated in Antwerp in 1605) to Charles County. Upon their arrival in 1790 Charles Neale, a Jesuit priest, gave them a tract of land.

The Carmelites owned a number of slaves who worked the land and whom they also instructed in the Catholic faith. As novices joined the Carmelites, they brought their slaves with them.

The Carmelite Sisters moved to Baltimore in 1831 and settled on Aisquith Street. Later they moved to Caroline and Biddle streets until the move in 1961 to Dulaney Valley Road in Baltimore County. Before the Carmelites left Charles County they sold their slaves.

The first Black Carmelite, Sister Barbara Jean LaRochester, entered the religious community of the Sisters of the Holy Family of Nazareth of Philadelphia in 1955. She transferred to the Carmelites in 1972.

The Confraternity of the Sacred Heart began to admit secular members in 1821. Included on the list were the names of some of the most noted Catholics of Maryland and the names of two Black women, Nancy and Susanna. They were not listed with a surname, and the word Negro was written beside their names.

Maryland always welcomed diverse religious groups because of religious toleration. Many Catholics came to the state from various areas of Europe seeking a safe place to worship.

Jesuits owned slaves, but they were not the only religious order to own slaves. The Sulpicians in Baltimore, who formed the nucleus of St. Francis Xavier Church, owned slaves. Many of the Catholic slaves who were owned by the Sulpicians were buried in Cathedral Cemetery. Several slaves belonging to Rev William DuBourg of the seminary were buried in the graveyard in 1809.

The baptismal registers of St. Peter's Pro-cathedral and of the Basilica of the Assumption, both in Baltimore, recorded entries of those who were Black and those who were slaves. Many of the entries indicated "the large presence of French-speaking Blacks in Baltimore at the end of the 17th century" ("Black Catholics in the United States," Father Cyprian Davis, O.S.B.).

The slaves attended Mass and received the sacraments in the same church that they helped build. They were delegated to a certain section for seating to hear the word of God, and they received Holy Communion after all the white parishioners.

Marriages took place in the fields or in the slave quarters, and burials were performed with a reading from the prayer book. It was a rare occasion when a Black received the sacrament of Extreme Unction. Certain Sundays were set aside for baptism.

Blacks have a unique position in the Catholic history of Maryland. They were there in the beginning and assisted in laying a solid foundation of faith and a course of devotion that manifests itself into the new millennium – 2000.

CHARLES G. TILDON, JR.

This Far by Faith

A merica has become a world leader in the field of human rights. This has been possible because the founding fathers recognized the value of religious freedom. It is ironic, and to many of us disheartening, that the concept of freedom and human dignity did not include some persons – particularly African Americans. American slavery was a cruel practice that embraced the principles of inequality and dehumanization. The American Catholic Church as an institution, as well as most of its members, supported slavery although its practice clearly contradicted the values on which this country was founded. Historically, the Roman Church directed the American Catholic Church not to practice slavery.

How great it is that God's love would not allow this practice to undermine His great purpose for all his children! God's word persisted, and African Americans have relentlessly persevered, as discouraging as it could have been. As early as 1634, records show that Blacks sought God's grace in the Catholic Church. Maryland served as the entry point for many Catholics seeking religious freedom and many of their Black servants were Catholics. By 1790 there was a congregation of Blacks that attended Mass in the basement of St. Mary's Seminary on Paca Street. A Catholic priest, Father John Souge, spoke out against slavery and called for an insurrection.

Circumstances that were unfair and debilitating could not prevent God's love from penetrating the Black community. The faith in God's word inspired the formation of the Oblate Sisters of Providence – an order of Black nuns in 1829. In 1843 a Black Catholic Organization was founded and met in the basement of Calvert Hall. This was the first Lay Catholic Organization in this country. Although the church hierarchy supported slavery, and the prejudice and Jim Crow laws that stemmed from it, there were priests and other church leaders who helped ensure that God's love and God's Word would be known to the Black population.

In 1889, 200 delegates met in Washington, D.C., at the first Black Lay Catholic Congress, where the theme was "You Shall Know The Truth and The Truth Shall Make You Free" (John 8:32). Black Lay Catholic Congresses followed in 1890 in Cincinnati, Ohio, and in 1892 in Philadelphia, where the themes were education of the race. The Fourth Congress convened in Chicago in 1893. Discriminatory actions in Catholic schools was the topic. This Congress concluded with a meeting attended by 5,000 people.

In 1894, the Fifth Black Lay Catholic Congress was held in Baltimore and ended with a ringing hope expressed by Dr. William Lofton that "the American people, the hierarchy of the Catholic Church and the laity shall rise up in their might and stamp out the prejudice which is destroying the life blood of this country."

In 1987, almost 100 years later, The Black Catholic Congress movement was re-instituted under African American Bishop John H. Ricard, S.S.J., in Washington, D.C. The Black Congress movement has become an integral part of the efforts by African Americans to respond to God's love, and those national meetings have been held every five years since and are scheduled to continue.

God's love and the demand for justice inspired the founding of the first official Negro parish in the country in 1863, St. Francis Xavier in Baltimore. This parish flourishes today at its third location.

The deep faith of Black Americans led to Black Vocations with the first Black Josephite priest being ordained in 1891, Father Charles Uncles, S.S.J.. This faith also led to the establishment of more Black parishes. Throughout the country African Americans were espousing Catholicism, and their faith was the overriding factor that kept them loyal to a church that was slow in discerning contradictions in its practices and its doctrine.

African American Catholics consistently and persistently participated in all aspects of the church. They joined the enlightened leadership in the American Catholic Church to examine its practices, traditions, errors, misconceptions and opportunities. They began to share the unique gifts that African Americans brought to the church.

In Baltimore, we could fast forward to the leadership offered by Lawrence Cardinal Shehan who used the power of his office to bring about changes in the church and in our society. Throughout this country leaders began to come to grips with the practices, the habits, the contradictions, the laws and, yes, the evil that ensured second-class citizenship in both the church and society.

The Indomitable Spirit

Although Blacks endured many years under the yoke of slavery, by their indomitable spirit they made significant achievements and contributions to the Church and American society. The deeds of the tenacious nature of their bondsmen striving for freedom attained national fame in their efforts to be free. Some of the noteworthy facts are discussed here.

African Americans numbered 3,638,808 out of a total population of 23,191,876, in the United States in 1850. About this time, the Fugitive Slave Act was passed by Congress, wherein runaway slaves were to be returned to their owners. In the same decade, James Augustine Healy, the first Black American Roman Catholic Bishop, was ordained a priest in Notre Dame Cathedral in Paris, France. At home, Booker Taliferro Washington was born a slave in Franklin County, Virginia. He attended Hampton Institute in Alabama. As early as 1834, a free Black man of Montgomery County, Maryland, Henry Blair, received a patent for his invention of a "seed planter." Several years later, he received another patent for a "corn harvester." Blair signed his name with an "X" signifying that he could not write.

The most celebrated case of the 1850's was that of Dred Scott and the U.S. Supreme Court Ruling. Dred Scott was born a slave about 1800. His second owner took Dred and his family to the free territories of Illinois and Wisconsin. Dred sued for his freedom based on the fact that he had lived on free soil for a number of years and therefore he was entitled to his freedom. Dred's case made its journey all the way to the Supreme Court. The Court ruled that a Black slave was not a citizen and hence could not sue in a Federal Court.

At the turn of the decade of the 1850's, the Black Catholics of Baltimore were having religious services with the Oblate Sisters of Providence at Richmond Street, since they did not have a permanent place of worship. At the time St. Ignatius Church was being built and the basement chapel was set aside for the Black Catholics and was named "Chapel of Blessed Peter Claver." Peter Claver was a missionary who worked among Black people.

Father Louis Miller, S.J., and Father Michael O'Connor, a former bishop of Pittsburgh, who became a Jesuit, collected $6,000 for a building on Calvert and Pleasant Streets, which was built in 1836 and later became St. Francis Xavier Church. It was dedicated on February 21, 1864, at the height of the Civil War.

Maryland held a Constitutional Convention, re-wrote the Constitution and freed all slaves within its borders on November 1, 1864. President Lincoln had issued the Emancipation Proclamation, January 1, 1863, which applied to those States in rebellion against the Union. This set the stage for Colored men to join the Army. The Secretary of War ordered Col. Birney to raise regiments of Colored Troops to add to Maryland's quota. The regiments were known as the United States Colored Troops. Maryland had six Black regiments. The 7th Regiment had the honor of having the highest-ranking Black officer, Dr. Alexander Thomas Augustus, in the Union Army. Dr. Augustus was born free in Norfolk, Virginia, and came to Baltimore as a youngster to be educated by tutors. He graduated from Trinity Medical School in Toronto, Canada, because the medical schools in the United States would not accept a Negro.

The Civil War ended in April, 1865 and the 13th Amendment abolishing slavery in America was ratified in December, 1866.

The decade of the 1860's held promising deeds. The 14th Amendment was ratified June 21, 1868, and made all Black folks citizens of the United States, although Blacks had been here for nearly 300 years. The 15th Amendment was sent to the Senate, on February 26, 1869, and was ratified on March 30, 1870. This Amendment gave Negroes the privilege to vote.

MELVILLE W. PUGH JR.

The Nucleus

Black Catholics came to America with the Spanish explorers in Florida in the 16th century.

Historians have carefully examined an event named the Stoner Rebellion in Georgia in the 1700s. Some of the slaves who participated in this rebellion were originally from the Congo region, part of what is now Angola. It is suggested that these slaves considered themselves Catholic. The Congo became Catholic in the 15th century when King Alphonso the Good converted to Catholicism.

Maryland was the home of the largest community of Black Catholics in colonial times and during the antebellum era. In 1785 there were 3,000 Black Catholics in Maryland.

In 1793 the core of Black Catholics arrived in Baltimore at Fells Point from Cape Francois. The 619 passengers and crew, Whites and Blacks, were fleeing the revolution occurring on the island of Santo Domingo, in the country now known as Haiti. The French-speaking Blacks eventually found a spiritual home in the lower chapel of the Sulpician seminary.

An important data source which helps to identify the Blacks and the slaves is the baptismal register. A perusal of baptismal registers of St. Peter Pro-Cathedral and the Basilica of the Assumption confirms the ethnicity of this population. It was particularly evident that there was a significant presence of French-speaking Blacks in Baltimore at the end of the colonial period.

On March 24, 1797, the ceremony of baptism was presented to an 18-year-old female of color, Jeanne Antoinette Sanite, born in Santo

Domingo; her sponsors were Judocus Schutte and Catherine Mary Le Monnier. The next month, in April, a six-week-old infant, John Gabriel, was baptized. He was the biological son of Marinette, a French Negro slave. Listed sponsors are Ambrose, a free Negro, and Mary Louise, Negro slave.

In 1797 Black Catholic families began to be more visible in Maryland. Such was the case with the Butler family. David Butler, infant son of Nancy Butler, was baptized. The godmother was Priscilla Berry, a slave of James McSherry. In May, Jane, the daughter of Clare Butler, was baptized. Henry, a slave, and Joanna Butler, a free mulatto, served as sponsors. The baptismal registers also reveal that the rector of St. Peter Pro-Cathedral, Father Francis Beeston, was a slave owner.

In his search of the Sulpician archives in Baltimore, Father Cyprian Davis, O.S.P., discovered a small notebook which sheds some light on the history of Black Catholics in the United States. It is handwritten, and the first page begins: "Journal of the Commencement and Proceedings of the Society of Colored People." This remains the oldest written document of a Black Catholic society in the United States, the Holy Family Society.

The Society included a number of different activities on the agenda of their meetings. Group singing was always included and generally included four hymns; it was not unusual to extend singing beyond four hymns and to engage in a practice session during the week. Occasionally, there were solo performances and the beautiful sounds of violin music. The prayers included the recitation of five decades of the rosary.

A copy of the ledger for Easter confessions for the cathedral parish in Baltimore from 1819-21 recorded names of Blacks. The following were members of the Society of the Holy Family: Edward Queen, Rosetta Livers, Harriet Berry, Mary Johnson and Mary Holland. Black Catholic family sponsors for baptism from 1822-24 are also recorded: Sidney Queen, Fanny Queen, Edward Queen, Sophia Queen, Lucy Butler and Mary Berry. Names of nine persons were entered into the baptismal register.

Evangelization was a continuous and positive force, stimulating the increase of Black Catholics in Baltimore. The Jesuits, the Josephite Fathers and Brothers and the Oblate Sisters of Providence (the "super" nuns) all played major roles in the remarkable religious movement.

Holy Family Society

A s we celebrate the feast of the Holy Family, I share a story of the Society of the Holy Family, the first Black Catholic lay society in the United States.

The society was formed as a devotional group of Black lay Catholics through piety, prayer and music to manifest their spirituality. The society gave the members autonomy and independence in ministering to their salvation.

The group's first meeting, December 3, 1843, was in the basement of Calvert Hall, then attached to the cathedral (now the Basilica of the National Shrine of the Assumption of the Blessed Virgin Mary in Baltimore). The first and second floors of the building were used by the Christian Brothers as a school.

It was at the second meeting that the members adopted the name Society of the Holy Family. At the third meeting the group elected officers. John Noel, a barber, was elected president; Mary Holland, first counselor; and Washington Ford, a stone cutter, first vice president. Other officers were Mr. London, Elizabeth Bury, George Holly and Mary Howard. Father John Hickey, a Sulpician, was instrumental in the formation of the society and acted as its director, secretary and treasurer.

There were more than 200 members including slaves as well as free Blacks. The society was made up of members whose occupations were varied such as white washers, washerwomen, cook, porter, carrier, drayman, proprietor of a coffee house, cooper, sawyer, laborer, waiter, laundress, stone cutter and barber.

The Calvert Hall meeting served as the site for the society in expressing their own spiritual, social and educational undertaking. The society held weekly general meetings, and the council met monthly.

The meeting opened with a prayer, the rosary and spiritual readings followed by a hymn, collection, advice, another hymn, night prayers and sometimes the Litany of St. Joseph. Father Hickey delivered sermons. Sometimes Jane Thompson would hold up the meeting by singing a hymn.

The Society of the Holy Family was not affiliated with a parish. The society was free-standing and independent, yet it had a devoutly religious identity. The organization helped the poor, had Masses said for the deceased and paid for the opening of graves. They also opened a library, purchased books and catechisms.

The organization was doing well, membership had increased, and each member paid six and a quarter cents a month. The group also made monetary contributions to the cathedral.

The closing of the organization was swift and complete. On September 7, 1845, the Society of the Holy Family went to Calvert Hall to find their meeting room packed full of lumber and carpentry equipment. It was then that they knew that the Christian Brothers had taken over their space. The priest offered them several other places for their use, but they respectfully declined.

Last minutes of the society were taken October 21, 1845. At this meeting the members transferred the library to St. Peter's for the use of colored children. The bookcases, benches, chairs and lamps were sold and the proceeds given to the poor.

This was the demise of the Society of the Holy Family. This was the first society ever organized by Black lay Catholics that stood independent of the church and whose records survive to pay homage to their indomitable spirit.

Pursuit of Self-Governance

For the longest time, I have been intrigued by the story of the "Holy Family Society" a lay organization of "Coloured Catholics of Baltimore." I thought the organization began in 1843. I was taught a good history lesson yesterday, as I spoke with Sister Reginald Gerdes, O.S.P., and roamed through files at the Associated Archives at St. Mary's Seminary.

In 1827, Sulpician Father James Hector Joubert's pastoral concern for Black Catholics motivated him to establish the Holy Family Society on December 25, 1827, in St. Mary's Lower Chapel. Undoubtedly Elizabeth Lange was connected to the initiation and support of such a society.

"This religious devotional society, formed with the approval of Archbishop Ambrose Maréchal, enrolled Black members exclusively. In 1833, Father Joubert sought and received special indulgences and papal favors for the Holy Family Society as well as for the Oblate Sisters of Providence." (Dr. Diane Batts Morrow, "Persons of Color and Religious At The Same Time: The Oblate Sisters of Providence, 1828-1860")

While founded by Father Joubert, in its early days and the provision of pastoral support of a director, Father John F. Hickey, in its latter days – the men and women of this society were the decision-makers and pursued self-governance. The principal object of the society was to "afford the Coloured people an opportunity of attending more particularly to their salvation and spiritual concerns," according to Father John F. Hickey's "Journal of The Society of Coloured People."

From 1843-45, meetings were held in the basement of Calvert Hall – near the basilica, then called St. Peter's Cathedral. However, in its early days, meetings were held at St. Mary's and the Oblates' convent

31

on Richmond Street.

Officers were elected, both men and women with John Noel serving as president for most of its existence. Mr. Noel was from Haiti and his daughter entered the Oblate Sisters of Providence. Meetings offered spiritual presentations delivered by the director, followed by the officers giving remarks or some exegesis regarding the religious topic. (That sounds like inculturation to me.)

Other elements of their meetings included singing, prayerful invocation of the Holy Spirit and the saying of the rosary. Officers held council meetings where discussion of dues, approval of new members and designation and distribution of monies were determined.

This organization put together a lending library (which says that reading and education were valued), hired musicians, attended to the poor, raised monies for "the only free school" led by the Oblates and evangelized. The journal kept by Father Hickey from 1843-45 shows evidence of the above with special mention of the interest and enthusiasm rendered for singing and invitations extended to Protestants to come as guests to "The Holy Family Society" meetings.

The above activity is significant in its historical context as Maryland was a slave state and the slave codes included the "prohibition of slaves to learn to read and assemble beyond three people."

In reading the Journal of "The Holy Family Society," I was mesmerized by the list of 270 names of members, many whose surnames appear on our parishes rosters today. A short list includes: Rosetta Bell, Louisa Black, Gabriel Brisko, Daniel Brooks, Anastasia Brown, Elisa Burgess, Henry Butler, Maria Carroll, Maria Clarke, Margaret Carter, Mary Casell, Joseph Davis, Henry and Mary Dorsey, Washington Ford, Julia Green, M.H. Gordon, Mary Elis Gustav, Mary Ann Hall, Ann Hammonds, William and Christina Harris, John Hardy, Rutha Hobb, Diana Hollen, Martha Holly, George Holly, Margaret Howard, Ellen Johnson (one of seven Johnsons listed), Guilbert Jordan, Harriet Jourdan, Bethea and Rachel Lee, Rachel Lloyd, Alexander Matthews, Mary McGhee, Amelia Mitchell, Nelson Morquet, Henry Nelson, John Noel, Owings Oliver (four Olivers listed), James Powell, Adeline Prit, Lucretia Queen, Harriet Queen, Grace Richardson, La Smallwood, Ephrem John Snowden, Nathaniel Williams, Mary Wilson, Elis and Mary Woods.

(Special thanks is extended to Simran K. Dhami at the Associated Archives at St. Mary's Seminary and Sister M. Reginald Gerdes, archivist of the Oblate Sisters of Providence, for their kind assistance.)

The Civil War

The Civil War years (1861-65) in Maryland are important because of the political and religious events that intertwined.

On the eve of the Civil War, Maryland had more free Blacks than any state in the Union. In 1860 there were more than 87,000 slaves and 83,000 free Blacks residing in Maryland.

Five states had seceded from the Union by March, 1861. The Union forces surrendered Fort Sumter to the Confederates a month later. This action was the start of the Civil War.

During the Civil War, Maryland was the center for Black Catholics, and Baltimore was a hub of activity. Blacks were engaged in many professional endeavors. They were caulkers, carpenters, waiters, barbers and workers in other areas of employment. They gave charitable affairs to support the church – selling oysters and holding fish and chicken suppers. In their eagerness to learn, they attended night school and borrowed books from the Jesuit library.

By 1861 a congregation of Colored Catholics attended Mass in the basement Chapel of Blessed Peter Claver at St. Ignatius in Baltimore. This congregation eventually became St. Francis Xavier parish, Baltimore, founded in 1863.

The Oblate Sisters of Providence continued their mission of instruction to Blacks through St. Frances Academy, an educational and evangelization oasis, also in the city.

President Lincoln issued the Emancipation Proclamation in January, 1863. This cleared the way for Black men to join the Union Army, and Maryland contributed six Black regiments, with the last formed in 1864.

They were known as the United States Colored Troops (USCT).

The General Assembly passed a law that awarded a bounty to every man who joined the Army as well as the owners. The slave owner had to manumit the slave to be eligible for the bounty.

Recruiting was brisk and lively at its location at Holiday and Baltimore streets. Men from all parts of Maryland came to join the Army, especially from the Southern Maryland counties where many of the slaves and freemen were devout Catholics.

Bishop Michael O'Connor, the first bishop of Pittsburgh, joined forces with Father Peter Louis Miller in the evangelization of Blacks. The dedicated pair noticed that the Chapel of Blessed Peter Claver was inadequate to accommodate the large number of Blacks who worshipped there.

Determined to see Black Catholics with a church of their own, the priests went door-to-door and collected $7,000 in donations. The funds were used to purchase a building that was once a Unitarian church and a public hall.

It was about this time that the 4th Regiment United States Colored Troops was sworn in at Baltimore. Dr. Alexander Thomas Augusta, a Black physician who was educated by tutors in East Baltimore and graduated from Trinity Medical College (Toronto, Canada), examined and provided health services for Colored soldiers. He was appointed chief surgeon of the 7th Regiment USCT and officially inducted for three years at Bryantown in Charles County.

Several important events occurred in 1864. St. Francis Xavier Church was dedicated in February with Father Miller as the first pastor of this historical church formed exclusively for Black people.

The state of Maryland took a noble step November 1, 1864, by rewriting the constitution of Maryland and freeing all slaves within its borders. This milestone event for Black people transpired more than a year prior to the passing of the 13th Amendment that abolished slavery throughout the United States.

In 1865 William A. Williams, a Black man who once studied for the priesthood, joined retired Bishop O'Connor and Father Miller in efforts of ministering to Blacks by publishing a journal in Baltimore titled the "Truth Communicator."

These events of history and religious matters made Baltimore fertile ground for the formation of Black priests and the home of the fifth Colored Congress led by Daniel Rudd.

Losing the Chance

During the Civil War, for the most part, the bishops of the United States maintained a position of "reticence and abstention" referring to the moral discussion of slavery.

Father Cyprian Davis, O.S.B., author of *"The History of Black Catholics in the United States,"* writes, "History since that time has taught us that no one can remain silent in periods of great social turmoil and still retain any moral authority. It has also taught that there is no such thing as a political issue without moral consequences. From today's vantage point, it can be said that the American bishops in the period of slavery made a bad choice. At the end of the Civil War, they were given a chance to rectify it."

That chance to rectify their choice made its way into the discussions and proceedings of the Second Plenary Council of Baltimore, held at the Basilica of the Assumption in 1866. Archbishop Martin J. Spalding actively promoted a national council, "to be held immediately after the war as a proof of the unity of the Catholic Church and to address the many problems arising from the altered condition of the country and the growth of the church since the First Plenary Council."

In a letter written to Archbishop John McCloskey of New York, Archbishop Spalding spoke about the objective of the forthcoming council in dealing with the question of African Americans. "I think it precisely the most urgent duty of all to discuss the future status of the Negro. Four million of these unfortunates are thrown on our charity … It is a golden opportunity for reaping a harvest of souls, which neglected may not return."

Rome gave final approval of the agenda and, in the same papal brief, named Archbishop Spalding as the leader of the council. Of the topics that were to be covered in the council, the eighth and last dealt with the evangelization of the African Americans. By the time this agenda item was to be discussed, time ran out. Thus this discussion appeared at "an extraordinary session" called after the Plenary Council had officially closed.

The discussions were bitter and long. Archbishop Spalding hoped for a unified national response to evangelization of African Americans. A preliminary schema was composed, titled "On the Care of Souls," proposing the consideration of special churches for African Americans, African American priests and missionary endeavors among Blacks.

Another schema, known as "Title 13 : no. 4," was also proposed for the appointment of a prefect apostolic for the spiritual care of African Americans. Archbishop Peter Kenrick of St. Louis, who had been in very bad humor throughout the council, "asserted that he would accept no such prefect; if one were forced upon him, he would renounce the episcopacy." The Sacred Congregation in Rome sent directives that "something special for Blacks was to be done."

In the end, the council fathers rejected the notion of an ecclesiastical coordinator or prefect apostolic. Nothing new was created to deal with the situation on a nationwide scale. It was decided that each bishop who had Blacks in his diocese should decide what was best and work in concert with others in provincial synods. It became the opinion of many that the opportunity for a harvest of souls was missed.

In the past, the moral question was slavery. Today, remnants of slavery remain with us – the bitter sting of racism. Sister Jamie Phelps, O.P., writes, "Many consider institutional racism a matter of political and social concern rather than the moral issue that it is. Many remain silent and inactive about institutional racism to maintain a false sense of peace and sinful security."

Let us as church, through our parishes, schools and charitable organizations, not allow racism to block (now and in the future) "a golden opportunity for a harvest of souls" of African Americans.

Celebrating

B efore the resounding echo of celebration May 19, 1870, had dimmed, Baltimoreans were still celebrating the passing of the 15th Amendment that gave suffrage to all Black folks.

It was one of the largest parades ever held in downtown Baltimore. It had front-page coverage by newspapers. It was a day of commemoration in which many organizations participated, including churches, social clubs, societies and lodges.

St. Francis Xavier Church was located along the parade route, and several societies along with the children of the parish marched in the historic observance.

It was about this time that Father Herbert Vaughan, the superior of the Mill Hill order, and four priests arrived at St. Francis from England. They began their religious activities immediately.

As the St. Francis congregation was preparing to enter the Advent and Christmas season, the newly arrived Father Vaughan was appointed to preside and preach at Mass on Christmas Day.

Further, in order to worship the newborn Christ child's birth, Father Noonan suggested that it would be necessary to practice singing hymns. Mr. Webb, a musician, offered to hold practice several times a week until Christmas.

It seems that Mr. Webb was the organist as well as the choir director. One of the older boys of the parish pumped the organ by working the pump handle up and down. Mr. Webb announced that "the singers should prepare their voices well so that the singing may be worthy of the Baby Jesus."

In seeking documentation concerning Mr. Webb, it was noted that he was listed in the Josephite archives with a surname only. However, other historical information indicates that there was a Harrison Webb, musician of 10 Low Street in 1871 and 1872. Harrison Webb also lived at 124 Orleans Street and later moved to 79 Spring Street. There is a strong possibility that Mr. Webb, the musician and choir director, is the same Harrison Webb of Low, Orleans and Spring streets in the early 1870s.

Another gentleman, Mr. Anderson, taught in the basement of the church for two years. He, too, is listed in the Josephite archives by a surname. Further research indicates that a William S. Anderson, teacher, resided at 8 Beaufort Street in 1871 and 1872. All of these addresses were in close proximity to St. Francis on Calvert and Pleasant streets.

Moreover, several organizations in the church combined their talent and creativity and decorated the exterior and interior of the church. The priests appealed to the congregation for evergreens, moss and other types of decorations.

The people of St. Francis were asked to help by bringing in their donations early in the week. The organizations and parishioners responded immediately. The Ladies of the Sanctuary weaved pinecones into bouquets for floral decorations for the main altar. Sprigs of holly were interspersed among the votive lights, while the sanctuary lamp burned continuously.

Some of the animals found around the crib were hand-carved of wood by the men of the parish. Cedar branches were joined and plaited to adorn the columns of the altar. Men from the congregation hung spruce branches over each door of the entrance to the vestibule of the church. Men called carters, driving horse and wagons, delivered pine trees and hay for the manger.

Solemn High Mass was celebrated at 10 a.m. Christmas Day. The church had standing room only with a membership of 3,500 parishioners. The choir sang melodiously under Mr. Webb's guidance. The St. John's Beneficial Society led the procession around the church and the St. Francis Society carried the Infant Jesus to the crib. The children of the Sunday school sang hymns as they marched in the procession.

The consequence of good deeds, religious celebrations and respect for civic responsibility has made St. Francis Xavier Church (the oldest Black Catholic community in the United States) a foundation of hope and love to serve the community.

St. Monica Church

Faith in God, prayers of helpfulness, determination of spirit and perseverance sought to make St. Monica Church a viable entity of the South Baltimore community.

South Baltimore was seemingly a transient community. It was a transportation and shipping center for Baltimore. It attracted new populations from various areas, including Charles and St. Mary's counties. People came for better wages and living conditions.

As they made progress and the white population moved to suburbs, colored folks moved into the vacated homes. St. Francis Xavier, located in East Baltimore, could no longer accommodate the extended Black Catholic community of Baltimore; therefore, it was imperative that a place of Catholic worship be created.

St. Monica had its beginning in a small building on Leadenhall Street known as the Chapel of the Sacred Heart in 1872. It was staffed by the Mill Hill priests who had recently arrived from England. The chapel did not prosper; after several years and it was closed.

The name chosen for the original church was St. Monica. St. Monica was the mother of St. Augustine of Hippo and the patron saint of Christian wives and mothers, and of women's sodalities.

On January 21, 1883, the original St. Monica Church on Hill Street was dedicated by then-Archbishop James Gibbons. This was the second Catholic church established specifically for Black Catholics of Baltimore. Many of the people who attended the first Mass were visitors from the 7,000-member congregation of St. Francis Xavier, the oldest Black Catholic parish in the country.

St. Monica on Hill Street and its pastor had a diverse history. It was first a Methodist Episcopal church. Later it came into the possession of the Colored Baptists, and then it was used as a barracks for the Salvation Army.

Father A.B. Leeson had been an Episcopalian minister in England and converted to Catholicism. He was ordained and accepted into the Archdiocese of Baltimore. He became the first pastor of St. Monica. The church remained closed for several years after his death in 1900.

When St. Monica opened its doors for worship again, it was three years after the death of Father Leeson. St. Monica was serviced by priests from St. Joseph Seminary, St. Barnabas and St. Francis Xavier until Cardinal Gibbons assigned the American Josephites to administer to the religious needs of the Black Catholics.

Father John Henry Dorsey, the second Black priest to be ordained in the United States (the first being Father Charles Uncles) became the pastor of St. Monica. Father Dorsey did an outstanding job, increasing the membership of the church and the school. The Oblate Sisters worked diligently with the students and parents.

Father Dorsey became ill and had to resign his pastorship in 1923. He died three years later. Before he resigned his position, he had purchased a Lutheran church on South Henrietta Street across the railroad tracks. The building consisted of a church, rectory and school.

In 1920, there were over 400 parishioners at St. Monica; by 1927, there were less than a hundred. In the 1930s and '40s enrollment rose and declined until 1958 when 135 people registered there. However, the priest, Oblate Sisters and the parishioners put forth effort and ingenuity to assure the continuous use of the house of worship.

St. Monica School was destroyed by fire in February, 1935. The old St. Monica that was used by the Italians had been closed for a few weeks. It was renovated and used as the new St. Monica School.

St. Monica Church took its place in history on April 6, 1959, when the funeral service for Mrs. Clementine Gross, the oldest member of the parish, was celebrated.

During urban renewal, the church and rectory were purchased by a chemical company and the old St. Monica convent and church were bought by a businessman.

AGNES KANE CALLUM

St. Barnabas Church

In recent years, St. Francis Xavier has had the honor of having Paulist Fathers as guests, visitors and associate priests. For the past several years, St. Francis has enjoyed at least three Paulist priests who have sojourned with the church.

However, about 96 years ago, at the dedication of St. Barnabas Church, a noted Paulist, Father Walter Elliott delivered the homily for the occasion. He was a dynamic speaker and orator. He came from the Apostolic Mission House, Brookland, Washington, D.C. In his address, he acknowledged the presence of two Colored priests: Father Charles Uncles, who served as deacon, soon to be priest, and John Plantivigne, a subdeacon. He hoped that they would be the advance guard of many more.

St. Barnabas was the fourth Colored parish in Baltimore City administered to by the Josephite Fathers. Its origin came about as a result of the growth of Catholicism within the Colored community of Baltimore. This necessitated a need for another church.

Ironically, St. Barnabas was first an Episcopalian church and when the Catholics purchased the church they did not change the name. This church structure was built in 1856 on the same area of ground that St. Pius was supposed to be built, Argyle Avenue and Biddle Street. There was an error in the plans and St. Pius was built several blocks to the West on Schroeder and Edmondson avenues. When the Episcopalians sought to build, it was on the land that St. Pius had originally chosen and they named it St. Barnabas.

St. Barnabas Church was dedicated as a Roman Catholic church

41

by Cardinal Gibbons, February 5, 1907. Many dignitaries were present at the Mass, including Baron Moncheur, the Belgian ambassador to the United States. The church prospered and the congregation grew to 1,600. The main altar was 15-feet high and made of polished oak. The two side altars were made in the Eddington, Penn., Training School conducted by the Christian Brothers. They were made of white oak. It had a life-size figure of Jesus on the cross with Mary and St. John at his feet. There was a large framed picture of Our Lady of Good Counsel hanging near one of the altars. The aisles were wide and spacious and the pews were left over from the Episcopal parish.

In the early 1920's, the neighborhood of St. Pius began a transitional period. There was an influx of Black Catholics and an exodus of White Catholics in the area surrounding both churches. Blacks began to encroach upon the Masses and services of St. Pius.

Also, there was unrest within St. Barnabas parish concerning Father Waring, the pastor, and the parishioners. The parishioners accused Father Waring of being an autocratic. He forbid the Knights of St. John to participate in the May Day procession in uniform because they did not attend a May Day service in church. Some of the Catholics explained to Father Waring that the May Day service was not a Holy Day of Obligation. This did not deter Father Waring from dismissing the choir and several organizations within the church.

Several vocal Colored Catholics felt that the clergy was prejudiced and treated them with arrogance. They resented the paternalistic attitude forced upon the laity by the priest.

In the meantime, the Josephite priests took over the spiritual duties of St. Pius V church on July 12, 1931. At the time, St. Barnabas parishioners moved into St. Pius V church and St. Barnabas was officially closed.

Evidence League

The Negro Catholic Evidence League in the United States had its beginning at St. Francis Xavier church in East Baltimore under the auspices of the Josephite priests: Father John T. Gilliard, S.S.J., Ph.D., and Father Samuel Matthews, S.S.J. The Negro Catholic Evidence League was a group of lay Catholics who were dedicated to spreading the word of God through lectures and example.

The Catholic Evidence Guild was an entrenched organization in England. The Catholic Truth Society of Boston was the equivalent of the Evidence Guild and its popularity was well known.

Father Gilliard felt that well-qualified Colored Catholics should be the lecturers. Father Gilliard hand-picked his potential lecturers and taught them the proper technique of communication and articulation. He tutored and renewed their knowledge of Catholic doctrine.

The first meeting of the league was September 8, 1932, in the rectory of St. Francis Xavier Church, the first Catholic church established specially for Colored people. The goal of the Colored Catholics was to train race speakers. These were the people who taught the chosen lecturers on how to address a Colored audience. This was not a difficult task since they were educated and many of them were already well-versed in public speaking. The program was to meet once a week. The study questions involved the catechism and catechetical instructions given by Father Gilliard. They were given the option of choosing a topic or being assigned one by a priest.

Father Gilliard said there were two levels of advancement in evidence work. First, one must have the ability to handle all questions adequately.

The second consisted of the ability to handle any topic of Catholic doctrine. A board of examiners had been appointed by Archbishop Curley for the purpose of qualifying those who came under Father Gilliard's training. A certificate was awarded to the graduates.

Many of the lecturers were members of St. Francis Xavier parish. Several people mentioned in archival records were: Mary Lansey, Mildred Robinson, Irene Blay, Eugene Briscoe, Vernon Robinson, Mary Sewell and Leo Woods. All lectures were delivered in the auditorium of St. Francis Xavier Church. These lectures caught on and soon Protestants and Catholics were attending.

The speakers were school teachers, intelligent, articulate, and coherent. The lectures became so popular that a musical selection by St. Frances Academy Band was performed before each lecture. In the meantime, Father Gilliard visited Catholic churches in Washington and New York, lecturing on "Colored Missions" and the "Negro Questions" before the Catholic Evidence Guild. He also spoke at the John Carroll Club of Johns Hopkins University. The speakers of St. Francis Xavier were delivering lectures to the local population, with such titles as: *"How Many Churches Did Christ Start?"* or *"Will the Soul Live After Death?"* Miss Irene Blay spoke on *"Does God Really Exist?"*

The audience was both receptive and alert and the work of the Colored Evidence Guild was manifesting itself in the conversion of newcomers. The Colored lay society was proving to be worthwhile. The attendance at the lectures was always in the hundreds. During Lent the Evidence Guild would visit Colored Catholic churches in Baltimore and Washington. The topics were so well-delivered and received that the Baltimore Negro Evidence Guild was called "Catholic Action" which made the lay members "convert conscious." Father Gilliard, S.S.J., started a religious movement that taught the doctrine of the Catholic Church through lay members, faith in God and devotion to the church. Father Gilliard died suddenly in January, 1942.

Freedman's Bank

The Freedman's Savings and Trust Company is a rare document, that has a rich source of data pertaining to the ex-slave immediately following the Civil War. It had a short life span but it left a plethora of information concerning the depositors, the family, and descendants.

Congress passed an Act of Incorporation for the Freedman's Savings and Trust Company and President Lincoln signed it into law on March 3, 1865. The Savings and Trust Company was chartered by Congress for the enhancement of the newly-freed slave, to teach them to save money for the future, to be thrifty and to be productive. The objective of the Savings and Trust Company was straightforward and clear. It was supposed to be a direct path to economic stability for the Negro.

A branch of the company was opened in Baltimore and became known as Freedman's Bank. Many organizations such as societies and clubs, as well as churches, became members. As early as 1870, St. Francis Xavier Church Sinking Society Fund had an account at the bank. The banking committee was John Peed, Cornelius Thomas and Paul C. Thomas. The pastor of St. Francis Xavier called a meeting of all of the societies and suggested that they initiate a plan to enable the priests as executor of the accounts, so that they could carry out different projects for the good of the Colored people.

As a response, St. Francis Xavier Sanctuary Society had an oyster supper and they deposited their proceeds in the Freedman's Bank. Their banking committee members were Cecelia Lee, Mary Ann Coates, and Mary A. Laker. In 1873, St. Francis instituted a Burial Society wherein the members were charged 10 cents a month and the monies deposited in the Freedman's Bank. The banking committee was John Peed and Anna Morris.

St. Francis reached out to the community and started to feed the hungry and motherless children in the neighborhood. Some of the parishioners of St. Francis Xavier commenced an Orphan Aid Society. They, too, saved their money in the Freedman's Bank with a committee of three, Ellen Johnson, Eliza Thomas and Mary Jane Heall. This society is a forerunner of St. Elizabeth Home for Colored Children, which had its beginning in the 1870s.

There is a possibility that other organizations in the church used the services of the bank, but they are not noted in the Freedman's Bank nor in the announcement book of St. Francis Xavier 1869-1882.

The announcement book of St. Francis contained the activities of the church and its members. It consisted of news and activities of the parishioners, such as, special occasions, benefits, entertainment programs, collections, prayers for the sick and the dying. Death notices and marriage banns were also recorded. Rarely were the societies mentioned except in meetings and in advertisements. The accounts with the savings bank were not listed.

Several years before the origin of the Freedman's Bank, the Black soldiers of the Civil War had been saving their monies in the Savings Bank of Baltimore, which had been established in 1818. This took place through an allotment system supervised by officers of the regiment. In the archaic files of the Savings Bank of Baltimore survives correspondence which lists the names of soldiers of the 7th Regiment United States Colored Troops and their transactions with the bank.

The Freedman's Savings Bank seemingly operated well. In 1870, the bank changed its policy of dealing with loans and investments. That created economic problems that caused a dilemma within the bank financial structure. Frederick Douglass joined the bank as its president in 1874 to boost the morale of the depositors. He soon realized that the bank was in trouble and could not survive. He recommended to Congress that the bank should close. Congress passed an Act to authorize the trustees to close the bank. By June of the same year, the extinction of the Freedman's Savings Bank was complete.

Without a Priest

In 1897, Father Daniel Berberich discovered a Black Catholic parish in a remote section of South Carolina named Ritter. It is 40 miles southwest of Charleston and is at the crossroads of the Charleston and Savannah Highway. At one time it was known as Thompson Crossroad and later as Catholic Crossroads. Bishop John England, the first bishop of Charleston, established the parish and it was given the name St. James the Greater in 1833 at its dedication.

However, the Catholic community had commenced in 1824 at Walnut Hill on donated land before the arrival of Bishop England. The community had a vestry, and Bishop England met with the group several times in 1831 and decided to build a church to accommodate the White plantation owners and their slaves.

Catholic owners of slaves were diligent in seeing that their slaves attended services and received the sacraments. There were many Protestant slave masters in the area that were soon converted to Catholicism as well as their slaves. Several hundred baptismal records listed the names of White and Black folks, slaves and free, at St. James the Greater Church in the 1830s.

Blacks came to Ritter as slaves of White owners. The slaves assisted in building a vestry as well as the 1831 church. They took care of the priestly accouterments. About this time Crossroads was known as Catholic Hill. The church burned to the ground in 1856 a few years before the Civil War.

This did not deter the slaves from gathering and saying prayers. This was led by a former slave named Vincent DePaul Davis. He owned a store and taught the children instructions in his store. The records do not show it, but there is a strong possibility that he held church services there also. He was a devout and pious person and lived an exemplary life. He was the leader in saying the rosary and reciting the litany. They observed the holy days of the church and gathered every Sunday for prayers. He and others read from the Bible and sang hymns. It was his effort and example that helped to preserve Black Catholicism, though no priest was present for 40 years.

Vincent DePaul Davis' descendants are still members of the church 160 years later. The Civil War years took its toll on the little Catholic community. The White population decreased, and since the church had burned, they felt no urgency in rebuilding another. In spite of the poverty and segregation, the Blacks never relinquished their faith in Catholicism. They remained true and loyal to the tenets of the faith. From 1856 to 1897, no record survives that can give positive insight into the history of the church. For 40 years, no Mass was celebrated. There were no sick calls, no baptisms, no communion, no extreme unction and no funeral services for the group.

When Father Berberich met the group in 1897, he was astonished. He baptized parishioners that were 40 years old. Father Berberich was impressed with the Black Catholics' unrelenting devotion to the church.

Immediately, he set about building a church and a school. These buildings are still in use. He celebrated Mass twice a month at St. James and arranged for a priest from nearby areas to visit in the intervening weeks. Father Berberich administered to the religious needs until 1909.

Father Cyprian Davis, in his book, *"History of Black Catholics in the United States,"* gives a microcosm of insight into a group of Black Catholics who unknowingly and unintentionally helped to extend Catholicism by their visible faith. This was accomplished without the assistance of missionaries but through faith in God.

NICHOLAS M. CREARY

TWO PART SERIES:

The Freedom Sought

The cultural values that the Federated Colored Catholics (FCC) espoused developed after the Civil War when growing numbers of African Americans succeeded in obtaining high school and university level education, and became part of the American urban professional class. Following the end of Reconstruction in 1877, the United States entered a period of aggressive racism: "Jim Crow" laws were passed throughout the South; the Supreme Court upheld the doctrine of "separate but [un]equal" facilities for Blacks and Whites; "lynching" of Black men was rampant, particularly in 1919, after the return of African American servicemen who fought in World War I.

Efforts to deny social equality to Blacks included the Catholic Church, which directed the overwhelming majority of its resources to the pastoral care of European immigrants and established (White) ethnic Catholic communities. Amazingly, within this context Black Catholics held five lay congresses from 1889 to 1894.

The organization that became the FCC began in 1917 when Thomas Wyatt Turner, a botany professor at Howard University, and four parishioners of St. Augustine's church in Washington, DC, formed the Committee Against the Extension of Race Prejudice in the Church. They initially organized to protest that Black Catholic servicemen fighting in World War I did not receive welfare services. American troops were racially segregated, as was the YMCA, which provided support services to Protestant soldiers, both white and Black, along racially segregated lines.

Similarly, the Knights of Columbus, whom the National Catholic

War Council charged to provide such services to Catholics, refused to accept Blacks into their fraternal organization. Turner and the committee met with Cardinal Gibbons, the archbishop of Baltimore, and with the Knights of Columbus director of welfare services, with the result that Black Catholics were placed in several of the Knights' cantonments, where they served until the war ended.

By 1919, the committee had grown to 25 members and became the Committee for the Advancement of Colored Catholics (CACC). In 1924, the CACC reorganized itself into the Federated Colored Catholics of the United States (FCC), which was an umbrella organization for local and parochial Black Catholic societies and guilds to unite and seek equality in the American church. It was also an avowedly Black American lay organization.

The FCC sponsored annual conventions which became a national forum in which Black Catholic leaders met and supported one another in their common struggle, voiced their concerns, and applied pressure for change on a national level. At its height in 1931-1932, the FCC claimed 72 separate chapters and 44 individual members from more than 20 states.

In 1928, William Markoe, a Jesuit from St. Louis, joined the FCC. Father Markoe wanted to transform the FCC into an interracial organization. The differences between Turner and Father Markoe concerning the fundamental nature of the Federation led to changing its name to the National Catholic Federation for the Promotion of Better Race Relations at the Eighth Annual Convention in New York in September, 1932. This was a compromise which had neither the words "Colored" nor "Interracial" in the organization's title.

Turner saw Father Markoe's efforts to change the direction of the FCC as an attempt by a clergyman to wrest control from its Black lay leadership. Father Markoe charged Turner with anti-clericalism. In April, 1933 the NCFPBRR split into the National Catholic Interracial Federation led by Father Markoe, and the Federated Colored Catholics, led by Turner. Although both organizations worked to improve Blacks' position in the church, the Catholic Interracial Council movement, which John LaFarge started in 1934, overshadowed them both.

This organization was dedicated to the integration of Blacks into the Catholic Church in the United States and not pluralism – the equal recognition of Black Catholics as a group on par with European-American groups – as was the goal of the Federation. During the dispute, LaFarge remained largely silent, but ultimately sided with Markoe – a fellow Jesuit – in promoting interracial action, rather than pluralism for Blacks within the church.

After 15 years of working directly in the southern Maryland missions (1911-1926), and a further seven working closely with African Americans, LaFarge became exhausted working for equality for Blacks in the Catholic Church on their own terms, that is as African American Catholics. By 1933, he had met White Catholics in New York who were willing to support work for Black Catholics, but on different terms: the work had to transcend the issue of race, and become an issue of Catholicity, of accepting all people equally as people; in short, of assimilating all peoples into the one fold of the church regardless of culture or color.

Although it was LaFarge's interracial movement that laid the foundation for Catholic participation in the Civil Rights movement, its membership and organization came largely from Turner's federation. More importantly, Turner and the FCC had made significant progress in presenting the concerns of Black Catholics on a national level, including a rare audience for laymen with the American bishops at their annual meeting in November, 1932. Any success that LaFarge and his movement may have had was clearly built on the 15 years struggles of Turner and the FCC.

As early as 1919, the Committee for the Advancement of Colored Catholics (CACC) sent a letter to the American Catholic bishops seeking to secure equality for African Americans within the church. In 1926, the Federated Colored Catholics (FCC) addressed another letter to the hierarchy deploring the general lack of progress made since the CACC sent its letter in 1919, particularly in the areas of African American clergy and education. The FCC's continued advocacy for the integration of Catholic institutions at their annual conventions provoked a discussion among the bishops in 1929 "on the Negro problem as it affects the activities of the [hierarchy and] concerning the attitude to take toward the Negro [sic] when he applies for a position, attendance at our schools, etc."

The crowning achievement of the FCC came, ironically, just as internal dissent cleft its national organization. In September, 1931, Thomas Wyatt Turner sought an audience with the hierarchy. Although they were not able to meet with the bishops formally, FCC members conferred informally with several bishops. In October, 1932, Turner submitted a letter exhorting the hierarchy to "repair the rent in the seamless garment of Christ [and] remove the sad division that exists in the otherwise glorious Catholic Church in this country," and requested "that in matters of national institutions, such as the Catholic University, and movements such as the National Catholic Welfare Conference, all bishops make it their personal concern that there be no exclusion of Colored Catholics either in theory or practice."

The bishops' Administrative Committee authorized Bishop Emmett Walsh of Charleston, South Carolina, and Archbishop John McNicholas of Cincinnati to meet with Turner and his associates about their petition. Prior to meeting with Turner, Eugene A. Clark, and H.M. Smith, Bishop Walsh expressed "the fear that Dr. Turner would try to force matters in an aggressive way."

When the sub-committee returned from their meeting with the FCC delegation, they reported "that they found these Colored Catholics to have a thoroughly proper attitude and that they were satisfied to do as the bishops wished." The Administrative Committee then authorized a survey "of the entire problem with regard to Colored Catholics" for 1933, and recommended that they find a priest "as soon as possible" to serve as an official liaison between the bishops and the FCC. Sadly, neither the survey was carried out nor a liaison appointed due to the FCC's split in 1932-1933.

After having labored so long and overcome such a variety of opposing racist views, it is tragic that the Federation was destroyed from within. Turner and his allies had gained some support for the Federation's program at the highest levels of the Catholic Church in the United States. One cannot help but wonder what the FCC could have accomplished had it remained a nationally unified force for change after April, 1933.

Shout Out

In 1889 Daniel Rudd did what we call today a "shout out."

Somehow, some way, Black Catholics needed to gather together to discuss the conditions of their people in America and within the Catholic Church.

Mr. Rudd was a noted and respected Black Catholic who was the founder of the first Black Catholic newspaper, "The Ohio Tribune," which was renamed that same year (1886) "The American Catholic Tribune."

As he traveled across the United States, covering stories, listening to his people and church leaders, he gained the idea of convening Black Catholic leaders.

Rudd was an activist who reminded the nation and the church that "the sacred rights of justice and of humanity are still sadly wounded," according to Father Cyprian Davis in his book *"Black Catholics in the United States."* With this rallying call, the Black Catholic Congress movement was established.

Cardinal James Gibbons was petitioned to lend support to this effort. Support was granted and history made. All bishops of the United States were invited to Washington, D.C., to stand with Black Catholic leaders as they created a plan to address both social justice issues and evangelization.

The congress members recognized that change must occur. First was education: "We pledge ourselves to aid in establishing ... Catholic schools." They singled out the need for trade schools, "where the hand of our youth may be trained as well as the mind and heart."

They made an "appeal to all labor organizations, trade unions, etc., to admit colored men within their ranks ... We appeal to all factory owners and operators, telegraph and railroad companies, store and shopkeepers, to give employment to colored people ... without discrimination and on the merit of their individual capacity."

They spoke of the children and the indigent, called for literary societies and the need of orphanages, hospitals and asylums. They urged for temperance "either individually or in the societies already existing in connection with the church," according to Father Davis.

Since this first congress in 1889, four more continued in the 19th century and three in the 20th century. Each congress designated a theme and created a plan of action.

The next Congress' (IX) focus is designed around leadership (in this new era of evangelization) to improve the spiritual, mental and physical conditions of African Americans. Under the theme, "Black Catholic Leadership in the 21st Century: Solidarity in Action," eight issues will be discussed – spirituality, parish life, youth and young adults, Catholic education, social justice, racism, Africa and HIV/AIDS.

Think about the eight issues proposed. What specifically needs to be addressed in these areas? They are broad topics, warranting specific discussion and action. What can be done to enhance ministry in those areas (on a diocesan and parish level)?

When Daniel Rudd did his "shout out" in 1889, who would have thought that his voice would be heard throughout the centuries into today? Some of the same issues that galvanized our people in the past still present challenges today.

Connections

Recently, I had the privilege to give a missionary talk to a parish in Louisville, Ky. Father Theodore "Ted" Sans, a teacher of some 26 years was my host. St. Albert the Great, has a very large school, three classes of each grade K - 6. One of the four local boys' high schools, Trinity High, has a freshman class of 394. The total enrollment is 1,382. I was impressed with the visible signs of Catholicism.

Since the Diocese of Louisville grew out of the Archdiocese of Baltimore, I made several references to the early priests, mostly Sulpicians, who were the pioneers in the wilderness, as Kentucky was called in the early 19th century. Stephen Badin, Charles Nerinckx, Martin Spalding, John Baptist David and Bishop Benedict Joseph Flaget were all from Maryland. The latter two were Sulpicians.

The Oblate Sisters have in their motherhouse chapel, a window honoring Bishop Flaget. The window depicts the bishop as he uttered a prophecy to the Sisters, "Today, you are four, in two years, you will be twelve." Sure enough, in two years the Oblate Sisters of Providence numbered 12.

Father Sans, being a history buff, offered to give me a tour of Catholic Louisville. After the noon Mass on Sunday, we headed for Bardstown, the seat of Catholicism in the Midwest. There I met Father Steve Pohl, pastor of St. Thomas parish. He was my guide.

Our first stop was the site of the first seminary of the diocese, an original log cabin. A sense of awe came over me when I stood on the holy ground once inhabited by holy men who migrated with Marylanders to minister to the Catholic population in Kentucky. The small space was unbelievable. The cabin originally belonged to a woman from Maryland named Ann Howard. When Bishop Flaget needed a seminary, Ms. Howard offered her home to the bishop and lived in one room on the bottom floor.

St. Thomas Church was the original seminary chapel. To my surprise, it is modeled after our own St. Mary's Seminary on Paca Street, smaller, but the same design. Because of the smaller size of the church, there are only 10 naves on the front of the building instead of 12.

We then traveled to Cistercian Monastery of Gethsemane whose location dates back to 1848. The original United States foundation was in Clementsville, Ky. In 1802, Father Vincent Smith, an African American, became a Trappist monk at Gethsemane and is buried in the cemetery. Also buried in the cemetery is Father Sans's great-great-great-grandfather, Zechariah Riney, who came to Kentucky from St. Mary's County, Maryland, in 1794 and was the first teacher of Abraham Lincoln.

Our next stop was Nazareth, where the Sisters of Charity of Nazareth have their motherhouse. Their chapel's architect designed the Louisville cathedral. Many of the buildings once used by the Sisters are now homes for the aging population.

The next site visited was St. Joseph's, the pro-cathedral of Bardstown. This was the first Catholic cathedral west of the Allegheny mountains. I was impressed with its Colonial-style architecture and the two statues on the front lawn. One statue was of Bishop Flaget and the other of Martin Spalding, who later became archbishop of Baltimore. It was Archbishop Spalding, who, in 1867 at the Second Plenary Council of Baltimore, pleaded with the American hierarchy to begin special efforts to evangelize the four million newly freed slaves. Archbishop Spalding's historic remark was, "If we lose this chance, opportunity may never happen again."

Another highlight of Bardstown is Daniel Rudd. Born into slavery in 1854, Rudd started a Black newspaper, The Catholic Tribune, and also started the National Black Catholic Congresses that continue to this day.

Singing the Song

As we enter a new millennium and celebrate Black history, "why not" answer the question, "Why does an organization called the National Black Catholic Congress exist?"

Why do people of African descent in the United States still ask the question, "how shall we sing the Lord's song in a strange land?"

In his book, *"Before the Mayflower, The History of Black America,"* Lerone Bennett, Jr. reported "the trials and triumphs of a group of Americans whose roots in American soil are deeper than the roots of the Puritans who arrived on the celebrated Mayflower a year after a 'Dutch man of war' deposited 20 Negroes in Jamestown."

The National Black Catholic Congress is part of the history of Black Catholics in the United States. As the Black Catholic historian, Father Cyprian Davis has written in his book, *"The History of Black Catholics in the United States,"* Black Catholics were a part of the settlements of the Spaniards and the French from the Gulf Coast and Florida to the Maryland plantations, from the Spanish Southwest to the Mississippi Valley and the Kentucky frontier.

There have been Black Catholics in this country from the time of the earliest settlers. During the earliest years in this country, Blacks have maintained their identity as African Americans and their pride in their Catholic identity.

The challenge to Blacks in this country has been to maintain their strong faith and to spread the good news among those of African descent who do not know the Lord. It was because of the many challenges which Blacks confronted that the Congress was born.

In a time when people of color were in many cases not welcomed in the church or into religious vocations, a group of lay persons with leadership provided by Daniel Rudd called for the first Black Lay Congress.

Daniel Rudd, born of slave parents in Bardstown, Ky., in 1854, became a strong and effective leader of the Negro race in the Catholic Church.

He was a newspaper publisher, a lecturer, a publicist and a well-known figure among the church hierarchy and among Catholic laypersons. He gave leadership to the movement which led to the convening of the first Black Catholic Lay Congress in 1889.

Four other Congresses were held in 1890, 1892, 1893 and 1894. The fifth and last Congress was held in Baltimore in 1894. Father Davis' book gives an excellent report on each of the Congresses, which addressed such issues as jobs, schools, housing, trade unionism, men's ministry, vocations, racism and Black Catholic theology. With these and other issues confronting Blacks in the 1800s, the 1900s reflected many of the same issues.

In the 1980s, almost 100 years after the first Black Catholic Lay Congress, the Congress movement was resurrected to provide a forum for the church serving persons of African descent to seek solutions to promote the concept that one could be Black and Catholic.

With three national Congresses being held in 1987, 1992 and 1997, the Congress movement, which through training, program development and networking, has opened many doors in the Catholic Church in the United States.

Persons of African descent are experiencing a new posture which proclaims that we are "strangers and sojourners no more." The Congress movement has been a force in "Opening wide the doors to Christ" so that those who work in parishes serving persons of African descent can now sing with increased pride at being Black and Catholic. "We can sing the Lord's song in a land which we have helped to build," to a rhythm that is understood by those with whom we share the good news of Jesus Christ.

Unfinished Business

About 3,000 African American Catholics and archdiocesan and pastoral Catholic leaders met at the ninth National Black Catholic Congress.

Their task is to complete some unfinished business that will promote African American leadership for the 21st century – forging solidarity in action.

In 1889 Daniel Rudd, the father of the Black Catholic congress movement, raised his voice to speak a new vision in hopes of creating a new plan of action for evangelization and leadership among people of color in the United States.

Rudd's idea of the Congress was to "gather and exchange views on questions affecting our race; then we can unite on a course of action. Let us stand forth and look at one another, forging bonds of community."

Why was such a gathering needed? Rudd wanted to get some business done because, "The Negro in this country is ostracized, abused, downtrodden and condemned; therefore, we need all the forces which we may bring to bear on our behalf."

Business was done at that first Congress. Delegates created a plan and declared a pledge: "We pledge ourselves to aid in establishing Catholic schools; to the practice of temperance; to address poor housing of our people; to speak and act on behalf of our children and indigents for the need of orphanages, hospitals and asylums; to appeal to all labor organizations so that fair employment of our people may be realized ... and to encourage the entire Catholic Church to work on these issues for the welfare of our entire people."

In addition to the above, the early pioneers of the Congress movement had a broad social justice agenda – attacking racism both here and in Africa. They were concerned with the plight of Africa and its people. Their business was also to deepen the spiritual lives of their people, to strengthen parish life and to promote the Catholic Church within the Negro community.

That's a whole lot of business to take care of, bearing on complicated political, sociological, educational and economic realities.

While there has been some progress, there remain many struggles that continue to bear on Black Catholics. Racism exists (articulated by Pope John Paul II), disguised yet accepted in many institutions, laws and policies both within the church and secular society at large.

Black Catholics continue to strive to be understood and appreciated as a people with a distinct spirituality impacted by culture. Parish life in the Black community is under siege as the clergy shortage becomes a reality.

Many of our youth and young adults feel underfed spiritually and are attracted to other Christian denominations. Too many of our people suffer under deplorable conditions, as poor education, joblessness and the string of illnesses brought on due to inadequate health opportunities as well as the violence that poverty causes.

Such conditions force Black Catholics to be clear and focused about a social justice agenda. The City of Baltimore has more cases of HIV/AIDS than all of the other counties and jurisdictions of Maryland put together. (Our people are suffering!) The plight of Africa, the home of our brothers and sisters as well as our ancestors, warrants our attention.

If Daniel Rudd would come back here today, I bet he would agree with me that there is still "some unfinished business to complete."

DANISE JONES DORSEY

A Sense of Urgency

"After this I looked and there before me was a great multitude" (Rev. 7:9NIV) more than 3,000 African American Catholics from Vermont to Texas and Florida to California. Lay leaders in the Roman Catholic Church proclaiming that "I'm Black, Catholic and proud!" Radiant, they were dressed in celebration clothes. Jubilant, they were ready to celebrate with deacons, priests, bishops and cardinals the word of God and the Eucharist!

As I looked out onto this multitude, I recalled St. John's revelation, "Then one of the elders asked me, these [in celebration clothes], who are they, and where did they come from?" I answered, "Sir, you know." And he said, "These are they who have come out of great tribulation; they have washed their robes ... in the blood of the Lamb" (Rev. 7:13, 14NIV). I thought, "Heaven must be like this!"

The National Black Catholic Congress was born more than 100 years ago out of the tribulation of Black Catholics. Although tribulation continues, undaunted African American Catholics convened for celebration and work!

During the days of the Congress, participants were called to develop a five-year action plan to implement eight principles. The principles are spirituality, social justice, parish life, Catholic education, youth and young adults, racism, Africa and HIV/AIDS. More than 3,000 participants had to be of one accord to adopt the action plan by consensus!

Bishop Eddie Long's book, "*Called To Conquer*," advises, "Just how do you get [3,000] people of one accord! Everyone must die to self.

The people of God must come to the point where they drop all of their personal agendas."

The designers of the consensus process allowed themselves to "die to self" and be used by the Holy Spirit to design a consensus model that accomplished the goal.

Two hundred people participated in the two-day workshop on the principle of social justice.

Father Bryan Massingale lectured on Catholic social teaching and the passion African American Catholics bring to the implementation of the teachings. Father Massingale concluded that passion is born of the lived experiences of African Americans in the church and in America!

The 200 passionate participants were asked to come to consensus on actions to be accomplished in one, three and five years. Motivated by a sense of urgency to address the social ills visited upon the "poor and vulnerable" in the dioceses, participants were committed to the goal of attaining one accord, creating the pathway to consensus.

The participants were to form their groups in the narrow meeting room. As a facilitator I wondered, "Oh Lord, how will the participants hear one another without disturbing the groups near them!"

Concerned, I thought, "The room sounds like a beehive! How will we ever get any work done?" Instantly, I realized the metaphor of a beehive was perfect. In spite of the sounds, emanating from the hive, the worker bees were focused and diligent as they accomplished the goal.

In the social justice workshop, the 200 participants came to consensus on the national action plan to be implemented by each diocese.

Within a year to plant the seed ... the participants agreed to initiate parish-based meetings to identify the social, economic and political needs of the parish community and ministerial ways to address them.

The sense of one accord, order and urgency spilled over to Sunday when the participants arrived for the 9 a.m. Mass. The final action plan was placed on each of the 3,000 seats in the auditorium!

Six weeks after the Congress, the sense of celebration, commitment to the eight principles, passion, being of one accord and the desire to accomplish the action plan is strong.

During a de-briefing meeting in Baltimore, participants who attended the Congress resolved "out of a sense of urgency" to work together. They "can't wait" to respond to the Gospel directive to address the needs of the poor and vulnerable in society.

MELVILLE W. PUGH, JR.

Sharing the Struggle

What is now the Archdiocese of Washington was originally part of the Archdiocese of Baltimore, the first archdiocese in the United States. In 1939 the Archdiocese of Washington was established and included the District of Columbia. Eight years later it was expanded to include the Maryland counties of Calvert, Charles, St. Mary's, Prince George's and Montgomery.

The Archdiocese of Washington marked its 50th anniversary in 1990. During this period, Black Catholics faced many challenges in their desire to be Black and Catholic. The theme of the anniversary celebration, "A Mosaic of Faith," symbolized the presence of several cultures in one faith. Black Catholics of the 21st century continue to articulate their concerns, to proclaim their rich heritage and to preserve it.

One struggle involved Catholic interracial and other social movements. The Catholic Interracial Council was designed to develop and implement strategies and programs to improve race relations within a particular parish. Thomas Wyatt Turner, a professor of biology at Howard University and a Black Catholic activist, called attention to the policies of Catholic education and racial segregation in church affairs.

The ministry of the Catholic Worker Movement focused on commitment to the poor and powerless regardless of race. Its co-founder, Dorothy Day, gave moral support to Black Catholic Llewellyn Scott when he began his lifework in Washington.

The Civil Rights movement of the 1960s found Black Catholics openly resisting all forms of segregation in America. The marches, protests, sit-ins, pray-ins and the inspiring leadership of Dr. Martin

Luther King, Jr. sparked a social revolution that shook the conscience and consciousness of America.

Another struggle involved the Black Catholic clergy, religious sisters and laity. The Civil Rights period stimulated a need for the Black community to join together for corrective action to fight the forces of poverty and prejudice.

Black Catholic clergy began to openly approach the church about racism and the need for Black Catholic leadership and visibility in the church in 1968. National Black Catholic organizations sprang up by the late 1960s – National Black Catholic Clergy Caucus and National Black Sisters Conference.

Acceptance of an archdiocesan secretariat for Black Catholics became a struggle. A group of Black Catholic leaders in Washington, D.C., in the 1970s met to form a united organizational project designed to assist the church in increasing its effectiveness in the Black community. This office was established in September, 1974.

At the same time, the archdiocese ordained its first Black Catholic bishop, Bishop Eugene A. Marino, S.S.J., as auxiliary bishop of Washington. The Archdiocese of Washington, with nearly 70,000 Black Catholics, represented the fourth largest number of Black Catholics in the United States.

Liturgical inculturation was celebrated at the first Black Catholic revival, "Jesus Made Us Free," in March, 1982. For four nights 1,000 worshippers went to St. Matthew's Cathedral for spiritual renewal in Christ led by a Black Catholic priest, the revivalist Father Giles Conwill. It featured the first gospel choir from combined parishes.

A few years prior to this revival there was serious discussion focusing on the desire of Black Catholics for liturgical expression uniquely suited to the Black cultural experience in America.

The final struggle has a national perspective, namely the National Black Catholic Congresses. These congresses affirmed the changed status and empowerment of Black Catholics. Five National Catholic Lay Congresses were held from 1889-94.

Nearly a century later, May 20-23, 1987, the sixth National Black Catholic Congress took place in Washington, D.C., at the Basilica of the National Shrine of the Immaculate Conception.

The national coordinator was Bishop John H. Ricard, S.S.J., then of Baltimore, and Therese Wilson Favors as executive director.

For Baltimore and Washington there are parallel struggles. Let us look to the future with hope, faith and love!

DEBORAH JOHNSON STERRETT

A Testimony of Faith

As a child I worshipped with my family in Apostolic and Baptist churches steeped in African tradition. But at 16, while attending St. Frances Academy, Baltimore, run by the Oblate Sisters of Providence, I converted to Catholicism.

At the same time I was undergoing a spiritual redevelopment in my new religion, I was also coming to grips with the racism and discrimination that peaked during the early 1960s. For the first time I was made keenly aware of my race, prejudice and injustice, and I immediately aligned myself with the cause of civil rights.

Answering the call to religious life that I first felt in my junior year, I joined the Oblates in 1965. I had not anticipated how much my journey of faith and service within religious life would be challenged by my efforts to fight against the racial injustice that permeated not only our society but also the Catholic Church.

Like many of my Black Catholic sisters and brothers, I sought to integrate my faith with my race, believing this surely could be realized in a church that has as its cornerstone the notion of universality and one body.

Many aspects of my faith were tested by the challenges of those early years in a church which I discovered was not very open to Blacks. Many African Americans were suspect of the church and its historical role in their oppression by acts of commission and omission.

And Black Catholics did not feel the church appreciated their faith, history or culture. I often found myself defending my faith to fellow Blacks and defending my Blackness to fellow Catholics.

When, in 1971, my faith journey took me from the convent to marriage and children, I joined several lay ministries of the church and instilled in my children a sense of duty to be active participants as well.

The mixed-raced Catholic church we attended, All Saints, was more welcoming of us and conscious of our heritage than the white churches we visited from time to time.

As my children grew in the faith, I witnessed their natural attraction to the Gospel Masses that were offered and to the homilists who would "preach like Baptists." Though they were Catholic all their lives, it was clear that they, like other Black Catholics, had a thirst for more African culture in the celebration of the liturgy.

This cause was addressed in the 1984 pastoral letter on evangelization from the country's Black bishops, "What We Have Seen and Heard." It sparked a greater sense of urgency in recognizing the benefits and obligations of Blacks in the church.

"There is a richness in our Black experience," the bishops told African Americans, "that we must share with the entire people of God." While urging Blacks to accept responsibility for evangelizing and teaching and witnessing to the faith, the bishops reminded us, too, that we should "not forget the devoted service that many white priests, vowed religious and laypersons gave to us as a people." They also encouraged the church to be open and responsive to the gifts and talents of Blacks, to take in the richness of Black culture.

As I have matured in my spirituality and taken many turns along my faith journey, I draw from the blessings of my uniqueness as an African American, a woman, a mother, a wife and as a Christian as I seek to live out my own salvation. I see the church growing in its consideration of all its members. I feel no conflict between my Blackness and Catholicism. I am a fully integrated individual. And I cannot help but marvel at this place of peace in which my spirit has settled, a place I would not be without my faith community.

By Leaps and Bounds

In the 1930s the Catholic Church was growing by leaps and bounds in Baltimore. Black Catholic growth was at an all-time high.

The year 1929 marked the 100th anniversary of the Oblate Sisters of Providence with Mother Consuella Clifford, O.S.P., serving as superior general. The Archdiocese of Baltimore included all of Baltimore, southern Maryland and parishes of Washington, D.C. (Washington became a separate archdiocese in 1939).

This was the same era in which St. Peter Claver parish would hold its May procession. Busloads of family and friends from St. Mary's County would travel to Baltimore to join thousands who would march in prayer and song along Pennsylvania Avenue.

At that time most Black Catholics worshipped in the city at St. Francis Xavier, St. Peter Claver, St. Pius and St. Monica (in South Baltimore, not far from Camden Yards). Staffed by the Society of the Sacred Heart – the Josephites – these parishes enjoyed growth in numbers and became central places for educational, social and cultural advancement of Black people.

The Josephites in these parishes were joined in ministry with the Oblate Sisters of Providence, the Franciscan Sisters of Glen Riddle and the Mission Helpers.

But, in Baltimore County, there was also a bustling, active group of Black Catholics in the small communities of Woodstock and Granite who worshipped at St. Alphonsus Rodriguez ministered by the Society of Jesus – Jesuits. The Sisters of Mercy provided religious education.

Local Historian Louis S. Diggs reports through interviews (from the book, "*Surviving In America*") some stories of Granite and Woodstock Black Catholics.

According to remarks by Josephine Jackson Tyler, in the 1930s most of the African Americans in Granite and Woodstock were Catholic. Other remembrances offered by Marva Bennett Kelly, Miriam Wilson Dorsey and Carmelita Wilson Ferguson paint an interesting account of how and why this area was so heavily populated by Black Catholics.

Marva Bennet Kelly's interview was loaded with historical information: "As far as I know, when the Jesuits came to Granite shortly after the end of the Civil War, my great-grandfather, Daniel Bennett, and his brother, Gabriel Bennett, came with the Jesuits from St. Mary's County, Maryland. I know that my ancestors were slaves to the Jesuits probably as long as the Jesuits have been in America."

Mrs. Bennett Kelly's great-great-great-grandfather was Harry Mahoney. Diggs' book reports a story rendered by Mrs. Bennett Kelly: "Harry Mahoney's heroic exploits during the War of 1812 are recorded in the histories of Maryland and St. Mary's County. While foreman at the Jesuit Manor at St. Indigoes, Mahoney single-handedly was responsible for saving the treasury of the Jesuit religious order at St. Indigoes from an attack by the British and leading to safety the women and children at St. Indigoes." Many Black Catholic families came with the Jesuits to Woodstock and Granite.

Two descendants of Gabriel Bennett, Miriam Wilson Bennett and Carmelita Wilson Ferguson, spoke of the religious devotion of their grandfather, Gabriel: "Our grandfather was truly a great man. He was looked up to and admired by all – both Black and White. All of the grandchildren wanted to walk down to his home and work in his garden.

"While you were there, you had to stop working and pray with him. He said his rosaries every day, and he always listened to the novena on the radio at 7 p.m. He worked at Woodstock College where he was the head cook. He sent all of his daughters to St. Frances Academy, and one, Mary Cecilia, became an Oblate Sister of Providence – Sister Theophane Bennett, O.S.P."

FATHER DONALD A. STERLING, D. MIN.

An Inclusive Era

Western European thought, traditions, values, secular affairs and pursuits have dominated the world for centuries. This "classical culture" was supposedly rooted philosophically and artistically in ancient Greece. Recent historiography, however, reveals that most of this Greek philosophy was based on Egyptian/African philosophy.

This classical culture developed a normative definition of God, society, family, church and state. The culture, values, traditions, and so on, of other peoples were considered savage or barbaric. Through the years preceding the Second Vatican Council, the church was a great preserver and reservoir of classical culture.

Historically and consistently the Catholic Church in the Americas embraced classical culture's mentality. Church prelates, religious communities and laity alike systemically participated in the oppression of minorities – directly or indirectly – oftentimes as racists, slave owners, progenitors of slave children, segregationists, oppressors and suppressors of cultures.

There was often a discernible difference of opinion and responsible action between the Vatican and the United States hierarchy with regard to slavery and race relations. The Vatican consistently directed the United States hierarchy to respond to these issues as agents of change rather than facilitators of the status quo.

The relationship of diverse cultures and religion must be addressed in order to construct a truthful and inclusive history. The pains and scars of racism rooted in slavery are deep and real throughout American society. The Christian community is not excluded. Truth has often been denied or erased. Yet centuries later, truth cries out for a hearing.

A consequence of classical culture is mis-education. For example, one of the best-kept secrets of history is the identity, role and prominence of Blacks in world history. Generally we have been led to believe that people of African descent became Catholic as a result of conversion in the New World. The reality is quite different.

According to Father Cyprian Davis, O.S.B., author of *The History of Black Catholics in the United States*, "the church originally was not European; it was Mediterranean ... Ethiopia was a Christian nation earlier than many nations in Europe. It was a Christian kingdom before Ireland was evangelized, before most of North Germany was evangelized and before Poland was a Catholic country."

Dark-skinned people were politically, culturally and numerically dominant in the ancient world and parented civilized society as we know it today.

Why the need to speak of Blacks or Black Catholics or Black Catholic history?

• All people, Black Catholics included, deserve the recognition and appreciation of their contributions to history.

• Black Catholics throughout history have enriched the Catholic Church and rightfully deserve recognition as do classical culture's children.

• Black Catholics have given great gifts to the Catholic Church that have been whitewashed (for example, monasticism (Moses the Black); martyrs such as Perpetua and Felicitas; the great theologian St. Augustine and others); popes (St. Victor I, St. Miltiades, St. Gelasius); and great saints including Monica and Maurice.

• Christians can be counted among racists.

• Ethnicity and race have been largely ignored in Christian education.

• Ignorance is at the core of racism.

• It is healthy to address the subject of race from the standpoint of information rather than emotion.

There can be no such thing as a color-blind society until the unique contributions of other cultures and peoples are affirmed, embraced and respected.

Today, we are literally witnessing a healthy modification of classical culture to include the reality of cultural diversity. Traditional Catholic history must include Black Catholic history.

MELVILLE W. PUGH, JR.

First Black Priests

The first Black priests in the United States were brothers, specifically three of the sons of Michael Morris Healy and Mary Eliza Clark. Michael M. Healy immigrated to Georgia from Ireland in 1816. He possessed a spirit of adventure, ambition to acquire wealth, sound business sense and he eventually became an owner of plantations and a number of slaves.

In 1829 he bought a 385 acre farm on the Ocmulgee River near Macon, Ga. Here he built a large family house and log cabins for his slaves. Michael married Mary Eliza Clark, one of his slaves. She was 16-years old, intelligent and became an ideal wife and mother.

The Healys had 10 children: James Augustine, Hugh Clark, Patrick Francis, Alexander Sherwood, Martha Ann, Michael Jr., Eugene (passed in infancy), Josephine, Eliza and Eugene (named for his deceased brother).

The Healy children were not reared as slaves. Michael Healy sent his sons to the North for an education as well as for freedom. It appears that Michael's friendship with Bishop John Fitzpatrick of Boston changed the life of his sons. Bishop Fitzpatrick encouraged Healy to send his sons to study at Holy Cross College in Worcester, Mass. The boys were enrolled in this Jesuit school in the summer of 1844 and baptized in November the same year.

James Healy (1830-1900) entered the seminary in Montreal in the fall of 1849. His mother died suddenly in May 1850, followed by the demise of his father in August. A devastated James arranged for the sale of the family property and the 57 slaves. Then he devised a plan so that his siblings would be able to have an adequate scale of living from the proceeds of the Healy estate.

In 1852 James transferred from the seminary in Montreal to the Sulpician Seminary at Issyles-Molineaux, Paris. Also, Alexander entered the same seminary in the fall of 1852. Hugh (1832-1852) saw him off and died from typhoid fever.

James was ordained a priest in the Cathedral of Notre Dame, June 1854. He became the personal secretary of Bishop Fitzpatrick, was named chancellor of the Boston diocese and later became vicar general. In 1875 James was named bishop of Portland, Maine, making him the first Black bishop in the United States. Bishop Healy was recognized as an excellent preacher. He participated in the Third Plenary Council of Baltimore in 1884.

Patrick Francis Healy (1834-1910) was ordained a priest in 1864 in Liege and stayed at the University of Louvain in Belgium one additional year to complete his study for a doctorate.

Patrick began teaching philosophy at Georgetown College in 1866. Later, at the same institution he became vice-president and in 1873 vice-rector and in 1874 president. He had a dream, which resulted in transforming Georgetown into a university model. At the center of his dream campus was a huge building, which would contain classrooms, science labs and dormitories. This structure known as Healy Hall is still a part of the campus.

Alexander Sherwood Healy (1836-1875) studied at the Institute of the Apollinaris, the faculty of canon law at the Lateran University. He was ordained in Rome on December 15, 1858, and two years later received a doctorate. Bishop John Williams of Boston selected Father Alexander as his theologian at the Second Plenary Council of Baltimore in 1866. He was gifted and talented, a popular preacher and canon lawyer.

The Healy Brothers were an unusual trio. Patrick concealed his African origins while James and Sherwood acted in an opposite manner. The Healy brothers were not solidly connected with the Black community or the Black Catholic community. They were silent on racial bigotry, equal rights and Southern violence against Blacks. Why did they avoid reaching out for justice and opportunity for people of African descent?

Three Pioneers

Father Charles Randolph Uncles, a native Baltimorean and parishioner of St. Francis Xavier, Baltimore, became the first Colored seminarian to be educated and ordained a priest in the United States.

He was ordained by Cardinal James Gibbons at the then Cathedral of the Assumption in Baltimore in December, 1891 and celebrated his first Mass Christmas Day at St. Francis Xavier.

Charles Randolph was the son of Lorenzo and Anna Marie (Buchanan) Uncles, who were born free and faithful Catholics. Charles Randolph had the desire to be a priest at an early age. He dedicated himself to acquiring an education and following the tenets of the Catholic Church.

He attended Baltimore Normal School for Teachers and taught in Baltimore County public schools. He was fluent in Latin, Greek and French. Father Uncles was sponsored by Father Slattery, who was the American provincial of the Mill Hill Order, to attend St. Hyacinthe College in Quebec, Canada. He finished his studies there with the highest grades in his class.

In the meantime, Cardinal Herbert Vaughn, who was the spiritual leader of the Mill Hill Order of England, arrived in America in 1871. By the latter part of 1888, Cardinal Vaughn formed St. Joseph Seminary in Baltimore, and Father Uncles was one of the first candidates. It was here that he received tonsure (the ceremony in which some or all of the hair is clipped as an entrance into religious status) by Cardinal Gibbons.

Father Uncles, along with four other priests, was instrumental in forming the Society of St. Joseph of the Sacred Heart, known as the Josephites, in 1893.

From 1891-1925 Father Uncles taught mainly in Epiphany College in Baltimore and Newburgh, N.Y. While residing at Epiphany College he fell ill and died July 21, 1933. He is buried at Calvary Cemetery, Josephite Plot, in Newburgh.

For the first time since its inception in 1893, the Josephites did not have a Black priest because Father John Dorsey, who was fully educated and ordained in the United States in 1902, had died in 1926. Father John Joseph Plantevigne had been ordained a Josephite in 1907 and died in 1913.

Father Dorsey, a Baltimorean, was baptized at St. Francis Xavier in 1875. Like Father Uncles, he, too, celebrated his first Mass at St. Francis Xavier. Father Dorsey was noted for his impressive and spiritual homilies and for his dedication in bringing converts into the Catholic faith.

In his tour of the south, he became friends with one of America's foremost Black leaders, Booker T. Washington, founder of Tuskegee Institute in Alabama. Father Dorsey was given the privilege to celebrate Mass at the institute the first Sunday of each month.

In February, 1905, Father Dorsey became the first Black pastor in the United States as the spiritual leader of St. Peter Catholic Church in Pine Bluff, Ark. He was also one of the founders of the Knights of Peter Claver, which commenced November, 1909. He was their national chaplain from its beginning until 1923.

Father Dorsey was the pastor of St. Monica in South Baltimore until his death, June 20, 1926. He is interred in New Cathedral Cemetery in Baltimore.

Father Plantevigne was born on a small farm in Louisiana. He received the vows of Holy Orders in 1907 as a Josephite. He celebrated his first Mass at St. Francis Xavier and later became the assistant pastor.

While at St. Francis, Father Plantevigne contracted tuberculosis and died in January, 1913 at age 42. There was not another Black Josephite ordained until 1941 with Father Charles H. Hall.

However minute or great the efforts of the three pioneers of Black Catholicism, Fathers Uncles, Dorsey and Plantevigne, their names and deeds are forever posted in the history book of time.

Somebody to Look Up To

He was one inch over six feet tall, but that did not make him someone to look up to. He hailed tall in many arenas of life particularly in the age in which he lived: freeman, journalist, priest, scholar – mastering four languages, historian and teacher.

A building at 607 Pennsylvania Avenue in Baltimore City was named after Father Charles Randolph Uncles, S.S.J., the first Black to study in and be ordained from a U.S. seminary on June 17. He was also co-founder of the USA St. Joseph's Society of the Sacred Heart. Father Uncles, a quiet and modest man, became somebody to look up to because of his walk of faith.

The archives at the Josephite Motherhouse under the directorship of Father Peter Hogan, S.S.J., are loaded with information about Father Uncles.

According to an article written by Father Hogan (in The Josephite Harvest – Winter 1991), Father Uncles was born on November 6, 1859, the son of Lorenzo and Anna Marie (nee Buchanan). Both of his parents were Catholic and free. Lorenzo worked as a machinist for the Baltimore and Ohio Railroad.

Father Uncles had one sibling, a brother – Norman Uncles. The family attended St. Francis Xavier – the oldest Black Catholic congregation in the United States. Although Father Uncles was born in 1859, he was not baptized until 1875. He was confirmed in 1878 and ordained December 19, 1891.

Given the hour of racial challenge, fluent bigotry, anti-Catholic sentiment, segregation and societal ambivalence in the United States,

Father Uncles as a young man "studied Latin, Greek and French in his free time."

For a sustained period of time, W.A. Willyam taught him in a Catholic school. Mr. Willyam once studied for the priesthood at Rome's Urban College from 1855-62 and organized a short-lived Black Catholic Journal titled "Truth Communicator" issued from St. Francis Xavier Church in Baltimore before Daniel Rudd's American Catholic Tribune.

For two years, the future priest attended a segregated public school. He worked part-time as a journalist/printer to finance his way through secondary school. In 1878, Father Uncles attended the Baltimore Normal School for Teachers and from 1880-83 taught in Baltimore County Public Schools.

"Participating in the life of Black Catholics at St. Francis Xavier Church … the idea of the priesthood took hold of Charles and he enrolled in St. Hyacinthe College, Canada, in 1883 where he studied until 1888. Always an excellent student, Uncles graduated first in his class" according to Father Hogan's article in The Josephite Harvest – Winter, 1991.

In 1888, Uncles began his theology studies at St. Mary's Seminary-Paca Street, here in Baltimore while residing at St. Joseph's Seminary on 607 Pennsylvania Avenue.

Uncles became the first student of color at St. Mary's Seminary. After ordination in 1891, Father Uncles dedicated his priestly ministry to teaching at Epiphany Apostolic College in Walbrook, Md. (the Walbrook Junction near St. Cecilia's) from 1891-1925. When Epiphany moved near Newburgh, N.Y., in 1925, Father Uncles moved also, teaching there until his death in 1933.

Father Uncles' jubilee became a grand occasion for Baltimore's Black Catholics. On January 7, 1917, Father Uncles celebrated solemn High Mass at St. Francis Xavier Church. The following day a reception was held in his honor at St. Peter Claver Church Hall concluding with evening vespers at St. Barnabas Church. Distinguished guests at the reception included church, civic and educational leaders such as Father John Henry Dorsey, the second Black Josephite; City Councilman Harry S. Cummings and Dean William Pickens of Morgan College.

Father Uncles did not build an edifice such as the one named after him this week, but he did build scholarly excellence and priestly formation within those whom he taught. He made his mark and today an edifice stands in his honor.

SISTER M. REGINALD GERDES, O.S.P.

Oblate Service

The Oblates Sisters of Providence were founded in Maryland in 1829. It was and is the first African American sisterhood in America.

Both the foundress, Mother Mary Elizabeth Lange, and the founder, Father James Joubert, S.S., were exiles from the French colony of St. Dominque. The slave revolt on the island caused a large influx of natives, both Black and White, to the shores of Maryland.

As early as 1796, Father William DuBourg started a class in Christian doctrine for the African American population of Baltimore in the lower chapel of St. Mary's Seminary. As time moved on, other priests were given charge of this project.

Finally, Father Joubert became the instructor for the catechism class. The children, being a generation removed from their native language and not fluent in English, had difficulty with the lessons.

The problem was solved when a young lady who conducted a school in Fells Point was recommended to Father Joubert. This woman, Elizabeth Lange, mentioned that she not only wished to help educate children in the love of God but also wished to dedicate her life to God as a religious.

Since there were no options available to Elizabeth Lange, she and Father Joubert decided to start a sisterhood for African American women. Thus, the birth of the Oblate Sisters of Providence.

Their year of preparation for the sisterhood took the form of starting a Catholic school for African American children. Today the school, St. Frances Academy, is still in existence on East Chase Street.

The sisters shared their home with widows and orphans. Academics, fine arts, household arts as well as rules of conduct for young ladies were part of the curriculum.

All classes were centered around religion. On Sundays, in addition to Mass, there were instructions, choir practice, recitation of the office and benediction. The chapel on Richmond Street (now the intersection of Park and Read streets) was the center for Black Catholic worship.

In 1832 the Oblates ministered to African Americans during the cholera epidemic. When times were hard financially the sisters were not looked upon with favor by ecclesiastical authorities. The Oblates continued their spiritual and corporal works of mercy by taking in washing and ironing. Gradually conditions improved.

From Richmond Street the sisters ventured out to minister to other areas of the city. In 1852, with the help of a Redemptorist priest, Father Thaddeus Anwander, the sisters built a school for boys. They also built a hall to hold meetings and other such events. In 1857 the Oblates purchased a building from the Redempotorist Fathers at St. Michael's parish and began a school for African Americans of the area.

Also in 1857, at the request of Father William Clark, S.J., the Oblate sisters took residence on Wayne Street. They began their first parish school at St. Joseph in South Baltimore.

The year 1864 found the Oblates, with the help of Father Miller, S.J., opening a free school for girls in conjunction with St. Frances Academy.

The following year the Oblates institutionalized their orphanage. There were now three institutions: St. Frances Academy, St. Frances Orphanage and St. Frances Free School. Also in the 1860s, the Oblates started a widow's home and a branch of St. Frances Academy in Fells Point.

The Oblate sisters worked with both the Jesuit Fathers and the Mill Hill Josephites in evangelizing and educating Black Catholics.

SISTER M. REGINALD GERDES, O.S.P.

TWO PART SERIES:

By Her Works

On July 2, 1829, four Black women met in a row house in Baltimore to pronounce simple vows. When the ceremony was over a new order of nuns, the Oblate Sisters of Providence, had been born within the Catholic Church.

This community, composed of free Black women living in a slave-holding state, came into being as a direct result of the San Dominique (Haitian) slave uprising in 1719. Because the slave revolt focused on property as well as plantation owners, many free mulattoes fled the island. Some of the refugees sought safety on nearby islands in the Caribbean. Others set sail for America.

Among those who fled the island was Elizabeth Lange. Oral tradition states that she sailed to Cuba, then Charleston and finally to Baltimore. It was in this antebellum city that Elizabeth Lange gathered women who were to defy the existing institutions and bring into being a school and religious community for Black women.

When Elizabeth arrived in Baltimore, she had four strikes against her: she was Black in a slave holding state, a woman in a male-dominated society, a Catholic at a time when it was not popular to be Catholic and she spoke French in an English city.

But Elizabeth was a spiritual and spirited woman. Her background and determination helped her to cope with those obstacles. The early works of the Oblate Sisters grew out of Elizabeth's willingness to serve the church and to serve her people.

At the time of Elizabeth's entry to Baltimore, there were many Black refugees from San Dominique. Their children were growing up in a slave society. Their traditions were being passed down onto youngsters as best they could. Seeing the lack of educational opportunities available for Black young ladies, Elizabeth Lange decided to take action. Fortunately, Providence provided Elizabeth with friends and benefactors who were foreign to American soil and themselves victims of violence from other revolutions. Such persons knew well the meaning of foreigner in a foreign land.

That Elizabeth Lange (later Mother Mary Lange) was a spiritual woman is evidenced by the fact that in her early years she sought spiritual direction. Her director turned out to be none other than the president of St. Mary's Seminary.

That she was an educator is indicated by the fact that she started a school for free Black girls. That she was a refined person is seen in the inclusion of music, classics and fine arts in the curriculum. School records from 1830s and '40s show students involved in choirs, concerts and recitals. Mother Mary encouraged her students to strive for excellence. The students competed for medals and awards in various subjects.

Faculty gave their yearly exams from St. Mary's Seminary in the early years and later by the Jesuits from Loyola College.

In 1828, it is recorded that Mother Mary took in children to be educated for free. Later, when news reached the Sisters that two little girls were motherless, she went to the house and brought the children to the convent. One year after the establishment of the Order, the Sisters began taking in widows and elderly women who had no place to go in their old age. The Sisters even helped nurse Black inmates in the almshouse during a cholera epidemic.

Scripture and religious instruction were offered to the young ladies as a legacy to pass on to others. Mother Mary opened her church doors to all for Mass, Benediction and other spiritual gatherings.

In addition to Sunday morning liturgy, there were vespers in the afternoon, religious instruction classes and sodalities. The first African American lay society took root at the Oblate Convent Chapel on Richmond Street.

In today's language, in celebrating the 175th anniversary of the Oblate Sisters of Providence, we can really say in African American parlance, that Mother Mary Lange was a woman who "walked her talk."

Mother Mary Lange by her works was a religious revolutionary. As such, her sufferings were great. Hardships of a special nature entered her life in the 1840s. Sulpician Father James Joubert, the Oblates' spiritual director died in 1843. Many of her French friends moved elsewhere. The financial picture was so bad that Mother Lange and her

Sisters took in washing, ironing and sewing as a means of support.

The then archbishop of Baltimore was a native of Maryland. His family owned slaves. Seeing the poverty of the sisters, Archbishop Eccleston suggested that the Sisters disband. Mother Lange said, "No."

During the mid-19th century, one can only imagine the "shocked" Catholic population when a Black woman refused to follow the suggestions of a White bishop. Yet, the archbishop did not dissolve the community. Providence provided for the young African American community.

What were the works of Mother Mary Lange? We know of her private school in the early 1820s, of her academy in 1828 and of her religious foundation in 1829. But, there was also an orphanage, a widow's home, spiritual direction, religious education classes and vocational training.

The early Sisters did home visiting and conducted night schools so Black adults could learn to read and write. When the Civil War was over, Baltimore was flooded with Black war orphans. Mother Mary gathered 60 of them and began a new era of caring for destitute children.

One knows Mother Mary Lange as a religious pioneer. A careful study of her life shows her as a social radical, a religious radical.

It was not easy to be a free Black teaching within the confines of the Catholic Church. At that time there were theologians arguing in Rome that Black people have no souls. On this side of the Atlantic, there was the archbishop telling Mother Mary to disband her community and become servant girls.

After the death of the first director, the Sisters had no one to minister to them spiritually. Deaths in the community were frequent. Mother Mary, humanly speaking, had grown weary and tired. A striking blow came when one of the original four members of the order abandoned the order.

Sister Theresa, a blue-eyed blond mulatto, left Baltimore for Monroe, Mich. Sister Theresa established a school and a new order of nuns. Both institutions founded by Sister Theresa became white organizations.

Within a year, another of Mother Lange's Sisters left for Michigan. Was the pain of being a free Black woman in slave Maryland too great to bear? Did the nuns who left find it easier to cross the color line and move geographically and physically into the white world?

A third nun had intended to follow the path to Michigan. However, while preparing to move westward, she received a letter saying, "Do not come for you are too dark of colour."

There were Catholics who thought it disgraceful that Black women should wear a holy habit. There were those who physically threatened the Sisters.

Mother Lange knew triumph, but she also knew ridicule. There were two incidents when an angry mob broke down the front door. In the 1860's, while teaching in Philadelphia, the Sisters were repeatedly forced from the sidewalks. She experienced many setbacks.

Each apparent failure and success was a step in the accomplishment of His work. She did not despair or become despondent because she possessed the combination of faith and hope. Mother Mary Lange knew that He who cares for the lilies of the fields and birds of the air would provide for her, her sisters, and her students.

The Pride of Baltimore

As the baton of leadership is passed among the Oblate Sisters of Providence, Baltimoreans step to the plate.

Sister Mary Annette Beecham, O.S.P., a former parishioner of St. Pius V and St. Edward, was installed as superior general and Sister Mary Ricardo Maddox, O.S.P., a former parishioner of St. Peter Claver, as assistant superior general. Both are 1961 graduates of St. Frances Academy, Baltimore.

In telling her story, Sister Annette shares "that all of my foundational knowledge and sense of spirituality is rooted in my family and the Oblate Sisters of Providence. God fashioned me through family in Baltimore, Wilmington and Virginia.

"The beginning of my calling started in the primary grades when I observed boys and girls in my class without adequate clothing, milk money or food for lunch. When I asked about this, I was told that these children were orphans. Many days I shared my lunch with them, deciding that one day I would own an orphanage and give children everything they needed.

"I believe that this desire was God's way of leading me to a life of service because it intensified and never left me. I was inspired by the Oblate sisters' strong sense of selflessness, the sincere, ever-present dedication and commitment manifested in their ministry of service to others.

"As I matured in my community, I noted that the Oblate sisters were women of prayer, and this full commitment of service to others that inspired me was not a surface activity but rooted in a relationship with

God. In a word, providence!

"My dream for the future of the Oblate sisters are rooted in our Pastoral Plan:

• To continue to live the legacy of Mother Lange and Father Joubert

• To live as true witnesses of Christ in these difficult times

• To follow the dictates of the Holy Spirit

• To emphasize the message of evangelization that Jesus is our Lord and Savior

"As Oblates, we face the challenge of radical conversion: to be true witnesses of Christ in these times of violence, racism, hopelessness and lovelessness; to be courageous and accountable women of integrity living the legacy of Mother Lange and Father Joubert."

Sister Ricardo is the 12th and youngest child of George and Augusta Maddox. "I came from a very supportive, faith-filled family," she said. "My parents struggled and relied on the Lord." Mr. and Mrs. Maddox came from St. Mary's County (where the Catholic faith flourished among Blacks) and were married in historic St. Augustine Church in Washington, D.C. Sister Ricardo served St. Augustine as a teacher for five years and as principal for 10 years.

In 1962 Sister Ricardo became the second daughter of the Maddoxes to become an Oblate. Her older sister, Sister Ann Joseph Maddox, O.S.P., led the way.

In grade school Sister Ricardo sensed the "spirit of a vocation, and in high school the thought became more prevalent. In addition to family, the Franciscan Sisters of Glen Riddle, parishioners and the Oblate sisters who trusted in Divine Providence shaped my vocation, in which I am blest." Her connection with the Catholic Youth Organization and the Legion of Mary gave great support. "I know that the Lord kept his hands on me all the time," she said.

"After graduating from high school and a year of employment, September 8, 1962 (the feast day of St. Peter Claver) my parents took me to the front door of the motherhouse on Gun Road – a dream fulfilled. I remembered thinking, 'I will always be able to carry the light of courage and faith that burned in the heart of Mother Lange' and 'Lord, make me an instrument of thy peace' became my motto. As an Oblate, I am looking for a preferred and better world in which I will continue to be an instrument of peace."

SISTER M. ANNETTE BEECHAM, O.S.P

God's Promise to Provide

In the midst of a rainy downpour, over 500 people joined the Oblate Sisters of Providence as we began a year of celebration moving toward the 175th anniversary of our founding. Celebrations of this nature always awaken within those involved a need to look back at the past, examine the present and do a little more than hope for the future. As I reflected on our history, our present day story and our vision and plans for the future, I was reminded of the scriptural reference from Isaiah, "You Lord give perfect peace to those who keep their purpose firm and put their trust in you."

Our purpose was made firm as we placed our trust in the Lord, through two distinct yet connected events. On June 13, 1828, 175 years ago, three pioneer Oblates established St. Frances Academy, the first formal day school for Black students under Roman Catholic auspices in the Archdiocese of Baltimore. Their focus was to offer an all-encompassing education. Their aim was to prepare students for life, encouraging them on levels of their day-to-day experiences. In this same year, Mother Lange and our founding Sisters began a year of spiritual preparation and training before professing vows of chastity, poverty and obedience.

The historic formal founding of the Oblate Sisters of Providence took place at 610 George Street during the 6 a.m. liturgy on July 2, 1829. It was in this setting that Sister Mary Lange, Sister Mary Frances Balas, Sister Mary Rose Boegue and Sister Mary Theresa Duchemin became a religious congregation, the first of its kind.

These courageous Oblate Sisters of Providence wore the distinctive garb of a religious in spite of some Catholics who resented seeing these women of color in a religious habit. They stood on God's promise to provide as they followed their desire to become members of a religious order and pursue their aspirations for the Black children under their care.

What a great vision they held in their hearts! What faith they manifested as they continually placed this vision before God, trusting in divine providence!

Today we spread the good news of Christ by the integrity of our faith, our love for God and our firm hope and trust in divine providence as we continue the legacy of Mother Mary Lange, O.S.P., and Father James Nicholas Joubert, S.S. The Oblate Sisters of Providence continue to serve God and God's people through ministries of education, child care, social and tutorial assistance, pastoral and Hispanic service, programs of spirituality and religious formation. We sponsor St. Frances Academy, Mount Providence Child Development Center, Mount Providence Reading Center and the Mary Elizabeth Lange Center. In all of these we share our charism which is to bring joy, healing and the liberating, redemptive love of Christ to those in need. This is the legacy passed on to us for this millennium.

Prayer, deliberation and discernment led us to develop a pastoral plan for the future. The goals and objectives in this plan assist us in maintaining our beliefs as Oblate Sisters of Providence and in fulfilling our mission to embrace and to serve others with the same compassion with which Christ embraces us, sharing with all the unconditional love of the Lord.

It has been 175 years and the Oblate Sisters of Providence still stand on God's promise to provide.

SISTER M. REGINALD GERDES, O.S.P.

Another Pioneer

Theresa Duchemin was superior general of the Oblate Sisters of Providence in 1844. As an African American community in slave-holding Maryland, times were hard.

The Sulpician founder of the Oblates, Father Joubert, had died a year earlier, and the sisters had no spiritual director. The archbishop of Baltimore had no use for the colored sisters, suggesting that they disband and find employment in the better households of Maryland.

Theresa was the first African American Oblate. Born in Baltimore in 1810, she was the mulatto daughter of a San Dominique mother and an English father. Her father, Major Arthur Howard, was a relative of the great John Eager Howard whose family sold the archdiocese the property on which the Baltimore Basilica was built.

Theresa's mother, like Mother Mary Lange, was a refugee from the island of San Dominique. Both were ardent Catholics, French-speaking and educated. Mother Lange operated a school for free girls of color in Baltimore.

Theresa's mother, Betsy, was a nurse. Whether Betsy and Mother Lange knew each other or not, we do not know. We do know that Betsy eventually placed her daughter, Theresa, in Mother Lange's school, located somewhere in Fells Point.

The basement chapel of St. Mary's Seminary was an official place of worship for laity, including African American Catholics. Here, the Sulpician fathers conducted a catechism class for children. When the newly ordained priest, Father Joubert, took over the class, he was at a loss in instructing African American youth. Coming to his aid was

Elizabeth Lange, an experienced educator.

During the course of the conversation, the idea of a religious community surfaced. Since there were no available options for women of color, the two decided to start a community for such women.

After Archbishop Whitfield gave approval for the community, Father Joubert and Mother Lange set up a plan of operation. The catechism class was expanded to a school. A house was rented at 5 St. Mary's Court, and in 1828 St. Frances Academy was born.

Theresa was 18-years old when she petitioned Mary Lange to become a religious, making Theresa one of the original Oblate Sisters of Providence. Well versed in English, Theresa taught languages in the newly created school. Her first love, however, was always French.

Having no priest to serve the community after Father Joubert's death in 1843, the Oblates resorted to walking to what is now the Shrine of St. Alphonsus, Baltimore, for their religious exercises.

Furthermore, the superior general of the Sulpician fathers ruled that the Sulpician priest free themselves of all ministries other than that of preparing young men for the priesthood.

Redemptorist Father Louis Gillet ministered for a time at St. James, Baltimore. Father Gillet was not fluent in German, so he served the French-speaking Oblates whenever possible. Father Gillet became a friend of Theresa and asked her to work with him in Michigan.

During the absence of a religious director, Father Czackert, another Redemptorist, became Theresa's personal spiritual adviser. When Father Gillet returned to Detroit, he made preparations for Theresa to start a school. She complied with Father Gillet's request.

On September 8, 1845, with the blessings of both the superior of the Redemptorists, Father Czackert, and the superior of the Sulpicians, Father Deluol, Theresa left the Oblate community and headed west. In November Theresa and another Oblate sister who followed her to Monroe made vows in a new community dedicated to the education of youth. This community became known as Sisters, Servants of the Immaculate Heart of Mary.

This congregation evolved into three separate communities: IHM Monroe, IHM Philadelphia and IHM Scranton. Today the Immaculate Heart sisters operate three colleges, many high schools and serve in a variety of ministries.

Theresa Duchemin, an African American woman, was indeed a pioneer in Catholic education.

SISTER M. REGINALD GERDES, O.S.P.

Providing a Catholic Education

Throughout the history of the Oblate Sisters of Providence, providence has always played a major role. Founded in 1829, in the slave state of Maryland, this congregation of mulatto women stamped the church of Baltimore with a new ministry – that of providing a Catholic education for the people of color.

Mother Mary Lange, a Catholic French-speaking immigrant from San Dominique, now known as Haiti, fled her country as a result of the slave uprising there. Providentially, this brave woman landed in Baltimore, took up residence in Fells Point and attended St. Patrick Church. Baltimore, at the time, was heavily populated with French immigrants.

In fact, there were three populations of French people. There were the true French, so to speak, the refugees from San Dominique and the Arcadians, themselves refugees from Canada. Most were Catholics. In addition, the French Sulpicians ran the diocese, had charge of the seminary and as early as 1796 established a catechism class for African Americans along with Sunday services for the Black Catholics. Providence led Mother Lange to the right city.

After teaching in the most exclusive school in Baltimore, James Joubert, another refugee from St. Dominique, decided to answer the call to become a priest. As a priest at St. Mary's Seminary, young Father Joubert was given the assignment of teaching catechism to the children of color. Many of the children being of French origin could not read and perhaps could not understand English either. Father Joubert needed help. His next move was to find some good women who could assist him with his classes.

The superior of the seminary, Father Marie Tessier, had just the right person: a Catholic, French, educated free woman of color who was conducting her own private school. When Lange and Father Joubert met, providence was in motion.

Elizabeth told Father Joubert that she would teach the children their religion but she really wanted to dedicate her life to God as a religious. Father Joubert and Elizabeth Lange decided to start such a religious community.

The two went to seek the permission of Archbishop Marechal who decided the time was not ripe. Archbishop Marechal died shortly afterwards and his successor, Archbishop Whitfield told the two souls to begin whenever they were ready. Plans for a congregation of African American women religious were about to become a reality. Father Joubert rented a house on St. Mary's Court and a program of formation began.

Three young women and an older student from Elizabeth's school were the founders of the Oblate Sisters of Providence. As part of their formation program, the future sisters started a school.

Elizabeth brought her experience from her private school for African American girls. Father Joubert used his experience from the Madam Lacombe School for wealthy young ladies. The school started with 21 pupils, nine of whom were orphans. Today that school is called St. Frances Academy.

Providing Religion

Who were those who stepped up to serve Black Catholics? They are a diverse and courageous collection of historical figures. Some of the major groups and individuals are noted here.

Sulpicians (1796–1843)

When the gentlemen of St. Sulpice came to America in 1791, their primary goal was to establish a seminary in the New World. Establish a seminary they did. They also established a college, became pastors of churches, were spiritual directors of women religious, held numerous positions in the hierarchy of the archdiocese and of special interest to African American Catholics, served the people of color in Baltimore.

Father William DuBourg, later archbishop of New Orleans, initiated catechism classes for the African American children. Father Marie Tessier took over the job. He expanded the ministry to include spiritual direction and a spiritual reading program that is documented as a lending library.

There was a Catholic lay society, moderated by Father John Hickey, S.S., called The Holy Family Society. Composed of both men and women, the organization was renowned for its good works. Because Father Tessier was such a detail person, he kept an excellent record of all his penitents' first Communions, Easter duties, confirmations and baptisms. Father Tessier was also instrumental in arranging the meeting between Father Joubert and Mother Lange, which led to the formation of St. Frances Academy and the Oblate Sisters of Providence.

Redemptorists (1847–1860)

In 1843, Archbishop Eccleston invited the Sons of St. Alphonsus to come to Baltimore to evangelize the growing German population of Baltimore City. The year 1843 was a significant one for Black Catholics. It was the year of Father Joubert's death and the beginning of the end of the Sulpician's special ministry to African Americans.

The Oblate Sisters' convent on Richmond Street was the center of worship for the Black Catholic community. Without a regular priest to offer Mass, the congregation eventually went elsewhere to worship. The above mentioned Archbishop Eccleston saw no reason for the colored nuns to exist. The Sisters who had no priest to minister to them walked down Park Avenue to St. Alphonsus for the sacraments.

In 1847, at the request of Father John Neumann, a Redemptorist was reluctantly given the permission to become the spiritual director of the Oblate Sisters. His name, Father Thaddeus Anwander. He encouraged the Oblates to open a school for the colored children in St. Michael parish. Father Anwander was able to build the St. Frances Male School, start various religious societies for the laity, recommend a young Black man for the priesthood, hold grandiose religious ceremonies for Confirmation, recruit women for the religious life and renovate St. Frances' Chapel.

In addition to Fathers Anwander and Neumann, other Redemptorists who served the Black community were Fathers Chazkert, Smulders, Porrier, Gillet, Seelos, Vogin and Krause. It is interesting to note that John Neumann is now St. John Neumann and Father Seelos is Blessed Francis Xavier Seelos.

In 1860, the Jesuits assumed the spiritual direction of the Oblates. The congregation continued, but at a different location. In 1866, Father Peter Miller, S.J., along with the Oblates Sisters initiated The St. Frances Orphanage. Most supportive of this endeavor were the priests and parishioners of St. Francis Xavier parish.

Josephite Fathers

In 1871, the Josephite Fathers of the Sacred Heart of Foreign Missions came to Baltimore from Mill Hill, England, to evangelize the African American. After 20 years of ministry, the group decided to divide its ministry. In 1891, the priests had a year to decide whether they wanted to return to England or to remain in the United States. Luckily, some men decided to remain in Baltimore. That group became known as the Josephite Fathers of the Sacred Heart. Their headquarters is here in Baltimore and their name and work is legend.

SISTER M. REGINALD GERDES, O.S.P.

Children of the House

From the very first day of St. Frances Academy's operation, the Oblate Sisters of Providence cared for homeless children. In 1828 the girls were called "children of the house." That phrase simply meant that the sisters would provide a home, an education and a spiritual life for the young ladies.

In the early days, begging was a way of financing their orphanage. However, it was under the Jesuit Father Peter Miller that the Oblates established a formal orphan asylum.

Following is an account of the establishment of St. Frances Orphan Asylum as written by Mother Theresa Willingham in 1866:

"In September 1866, Rev. Peter Miller, S.J., director of the Oblate Sisters of Providence, seeing the great need of an asylum for children, who had no one to care for them, engaged the sisters to open a home for orphan girls.

"A house in the rear of the convent on Richmond Street (now Read Street) was selected, as it was convenient for the sisters to go from one house to the other. Tyson Street was a back street. In a short time, everything was arranged to open the asylum."

The asylum opened October 2, 1866, with six orphans. Two nuns, Sisters Bernard and Agatha, and a postulant were appointed to take charge.

Soon the house on Tyson was too small, so the sisters moved to Richmond Street, next to the convent. Father Miller, pastor of St. Frances Xavier Church, interested the congregation in the work. He also established the St. Frances Orphan Relief Association.

The ladies did their duty with heart and soul. Father Miller also gave all he could to help the work. He used to call the asylum his joy.

In 1870 the sisters were compelled to leave Richmond Street, as the city extended Park Street through the buildings. They were obliged to build not only the convent and academy but also the orphan asylum.

In August, 1870 they left Richmond Street for their new home. It was in an unfinished state, rooms unplastered and others only floored, in a vacant lot with no fence. For a long time, the sisters could do nothing to remedy this. When Father Miller died September 26, 1887, it was a day of sorrow and general mourning.

In 1884 Father Alfred B. Leeson, a Mill Hill Josephite, was appointed director of the Oblates. Father Leeson played a great part in finishing the building. The building was plastered, painted, and much needed rooms were made such as dormitories, clothes room, kitchen and dinning room for the orphans.

Later, at his suggestion, many other improvements were made. The orphans now numbered 90 children. The only support besides the sisters was the alms of the charitable public.

An interesting note in the Oblate sisters' care of orphans is the New York connection. In 1875 the Sisters of Charity of New York made an arrangement with the Oblates to care for African American female orphans once they grew out of babyhood. The children were transported to Baltimore, and the only identification was a white wristband bearing the name of the child.

The orphanage continued until 1926 when Archbishop Michael J. Curley put all orphans under the bureau of Catholic Charities. Then the Franciscan Sisters of Baltimore took over the care for orphans, although the Oblate sisters continued to care for orphans in other parts of the United States. The Oblates in Baltimore then made teaching their priority in Baltimore.

For more information about the story of Black Catholics in the United States, read the book, *The History of Black Catholics in the United States*, by Father Cyprian Davis, O.S.B.

SISTER M. REGINALD GERDES, O.S.P.

Slavery to Freedom

O n the third shelf in Archives "B" room at Mount Providence Convent in Arbutus there is a box titled, "manumission papers."

A manumission paper was a legal document issued by a government agency during slavery times, stating that the person whose name appeared on the document was no longer a slave and entitled to the privileges of a free person.

In the history of the Oblate Sisters of Providence, there has been many a woman whose freedom came from a manumission paper and not from a birthright. In the days of both the Oblate community and St. Frances Academy, the concept and reality of slavery played a major role in accepting women for the religious life and others as pupils for the school.

Two little girls cared for by their grandmother enrolled in St. Frances Academy. Their grandmother became ill and was concerned about the children's future. This situation worried Father Joubert who had a special interest in the family. The children's grandmother had been a slave and not knowing whether or not the children were slaves, Father Joubert bought them and then set them free by obtaining a document of manumission for 50 cents.

The year was 1832, and the girls, Angelica Gideon and her sister, Sarah, were able to live with the sisters and attend St. Frances Academy. Angelica became an Oblate Sister of Providence. Although Father Joubert did not live long enough to see it happen, Sister Angelica became the principal of the Oblate's first school for boys, located on what is now Tyson Street. Sarah eventually moved to St. Louis, lived there until her death and remembered the sisters in her will.

Another interesting manumission story is that of the Finnall children whose owner, and probably father, had enrolled them in St. Frances Academy. Following is the manumission document of Elizabeth Finnall.

"Be it known by those present, that I, William Finnall, of the county of Warren in the State of Mississippi, now being present in the City of Cincinnati in the State of Ohio for and in consideration of the sum of five dollars in hand paid the receipt of which I do by acknowledge, set free, emancipate and fully and forever discharge from any [sic] and claims of servitude of slavery, Elizabeth Finnall.

"The said Elizabeth is the daughter of a Mulatto woman named 'Peggy' now deceased whom formerly owed service to me under the laws of Mississippi as a slave. Elizabeth Finnall was born on the fourth day of April in the year Eighteen forty-nine, is of fair complexion with regular features and has straight Black hair and Black eyes. She has no special marks.

"The said Elizabeth Finnall is in the City of Baltimore, in the State of Maryland, and is a pupil at St. Frances School at 48 Richmond Street in said city. And it is my intention to manumit and discharge her, Elizabeth Finnall, from any servitude of slavery either to myself, my heirs or to any person or persons, as she, the said Elizabeth Finnall, shall be henceforth to all intent and purposes, a free person and entitled to all rights, privileges and amenities of a free person of color in any of the States of this Union or elsewhere.

"In testimony whereof I have hereunto subscribed my name and affixed my seal at said City of Cincinnati in the State of Ohio, on this third day of September in the year Eighteen hundred and fifty six."

"In presence of F. Bungoyane, J.M. Mitchel. William Finnall"

The same type document manumitted Elizabeth's brother, James, also a student at St. Frances Boys School on Tyson Street.

DR. KIRK P. GADDY

Continue Marching

November is a time that Catholics discuss our saints, remember our deceased brothers and sisters and prepare for Thanksgiving. November is also the month designated as Black Catholic History Month. This month is a time to celebrate and retell the stories of faith, struggle and victory of the "saints" that marched before us.

Historian Father Cyprian Davis, O.S.B., gives much to ponder in his book, *The History of Black Catholics in the United States*. The stories reported unveil a series of actions by people of faith who marched through the centuries advancing the faith and the church within the Black community.

He poignantly reports that Black Catholics in the United States have continually blessed the Catholic Church with their time, talents and treasures. "Faithful soldiers" such as Mother Elizabeth Lange, Daniel Rudd, Pierre Toussaint, Henriette DeLille, Lincoln and Julia Valle, Father Augustus Tolton, William Henry Smith, William S. Lofton, Father John Dorsey, S.S.J., Father Charles Uncles, S.S.J., Mathilda Beasley and Maria Becraft marched down through the centuries, promoting spiritual and religious reform as well as social, educational and economic justice.

The "saints" were about overcoming racism, sexism and bigotry. They were also about establishing community, dignity and spiritual refreshment for their people and the church at large. Under the collective banner, "If I can help somebody along the way, if I can show somebody that he's travelin' wrong, then my living shall not be in vain."

Mother Elizabeth Lange spoke for herself and defined herself at a time when Black women were not respected and appreciated. She marched through evil and ignorance and became the foundress of the Oblate Sisters of Providence.

Daniel Rudd rallied people of color to speak for themselves and to call the church to be what the church is – a universal church – through the Black Catholic Congress Movement.

Pierre Toussaint, born in 1766 in Santo Domingo, was a helper of the poor in New York. At his funeral in 1853 there was talk about his cause for sainthood by mourners both Black and white.

Henriette DeLille opened in New Orleans a school for young girls, daughters of free people of color, who were educated by day while slaves received religious instruction at night. This was at a time when it was illegal for people of color to assemble.

Lincoln and Julia Valle were probably the first husband–and–wife evangelists who were Black and Catholic. They were administrators of a mission in Milwaukee that eventually became St. Benedict the Moor parish in 1910.

Father Augustus Tolton, born a slave in Ralls County, Mo., in 1854 gave witness of faithful endurance. Tolton became a priest in 1886, ordained in Rome to minister in the United States. His mother, Martha Tolton, is a strong example of a mother seeking freedom "at all cost" for her children.

In the 1880s two men joined Daniel Rudd in the congress movement: William Henry Smith and William S. Lofton. Both were Black Catholics from Washington, D.C., with distinguished professions. Mr. Smith was a librarian of the House of Representatives Library and Mr. Lofton, a dentist.

Fathers Charles Uncles and John Dorsey, both Josephites and Baltimoreans, marched through rough times to make a path to the priesthood for future Black men.

Mathilda Beasley of Savannah gave money and land to build a church in 1878. She established a convent and orphanage for people of color in Wilkes County, Ga., in 1891.

Maria Becraft (1805-33) marched through Washington, D.C., opening a school when she was only 15-years old. Her father had been a slave in the household of Charles Carroll of Carrollton.

There is so much more to share. Please read *The History of Black Catholics in the United States* and witness for yourself the stories of the "saints, marching through" the centuries.

SISTER M. REGINALD GERDES, O.S.P.

The Noels

When I was an eighth-grader at Corpus Christi School in New Orleans, a Sister of the Blessed Sacrament gave me a book. Its title was *"The Family That Overtook Christ."* This story was about a Trappist monk, St. Bernard of Clairveaux, and his very religious family. This article is about another family who overtook Christ. A Black slave refugee family from San Dominique overtook Christ right here in our own city of Baltimore. The family's name was Noel.

Just as St. Bernard was the key figure in his family overtaking Christ, Mother Louise Noel is the key figure in the Noel family that overtook Christ.

When the refugees from San Dominique arrived in America, many plantation owners brought their slaves with them. One such plantation owner was William Harmon who gave his slaves, Andre and Laurette Noel, their freedom. In addition, Mr. Harmon endowed the Noels with abundant property in one of the most elite and wealthy sections of Wilmington, Del.

The Noels lived on French Street and had an inn at the end of their property where travelers stopped on their way north. The Noels acquired the property in 1816 and one year later their daughter, Louise, was born. The Noels also had another daughter, Laurette, and one son. The father, Andre Noel, worked as a barber catering to the elite.

Among the people who lodged at the Noel's Inn were Bishop Francis Kendrick and Michael O'Connor, who later became bishop of Pittsburgh and eventually joined the Jesuits. Father O'Connor was stationed in Baltimore and was responsible for raising funds for the formation of the first building of St. Francis Xavier parish.

Sulpicians who stayed at the Noel's Inn included Fathers Tessier, Joubert and Dubourg, later bishop of New Orleans.

The Noel's Inn can actually be called the first rectory in the Delaware and Chestnut Hill area. Patrick Kenny, the first priest in the diocese, lived with the Noels while doing missionary work, but boarded his horse elsewhere.

At the request of Bishop Kendrick, the Noels took in as a young priest, George Carroll, who later became the first bishop of the Diocese of Covington.

Originally educated as a Quaker, Marie Louise Noel was placed as a boarder with the Oblate Sisters in Baltimore. Later, Madame Noel and the 10-year-old orphan she cared for decided to board with the Sisters. The orphan's name was Athanase De Mourier. In time, both mother and daughter decided to become Oblate Sisters. On May 18, 1834, Madame Noel turned all her possessions over to the Sisters.

The family brought more than wealth to the community. They were educated by the Quakers and were excellent needle workers. Madame Noel's other daughter also became an Oblate Sister.

In religion, the Noels had the following religious names: Madame Noel became Sister Chantal; Laurette became Sister Mary James after Father Joubert; Marie Louise; became Sister Louise; and Athanase became Sister Mary Joseph. Sister Chantal served as assistant superior just three years after taking vows. She was nominated for superior general in 1841 but died on the eve of the election day just four years after the death of her daughter, Sister Mary James.

Sister Louise was elected superior general in 1844. Mother Louise ruled the Oblate community for 45 years as superior general. Her rule of life was, "Never take back what you once have given to God."

Mother Louise died on March 27, 1885, at the age of 68.

The Fire of Faith

William Augustine Williams was born in Forksville, Va., of free parents about 1836. He loved to study and had an instinctive feeling for the Catholic faith. He showed a love of God and worship that was noticed by missionary priests from Baltimore. He converted to Catholicism and was baptized at age 14. He proved to be a brilliant student and as a young man voiced his aspiration to be a priest. He was encouraged to move to Baltimore to continue his education.

Williams' stay in Baltimore is not well documented, in fact, material concerning his life is scanty and exiguous. His desire to be a priest was so profound that several of the ecclesiastical hierarchy of Baltimore suggested that he attend Propaganda Fide in Rome, Italy. The Propaganda Fide, started in 1625, prepared men for the priesthood.

Father Thaddeus Anwander, a Redemptorist who had been the spiritual advisor for the Oblate Sisters of Providence, wrote a letter to the college inquiring about the acceptance of Williams for the novitiate. Archbishop Francis Patrick Kenrick of Baltimore signed the letter and attached a letter of recommendation. Bishop Amadeus Rappe of Cleveland, Ohio, also sent a letter of recommendation to Propaganda Fide. All inquirers were informed that Williams had been admitted and would commence his studies in the fall of 1855.

Archbishop Kendrick corresponded with the prefect of the college stating that Williams could not find a position as a priest in the United States because of race prejudice. In another letter in 1859, Bishop Rappe, suggested that Williams should be assigned to Haiti, where prejudices against Negroes were not so strong. He was offered a place

101

in Liberia after ordination. Williams declined the offer, proclaiming his desire to be a priest in his native land.

Williams studied at the college for six years but never received the sacrament of holy orders. He was constantly reminded of his status as a Negro. After careful deliberation and the advice of his instructors, he came to the conclusion that he had no calling for churchly duties, so he prepared to return to the states. He found work in Liverpool, England, and later attended All Hallows College in Dublin, Ireland.

Williams returned to the United States and periodically wrote letters in Italian to the Propaganda Fide concerning his activities in Baltimore. He told of his present position as a teacher at St. Francis Xavier Church School. He told of establishing a school for Negro boys. He spoke of the condition of the Negro since emancipation and that he was publishing a newspaper named the True Communicator for their benefit. He wrote of his desire to be a priest.

In his lectures, he spoke of his stay in Rome. Each day the students would take a walk around the streets of Rome. They frequently met Pope Pius IX taking his daily constitution. The pope singled out Williams for a salutation. The pope referred to him as "The pope's little Black." Williams said this was one of his dearest memories of his stay in Rome.

In some instances, his surname is spelled Williams, Willyams and Willyms. In the Baltimore City directory, Williams is identified as being a teacher and living on West Biddle Street. In the 1870 census, he was listed as a Black male school teacher born in Virginia and living in the ninth ward of Baltimore City. He was hired by Enoch Pratt as a cataloger and later became an assistant librarian at Catholic University in Washington, D.C.

Further, his obituary survives with title emblazoned: "A Famous Colored Catholic." In smaller print: "Death of William A. Williams, once Propaganda Student in Rome." He died in May 1904. The funeral Mass was held at St. Benedict the Moor Catholic Church where he had been the sacristan for several years.

Williams possessed impeccable character, a love for his race and a deep desire to be a priest. He was a linguist and was in the process of translating the life of St. Benedict from Italian to English.

DR. BEVERLY A. CARROLL

Emulating Our Ancestors

February is Black History Month. It was created by Dr. Carter G. Woodson, an historian, in 1926 as Negro History Week in response to a lack of information about the contributions of Black people in America.

Traditionally it is a commemoration of the past, directed toward honoring and emulating the ancestors and understanding the meaning and obligations of our history. It is Fannie Lou Hamer who taught us that there are two things we should all care about: never to forget where we came from and always praise the bridges that carried us over.

Many African Americans celebrate Kwanzaa and on the fifth day the principle, Nia (purpose), captures our attention and reflection. Nia calls every African American to focus his or her life on a purpose, one that strengthens and builds up people and the community-at-large.

Nia embodies the intent of Black History Month. When we celebrate Nia we are called to embrace this principle by commemorating the past in pursuit of its lessons and in honor of its models of human excellence, our ancestors. The practice of Nia offers, too, a time of recommitment to our highest cultural ideals in our ongoing effort to always bring forth the best of African cultural thought and practice.

Black History Month celebrations aim to achieve the above, not for a 28-day study, but for long-term effects toward rebuilding, transformation and liberation. This kind of an agenda must not get lost March 1, especially now when we are all struggling with the many changes forced upon us. Especially now when the question arises (by some) "of the value of Black life" at the same time when our Catholic teaching clearly purports that all life is sacred. For these reasons why not celebrate the lives and contributions of African Americans throughout the entire year?

Everybody studies history in a different way. Some of us appreciate a study of past events; others find particular interest in the life and development of an individual, a people or an institution. All is worthwhile investigation for reflection.

Desmond Tutu once said, "history is like beauty; it depends largely on the beholder." We behold that history is being made now by those who walk among us. Let us lift up their lives and learn from their footprints. In understanding these stories we gain hope, recognize progress and allow history to "carry us over."

ELLEN T. DUTTON

A People Story

Notable Black Catholics were asked to share their answers to two questions: What did it take for you to get where you are today? What or who strengthened you along the way?

Their answers revealed that they constantly defined, redefined and evaluated their purpose (Nia) to bring about progress, success and strength, not just for themselves but for their family, church and community.

Booker T. Washington wrote, "To be successful, grow to the point where you completely forget yourself; that is, to lose yourself in a great cause."

Councilwoman Agnes Welch, a parishioner and corporator at St. Edward, Baltimore, has lost herself in many great causes. Her special interest in the elderly, children, Black adult male health programs and women's issues makes her a "change-maker" within the community and the church. She made her mark as a delegate to the Democratic National Convention and served three terms on the Electoral College.

In the 1960s Councilwoman Welch actively worked to establish equal opportunities for Black staff, students and teachers within our Catholic school system. She reports that her "thrust into national, regional and local politics stems from her faith and belief that with God a single person and a single act of faith makes the difference." It is the combination of single acts of faith which has contributed to the public service career of Councilwoman Welch.

Herman Williams Jr., chief of the Baltimore City Fire Department and a parishioner at St. Cecilia, Baltimore, said "hard work and dedication" set the stage for his success.

He entered the Fire Department during the days of open segregation and discrimination. Struggle for him became a form of education. Father Marion Bascom, appointed as a commissioner of the Fire Board, made the first promotion of Black firefighters and was responsible for changing many existing policies. Chief Williams benefited from the advocacy of Father Bascom but not without using his own personal gifts of leadership.

Chief Williams gives credit to the Urban League and George Russell, the first Black judge on Maryland's Supreme Court, for their contributions to open opportunities of service at every level for all Americans. "My faith in God sustained me in those early days of segregation and prejudice," Chief Williams said. "God continues to give me the strength to do his will as I face another plateau in my life – retirement."

Dr. Marcellina M. Brooks gives great direction to others through her various education missions. She was a teacher, principal and the first Black woman to become president of Bowie State College, Bowie (1983-90). Dr. Brooks, director of The Center of Excellence in Urban Education at Coppin State College, University of Maryland System, Baltimore, serves as a leading voice, advocate and "bridge builder" in the various halls of education within Maryland.

This "love for learning" came from devoted parents who stressed the importance of faith and education to their 10 children. Dr. Brooks completed undergraduate and graduate work at Loyola College in Baltimore, at a time when very few Blacks walked the "halls."

Today she is very proud of her work on the board of Cardinal Shehan School, Baltimore, and her role as the newly elected chairperson of the Mother Lange Guild promoting the cause of Mother Lange's beatification.

"I am strengthened by God," said the St. Pius X, Bowie, parishioner, "and the belief that we are put here on Earth to serve God, our church and community."

These stories give witness to the power of parental example, working together and direction of purpose. But they also lift up the value of "connections." Hortense Canady writes: "Examine the histories of successful Black women and men who are in the forefront of serving their community or country; almost without exception, one will find a strong connection to the Black college, the Black church or both."

The Effect of Inspiration

Inspired by the lives of honorable people and the way they go about forging change and advancement can cause a domino effect.

What caused a person to get politically involved when Black women were not supposed to be so bold? What causes one's dedication to a business in the midst of rapid change and getting through the Depression? Victorine Quille Adams and J. Albert Maddox Sr. were inspired.

For Mrs. Adams, it started at a meeting in the Elk's Hall where Adam Clayton Powell and William Dawson were guest speakers. This took place in the late 1940s when an elected Baltimore City official said publicly, "I know I'm going to win re-election, but I want the Negro vote for the plurality it offers."

Mrs. Adams was infuriated at the man's gall in assuming Blacks had little political savvy about registration and voting. This negative experience gave way to inspiring Mrs. Adams to do something which had not been done before.

It was then that the idea of organizing Negro women in Baltimore was born. Friends who became loyal supporters helped form the Colored Democratic Women's Committee in 1956. The late Lloyal Randolph, president of the Democratic Men's Committee, was a staunch supporter.

In 1958 Dr. Carl Murphy, The Afro-American's publisher and CEO, and Dr. Willard Allen felt that a strong movement was needed among the women that included all women.

The late Ethel Rich along with Mrs. Adams conceived the concept of "woman power" as a means of mobilizing all women for political information and power. They trained members as registrars to register prospective voters, campaigned as an independent bipartisan organization, initiated "citizen alert" to keep the public informed of issues, initiated the first Fuel Fund in Baltimore and visited regularly the General Assembly and U.S. Congress to lobby.

All along this group of women did their part in the advancement of the civil rights movement. Now "woman power" is in its 43rd year of service to the community.

Mrs. Adams was an organizer within our parish – St. Peter Claver, Baltimore – in which she led several fundraising initiatives. As a life-long member, Mrs. Adams chaired the earliest Woman's Day celebration and was an integral part of the altar guild.

Mr. Maddox was inspired by his father, Gabriel B. Maddox. He said that this kind of inspiration and faith in God can take you a long way.

In 1907, Mr. Maddox's father established Maddox Printing Company on Druid Hill Avenue in West Baltimore. This was a Black-owned and operated business, family-centered, with special outreach to the faith communities.

Mr. Maddox grew up in the family business along with his brothers. During World War II, Mr. Maddox was drafted into the Army. When he returned home in 1946, his father had passed. Mr. Maddox and his two brothers, Gabriel Jr. and Frank, joined forces and operated their father's business.

For several years Mr. Maddox worked for The Afro-American. In 1954 he and his brother, Frank, established Time Printers Inc. In 1980 Frank Maddox retired. J. Albert operated the business with the help of his children, both male and female.

Today, the business is operating with four generations of the Maddox family.

"Know your craft, apply yourself, have faith in God" are Mr. Maddox's words to live by. "As we entered this new century, we are mindful of the fact that within the matter of less than six years, the Maddox family will celebrate a full centenary of association with the graphic arts in Baltimore. It takes dedication, diligence and discipline to stay in business for this length of time," Mr. Maddox said.

Inspiration is a powerful gift, and it indeed has a domino effect. Look at how many lives were inspired through the inspiration gained by Victorine Quille Adams and J. Albert Maddox Sr.

Lives of Inspiration

B lack History Month offers the opportunity to share a story of a people – past and present. The lives and experiences of Black Catholics today who are making history right in front of our eyes provide inspiration and revelation on "how success was gained." A proverb from Botswana says, "A person is a person through other people."

Barry X. Simms, anchor/reporter at WBAL-TV 11, talks about many people who gave shape to his thinking and aspirations.

On entering Mount St. Joseph High School, Baltimore, Mr. Simms knew what profession he wanted to pursue. He remembers looking at the news and saying to himself, "I can do that," and went about making decisions and connections to achieve this goal.

His first high school counselor encouraged him to pursue a career in print journalism. Mr. Simms wanted to be in television news so he switched counselors. His second counselor proved to be the right match.

While in high school Mr. Simms was introduced to several movers and shakers in radio and television. Mary Claiborne, noted radio celebrity at WWIN, became a mentor. "Ms. Claiborne opened doors for me. She talked with me. She walked with me," Mr. Simms said. Another individual who made a difference was Phyllis Shelton, formerly with WJZ-TV who coordinated a program for young people interested in the media. Many others assisted him during internships and at WISN-TV in Milwaukee.

He also speaks of his parents' consistent advocacy in acquiring a good education. For them, education was power.

Today Mr. Simms spends significant time in mentoring and encouraging young people. Many of his speaking engagements promote self-determination, fulfilling educational goals, developing a personal relationship with God and giving back to the community

Her fascination and intrigue with the trial of Angela Davis made a mark on Glendora C. Hughes, general counsel for the State of Maryland, Commission on Human Relations.

"My family was living in California in the '60s and early '70s, and although very young I became interested in Angela Davis' story as well as what was going on with the Black Panthers," Ms. Hughes explained.

She shared this interest with her father, Elwood P. Hughes, who taught and affirmed her in being an independent thinker. Her father cautioned her that one who "listens to the beat of their own drum can sometimes find themselves in a dangerous enterprise, take the risks and see what happens."

While in college Ms. Hughes decided to pursue a career in law. She remembers thinking, "I've never seen a Black lawyer."

Anchored by her father's confidence that "there isn't anything you cannot do," she studied law and met a great influence in her life – Judge Milton Allen.

Judge Allen was not only a lawyer but also a judge. He took a particular interest in Ms. Hughes and in many Black law students. He selected Ms. Hughes to serve as his law clerk. This gave her invaluable experiences and introduced her to numerous resources.

All of these connections and experiences led Ms. Hughes to the position she now holds. She is an activist outside the courtroom, too. Her faith compels and supports her. She is involved in many projects and forums that challenge racism and encourages racial healing.

These two "people stories" and others reported have led us to the insight that "when success is gained, it is crafted by the community and not merely by individuals."

Mr. Simms and Ms. Hughes realized success because the family, community and church chose to get involved with their careers. People had faith in them.

Benjamin Mays wrote: "We live by faith in others. But most of all we must live by faith in ourselves – faith to believe that we can develop into useful men and women."

A People Story

Here are two stories of successful and notable Black Catholics of Baltimore.

"A look at death can change you" says Julia Roberta March of March Funeral Homes.

At age five, two of her dear playmates' mothers died, and the children's suffering left an indelible mark on Mrs. March. She became afraid of the dead.

Eventually, Roberta married William C. March. While working at the Post Office, one evening William shared with his wife his interest in going to school to be a mortician. This troubled Roberta for her fear remained. They had an honest conversation and Mr. March assured his wife that if her strong feelings continued, he would withdraw from school and not pursue a practice.

Mr. March completed school and opened a small business in the basement of their home. One day, Mr. March needed someone to do the hair and dress a woman. His first contact disappointed him with unsatisfactory services. He shared this with his wife and then went on to his other job at the Post Office. While Mr. March was at work, Mrs. March got to work! "I do my own hair and I can help out."

On arriving home, William was pleasantly surprised at the care rendered by his wife. Her husband encouraged her to become a licensed and certified funeral director.

"It wasn't easy," says Mrs. March. "We were still raising our children and new in the business but I had some wind beneath my wings – my husband."

Mrs. March shared another significant move for the family business. "Witnessing the untimely death of youth and reaching out to hurting families, our daughter, Annette March Grier, RN, suggested that counseling services were needed." We agreed and now provide counseling sessions at no cost. "After all, we shaped our lives and our business on the golden rule, *Do unto others as you would want done unto you*," says Julia Roberta March.

Growing up in Trinidad, educated by the Holy Ghost Fathers and being hospitalized with eczema all impacted the career path/vocation of Dr. Laurence Scipio, director of Medical Affairs at Bon Secours Hospital and parishioner of St. Mary's in Annapolis.

At age seven or eight Dr. Scipio found himself in the hospital with eczema. "I remember sneaking down to the first floor and peaking through the Operating Room and being fascinated about the workings inside. But up until high school I contemplated the priesthood," said Dr. Scipio.

However, the vicar for the Holy Ghost Fathers shared, "you have a calling, not priesthood but one that works for the healing of people in another way."

Dr. Scipio found himself struck with these words and remembered his attraction to healing in his early years. "Coming from the Caribbean, I saw many sick and impoverished people. I could reach the masses of people through the healing ministry."

At Howard University Hospital, Dr. Scipio interned with Dr. George W. Jones. "Dr Jones and I automatically connected. We had many meaningful exchanges and upon graduation, he offered me a position in urology with him."

Today Dr. Scipio serves the masses in need of healing at Bon Secours Hospital and through his private practice in urology.

Oprah Winfrey said, "For everyone of us that succeeds, it's because there's somebody there to show you the way out. Sometimes that light comes from your family, other times from teachers and ministers." Our stories support this truth. There are many notable Black Catholics who tell of the light given as they journeyed in their professions.

Financiers of Service

In 1920, just after World War I, times were tough for Black people. For the most part, Baltimore was a city practicing segregation within its neighborhoods and churches. The summer of 1920 was filled with racial tension, race riots swept Chicago, the rise of the Klu Klux Klan and an outbreak of several anti-Semitism riots spread throughout the country.

While there were many Black laborers willing to work, industries were reluctant to employ people of color. This plight of limited financial resources placed extra strain on Black families and the community at large. It was at this stage in history that T. Wallis Lansey opened Ideal Federal Savings Bank in 1920, the oldest African American bank in Maryland.

Yvonne F. Lansey, president and CEO of Ideal says "My father's faith in God was a powerful mobilizing force. People's faith, dreams and vision create institutions however, hard work, conservative investments plus experience gives longevity. I am the third generation of Lanseys in the business." Now 81 years later, Ideal continues to operate and serve the under-served.

Ms. Lansey knew that knowledge was power and that experience is twin to knowledge. Educated at Morgan State University and later receiving a MBA in finance, she led Ideal into a new age of computerized systems and comprehensive services for customers. She worked and she worked hard from her early years at Druid Hill Laundry, to the Federal Reserve Bank to Westinghouse. Her experiences at these institutions laid the foundation for her present role as a bank executive.

Ms. Lansey has used her business and financial expertise to help Immaculate Conception Church in Baltimore through the Heritage of Hope Campaign. A lifetime member, Ms. Lansey yearns for the day when our very own archdiocese increases support of Black financial institutions.

Growing up in a large family and seeing your father work three jobs (one full time, one part time and one weekend job) marked Thomas A. Wilson, Jr. for life.

From childhood, Mr. Wilson had an interest in money – a kind of money (not greed) that would make life a bit more comfortable for his parents and his people. While at St. Cecilia's elementary school, he grew in confidence that he was "good with numbers." But always in the back of his mind rose the question "how can things get better for my people?"

"I wanted to learn more about, stocks, bonds and taxes," said Mr. Wilson. "So, when I entered college, I knew that business administration would be my major."

At the same time, he remembered contemplating on a musical hit sung by Lou Rawls with a line that kept him focused and remembering his people, "I'm tired of breaking my back so I'm going to start using my mind." Stocks, bonds, taxes tugged at Mr. Wilson's mind. He was convinced that dealing with these financial enterprises could provide benefits and savings for his parents and his people.

Today, Mr. Wilson is chief financial officer-senior vice president of Industrial Bank of Washington, the third largest Black owned bank in the United States, where he deals with stocks, bonds and taxes.

At Immaculate Conception Church in Baltimore, Mr. Wilson serves as chairman of the finance committee, organizing the books and seeking ways for the church to save. He also makes himself readily available to parishioners providing tax and financial consultation when sought. "It's the people, I want to help," says Mr. Wilson. "I've been taught … that our love for people is a measure of our love for God."

Just Souls Shine Forever

On All Souls Day, we think of our ancestors who were towers of strength in the African American Catholic community. Listen to their stories and gain from their strength. For these are the ones who left footprints of faith, fortitude and wisdom.

Dr. Rebecca E. Carroll, lifetime member of St. Pius V Church, Baltimore, was short in stature but a giant among many. Dr. Carroll was wife to James L. Carroll and mother of Dr. Constance M. Carroll. She was a scholar, educator and humanitarian. She worked on various archdiocesan committees in the area of finance and education, receiving the papal medal, "Pro Ecclesia et Pontifice."

Dr. Carroll was the first African American woman to receive a doctorate from the University of Maryland and retired as deputy superintendent from Baltimore City Public Schools.

Family was important to her. During her lifetime, she had the support of her parents, aunts, husband and sister, Elmira E. Harris. Dr. Carroll was founder and organizer of the Baltimore Council on Adolescent Pregnancy, Parenting and Pregnancy Prevention, Inc, and she was past president of the Baltimore Chapter of Delta Sigma Theta Sorority, Inc.

Her life epitomized integration of education and religion, the foundation of her relationships that contributed to her happiness, sense of self and success. Her book, "*Snapshots From the Life of An African American Woman,*" describes her legacy.

Marian B. Dixon always extended her voice and muscle for the work of justice. Born in Hollywood, St. Mary's County, from a long line of Catholics, she worked for the poor and disenfranchised. She was an activist and past president of Baltimoreans United In Leadership Development. She was acting office manager for B.U.I.L.D. at the time of her death.

Irene Mallory, her sister, said, "Because of her love for people, Marian was involved in many projects and did whatever she could to help anyone in need." Mrs. Dixon gave tirelessly of her time at St. Ambrose, Baltimore, where she was a eucharistic minister and lector. She served on archdiocesan and regional committees and was a member of the Ladies Action Society. She was married to the late Charles Dixon and had two children.

Mr. and Mrs. Frank Sewell, parents of nine children, worked as a team to help the poor and those in need. It began with a family turkey dinner and a pot of spaghetti in 1963. Since then, hundreds have been fed at this present family and church tradition which continues today.

Cecilia Sewell was a homemaker who worked in St. Peter Claver's school dietary department. She visited nursing homes during holidays and cheered the residents through songs, prizes and gifts.

Mr. Sewell was a key player in B.U.I.L.D., advocating for reasonable housing for the poor. He was instrumental in the formation of the Nehemiah Housing Project. Active in both his parish and archdiocesan St. Vincent de Paul Society, Mr. Sewell was chairperson of St. Peter Claver's food pantry where they distribute to 50-70 families per week. "Frank Sewell Way," located in the Sandtown-Winchester section of Baltimore, is named in honor of him.

The Book of Daniel says, "Those who work for justice shall shine like the stars forever. Let the light from these 'just souls' penetrate your life and give guidance."

Defending Advocates

S trong shoulders and a compassionate heart are noteworthy personal attributes. Add to these the virtues of Christian service, grace and steadfastness, and you will come to know these ancestors of faith – Judge Robert B. Watts, Anita R. Williams and Deacon Thomas A. Wilson Sr.

Judge Watts was a pioneer in the civil rights movement in Baltimore. Along with Attorney Juanita J. Mitchell, he defended hundreds of Morgan State College students who had been arrested while picketing for public accommodations.

He also was the longest sitting judge in the Circuit Court of Baltimore City where he presided as a specialist in domestic relations and introduced a number of reforms. He, too, served on many boards including the Urban Commission. He was a lifetime member of the NAACP.

Judge Watts' faithful membership at St. Gregory the Great Church, Baltimore, was followed by membership at New All Saints, Baltimore, where he served as an usher. In his latter years he became a member of the Cathedral of Mary Our Queen in Roland Park. Judge Watts was the husband of Jacqueline Watts and the father of three.

Anita R. Williams, the granddaughter of a Baltimore County slave, was the first African American social worker in Catholic Charities in the United States. She was a member of St. Pius V Church, Baltimore, charter member of the Baltimore Urban League and NAACP, founding member of the Catholic Interracial Council, one of the founders of Provident Hospital and the first African American on many social worker boards.

Her encounters with racial restrictions didn't deter her dedication to service. During the Depression, while serving on the Baltimore Emergency Relief Commission, there was some objection to Ms. Williams' presence as a representative in the trained delegation of supervisors lent by Catholic Charities. Father Leonard threatened to withhold the other Catholic workers, which caused the end of segregated social work in Baltimore.

Deacon Thomas A. Wilson Sr. served God and people in a quiet yet profound way. He once studied for the priesthood in Bay St. Louis, Miss., understanding that everyone should serve God in one way or another.

Married to Margaret R. Wilson, together they desegregated St. Cecilia Church in Baltimore in 1952 where he served as sexton, youth adviser, instructor for acolytes and eventually as deacon.

Always ready to pray and praise God, he encouraged others to "take a closer walk with Jesus." He was the founding member of the Legion of Mary at St. Peter Claver, Baltimore, in the early 1950s. Deacon Wilson was a distinguished pianist and would oftentimes compose songs for retreats and liturgical celebrations. He taught many lessons in life – about family, faith and service.

Deacon Wilson retired from the United States Post Office and was the father of seven children.

There are so many more stories of "the souls of the just" from the African American Catholic community. There are so many lessons to be learned from our ancestors.

Certainly, we won't forget the impact made by Katherine Wilson Brown, Rose Butler, James Carroll, Guilbert Daley, Ronald Dixon, Daniel Dember, Charles Dorsey, Mabel Dillworth, Barbara Ferguson, Joseph Garner, Beatrice and John Gaddy, Sister Michael Grant, O.S.P., Judge John Hargrove, Elmira Harris, Faye Wilkes Perry, Beulah Pinkney, Loretta Rose, Christine Scherrod, Charles and Etta Simms, Sylvia Wesson, Sister Juanita Ward, O.S.P., Catherine Woodland, Thomas Yorkshire, Annie Young and so many more.

Our African American ancestors were excellent role models, with deep faith that was passed onto their families. They gave generously of their time and talents. It is up to us to perpetuate their legacies for they lived Christ's love. Jesus told us that his followers are those who love one another.

Wonders Never Cease

Celebrating Black history is an opportunity to affirm one more time that wonders never cease.

The gatherer of Black history in the United States is Dr. Carter Godwin Woodson. Dr. Woodson was serious about education, not just elementary education or high school education or higher education, but comprehensive education that would affect the psyche in such a manner that it would produce positive self-esteem, pride and productivity.

Dr. Woodson was about developing minds of Black people wherever they were in life, and in this developmental process it would be an awakening and testimony of the history, progress and richness of African American achievement.

In 1926 Dr. Woodson designated an observance of Negro History Week. He chose February because Feb. 12 was Abraham Lincoln's birthday and Feb. 14 was the accepted birthday of Frederick Douglass.

By the 1970s Negro History Week had expanded to become Black History Month.

Dr. Carter Woodson dedicated his life to correcting the "miseducation" of the Negro and gave strong direction in employing Black history – "if a race has no history, if it has no worthwhile tradition, it becomes a negligible factor in the thought of the world, and it stands in danger of being exterminated."

There is so much tradition and history in the Black community, and there is equal history to be shared about Black Catholics in America as well as within the Archdiocese of Baltimore. Our rich legacy is a public sign of a refutation that "we are not empty-handed, therefore we fear not extinction."

The Acacia Tree

Throughout the United States, Black Catholics have lifted up the Acacia Tree, as a symbol of inspiration and hope. It is the official symbol of the National Black Catholic Congress.

The Acacia Tree is native to Africa. It is mentioned in the Bible in the Book of Exodus and in the Book of Isaiah. The wood of the tree was used to build the Ark of the Covenant. It is mentioned in Isaiah as a sign of the Messianic restoration in Israel.

The Acacia Tree has deep roots, and survives through drought, dryness and famine. It is a strong tree which provides shelter for animals from the soaring heat of the sun and it also provides food and nourishment.

Since biblical times, the Acacia has been a symbol of stability and resilience. The tree is still found in many areas of Africa and has been a symbol of that land.

Crosses made from Acacia were distributed to all participants of the Sixth National Black Catholic Congress in May, 1987.

Women of Influence

When listing notable women, two African American women of influence come to mind. Harriet Thompson began a letter writing campaign in 1853 appealing to Pope Pius IX to break down walls of prejudice and racism within the church in New York City.

Almost 100 years later, Sister Antona Ebo, F.S.M., made an appeal to the American government for equality for people of color as she walked in the Selma, Ala., demonstration. The day after the demonstration, Sister Antona received a personal call from Vatican News.

What a difference a woman makes!

Imagine calling the church to justice in 1853 in New York City where Blacks received a steady dosage of inferiority from priests and religious women. Free Blacks were in competition with the Irish. The Irish saw Blacks as labor scabs who threatened their jobs.

Harriet Thompson was an organizer who challenged the church of New York to be church for all people through her appeal that children of color be allowed to attend Catholic schools. This appeal eventually went to Rome. "Most Holy Father Visible Head of the Church of Jesus Christ, I humbly write these lines to beseech your Holiness in the name of the same Savior, if you will provide for the salvation of the Black race in the United States who is going astray from neglect on the part of those who have care of souls."

This letter laid out a list of racist practices of those within the church. The letter continues … Archbishop John Hughes of New York "did not recognize the Black race as part of his flock … it is well known by both white and Black that he (hates) the Black race so much that he cannot bear them to come near him."

Twenty six Black Catholics signed the letter. For the first time, but not the last, Black lay Catholics had spoken out for themselves expressing both loyalty and love for the church and anger and dismay at the racist practices of those within the church. Eventually, a short-lived, segregated school was established.

Elizabeth Louise Ebo was born into a Baptist family in Bloomington, Ill., in 1924 to Daniel and Louise Teale Ebo. Following the death of her mother, Elizabeth (fondly called Betty) and her older brother and sister entered a county home for "colored" children in Bloomington. She was only six-years old.

While living at the home, Betty's interest in Catholicism was sparked by a childhood friend who had an intense devotion to Jesus in the Eucharist. At age 18, Betty was baptized and several years later entered the Sisters of the Third Order of St. Francis (now known as the Franciscan Sisters of Mary). Betty took the name of Mary Antona and was one of the first three Black women to be received as a postulant of this order.

Sister Antona's contributions as a religious and in the struggle for human rights for African Americans are many. When she marched for civil rights in Selma, she was the first Black Sister to do so.

"They asked the nuns to march in the front, leading the crowd towards freedom. Before the demonstration, they asked me to speak at Brown's Chapel. God was with us," says Sister Antona. She was the first Black Sister/administrator of a Catholic hospital in the United States, St. Clare Hospital in Baraboo, Wis.

In 1968, Sister Ebo participated in the founding of the National Black Sisters' Conference. Today, at the St. Louis Archdiocesan Pastoral Center, a seminar room is named after Sister Antona Ebo, F.S.M.

These stories remind us that when you say yes to Jesus your life can be of influence – a positive influence.

Harlem Renaissance Writers

I have always been impressed with the many talented African American literary writers, especially those of the Harlem Renaissance period. Their writings, involvement and contributions in the African American community had a major impact. They had the courage to leave a record of whom we are and where we have been. They had the courage to write the story of our African American heritage. They had the courage to write about race and the African Americans' place in the American life during this period – the Harlem Renaissance.

More profound are two 20th century intellectuals, Ellen Tarry and Claude McKay who both converted to Catholicism, and are considered a part of the history of Catholicism, two African American Harlem Renaissance icons.

Ellen Tarry was born in Birmingham, Ala., in 1906. Ellen converted to Catholicism while she was a student at Rock Castle Academy in Virginia, which was operated by the Sisters of the Blessed Sacrament, a community founded by St. Katharine Drexel. She attended Alabama State Normal School and taught in Birmingham Public Schools before moving to New York in 1929 to pursue her passion and dream of becoming a writer.

Upon arriving in New York, Ellen formed an association with several prominent literary giants of the Harlem Renaissance, including Claude McKay. It was Claude who encouraged Ellen to continue to pursue her passion of writing. In addition, Ellen worked with the staff of Friendship House and wrote for Catholic periodicals.

Today, Ellen lives in New York and is an active parishioner at St.

Mark the Evangelist Church. Ellen has written a number of books for young people, including the biography of James Weldon Johnson. Her strong belief in the Catholic faith has allowed her to write books on individuals who have helped others in the Catholic faith.

One of Ellen's books suggested for young readers, "*Saint Katharine Drexel: Friend of the Oppressed*," is a true story of an American heiress and recently canonized saint who selflessly surrendered her life and her fortune to God by serving the less fortunate in America, especially Native Americans and African Americans. Ellen knew St. Katharine Drexel.

Born in Jamaica in 1890, Claude migrated to the United States in 1912 to attend Tuskegee Institute. However, he only stayed there for a few months, leaving to attend Kansas State College to study agriculture. After spending two years at Kansas State College, Claude journeyed to Harlem to pursue a literary career and joined other writers of the era. In Harlem, he turned his attention to the teachings of various spiritual and political leaders.

An intriguing poet, novelist, essayist, critic, and political activist, McKay was considered one of the great novelists and poets of the Harlem Renaissance. His book, "*Home to Harlem*," a vivid picture of an African American soldier's life in New York after returning from World War II, became the first best seller and the most popular novel written by an African American during the Harlem Renaissance period.

Claude moved several times in his lifetime. He moved from Jamaica to Alabama, then from New York City to various countries in Europe on to West Africa, eventually returning to the United States.

Each time Claude moved, he did so for a specific reason. He moved to Europe because he felt Communism was an effective solution to the poverty he witnessed in the United States. While traveling in Europe, Claude visited several Catholic cathedrals and began to draw closer to the Catholic faith. Claude eventually changed his opinion about Communism, moved back to the United States and became a U.S. citizen. Through his friend Ellen, Claude received medical help at the Catholic-run Friendship House in Harlem. Having experienced several religious beliefs, Claude found that Roman Catholicism offered him peace, order and truth.

These two Harlem Renaissance writers have contributed much to our story and the Catholic faith.

CHARLES G. TILDON, JR.

A Testament of Hope

In the coming weeks, we will spend time reflecting on God's greatest gift to the world, his Son, Jesus Christ.

Hopefully, we will be inspired by his example and remember that we need to redirect our lives. Hopefully, our leaders will be inspired to bring peace and justice to the world. Hopefully, our church will vigorously face the many opportunities to carry out the plan that Jesus shared with us through his life and the Gospels that left with us a blueprint for living and for salvation.

In the coming weeks as we celebrate the life of one of God's messengers, Dr. Martin Luther King, Jr., we should review his life, his work and his vision. We will be inspired by his commitment to end injustice, inequity, inconsistency and inhuman treatment.

I was fortunate enough to have attended Morehouse College with Martin L. King, Jr. He was an intelligent, quiet and studious student. We knew he planned to be a minister. I doubt, however, that few of his schoolmates would have predicted the impact that he would have on the course of history in this country and the world.

We yearn for some insight as we search for ways to realize "the dream" and honor King's memory. Perhaps we should be asking ourselves some soul-searching questions that would lead us to an understanding of his dream, its relevance today and ways to achieve it. What was Martin's dream? How did he express it? What can we do to achieve it?

Scientists and historians have reviewed his writings, speeches and other works, as well as chronicles of his life, to answer these questions.

The answers will undoubtedly be shaped by those who are doing the reviews.

I believe that all reviews will lead to Dr. King's understanding that Jesus left us with a prescription for a world where hate has no place and where love is the only true path to peace and justice.

As we look constantly for ways to share God's love with each other, we hope that we can use Dr. King's legacy as a guide to eliminate racism, remove stereotypes, force change, understand the roots of poverty and destroy those roots.

We sincerely hope that the majority population will recognize that shared power is not only morally right but that it is in the self-interest of all people. A powerless people is a hopeless people. Hopeless people become desperate people. Desperate people become irrational and therefore a people whose behavior is counter-productive for all.

We believe that the faith that Dr. King expressed in so many ways should be shared with all as we work to make this country and this world a place where freedom and equality are a reality. Yes, that faith that Dr. King expressed gives us hope.

His life is an example for us. His words are instructions for us. His sincere, inspiring leadership is a reminder of what is expected of us.

His death is a warning for us to be ever aware of the forces of evil that would attempt to thwart our efforts to develop a just society. His memory must serve to keep us vigilant, determined and committed to bringing about social, economic and political reform.

In short, his memory must be the stimulant that causes us to continue to demand that America and the world must change. We must become a world that keeps hope alive – hope for peace and justice.

Dr. King expressed it best at the end of an essay, "A Testament of Hope":

"A voice out of Bethlehem 2,000 years ago said that all men are equal. It said right would triumph. Jesus of Nazareth wrote no books; he owned no property to endow him with influence. He had no friends in the courts of the powerful. But he changed the course of mankind with only the poor and the despised.

"Naïve and unsophisticated though we may be, the poor and despised of today will revolutionize the era ... We will fight for human justice, brotherhood, secure peace and abundance for all. When we have won these – in a spirit of unshakable nonviolence – then, in luminous splendor, the Christian era will truly begin."

MELVILLE W. PUGH, JR.

TWO PART SERIES:

Claude McKay

A frican Americans were visible as residents of Harlem, New York City, at the onset of World War I, 1914. By 1920 Harlem was recognized as a city within a city, a "Black metropolis."

From 1919 to 1929, as the poet Langston Hughes wrote, "Harlem was in vogue." Black painters and sculptors joined their fellow poets, novelist, dramatists and musicians in an artistic outpouring that established Harlem as the international capital of Black culture. This was the Harlem Renaissance!

Noted writers were encouraging aspiring writers to hone their skills. A proud and independent writer and poet named Claude McKay provided encouragement and support to several writers. He was one of the Black personalities who helped launch the Harlem Renaissance.

McKay was born in Jamaica on September 15, 1890, in a farm family of 11 children. In 1912, he emigrated to the United States for study at Tuskegee Institute. After a few weeks, he transferred to Kansas State College, where he remained for two years and in 1914 moved to New York City.

In Jamaica, he had already written two volumes of poems in Jamaican Creole before he came to the United States. After arriving in New York City, McKay married a young Jamaican lady and entered the restaurant business. He soon lost the restaurant and his wife. She returned to Jamaica, pregnant with a daughter.

After World War I, McKay worked numerous jobs, the longest as a railroad dining-car waiter. He began writing poetry and became involved in the political arena. The severe racist structure of American society was unlike what he had experienced in Jamaica, and in the period after World War I, when resentment of Blacks began to explode, McKay, as did a number of young Blacks, became attracted to Marxism.

As the situation became more violent and Blacks more victimized, his poetry became more militant. He became widely known, to his own despair, for a single poem, called. "If We Must Die," published in the summer of 1919 in the Liberator. The poem calls for militant self-defense against white rioters.

It was perceived as a statement of racial defiance. Many have proclaimed this poem universal and Winston Churchill is said to have quoted it as an expression of British defiance to the Nazis in World War II.

McKay went to England in 1919 and spent some time studying Marx and learning about Socialist ideas and leaders. In 1921 he returned to Harlem only to cross the Atlantic Ocean again in 1922 with the Soviet Union as his destination.

Here, he became the unofficial spokesperson on the question of Blacks and the Communist Party in the United States. Later, McKay insisted that he was never officially a Communist.

In 1923, he left the Soviet Union and traveled to the Mediterranean coast of France and for a few years drifted to Toulon, Marseilles, Nice, Barcelona and Tangiers. In these port cities, he learned about the real life of dockers, sailors and prostitutes from Africa, the West Indies and the United States. He drew upon these experiences in the novels that he wrote.

McKay returned to the United States with physical ailments, including high blood pressure.

In 1944 he broke the news to Max Eastman, a friend, that he had been baptized a Catholic. He said that he yearned to belong to some religion, "now ... I have chosen the one that meets my needs."

After returning to Harlem he was never accepted. It was difficult to get his writings published and his health was deteriorating. In 1942, he was stricken with influenza, complicated by high blood pressure and heart disease. In the summer of 1943 working as a riveter in a shipyard, he suffered a stroke.

He moved to Chicago in 1944 and renewed his association with Dorothy Day and the Catholic Worker Organization. Also, he did some work with the Catholic Youth Organization and some lecturing at Catholic Schools.

Why did Claude McKay convert to Catholicism? He stated that he had fallen in love with the "Catholic way of life" while in Spain and that he had an "intellectual sympathy" with Catholicism. He had read the history of the Catholic Church and believed the church was a true international organization recognizing all as members of one global family.

In 1945, McKay spent two weeks at St. Meinrad's Abbey, a Benedictine monastery in Southern Indiana. During the next three years he was constantly signing in and out of hospitals. Then he signed in to the Alexian Brothers Hospital in Chicago, where he died on May 22, 1948. He was 57.

Some found McKay's conversion impossible to accept. But Wayne Cooper, his biographer, notes that in McKay's later years his loneliness and minimal personal resources motivated him to turn to the Catholic Church as a last possible benefactor.

Father Cyprian Davis in *"The History of Black Catholicism in the United States"* states that no one can fathom the heart of another and motivations are often complex. In an undated letter after his baptism, McKay notes that not many people understood just how much he had changed. And that others made their judgment from the outside. Then quoting scripture, he states, "The kingdom of heaven is within you."

In the final analysis, isn't conversion a change and isn't faith a leap?

And finally, McKay articulates his thoughts in his own creative manner:

"And so to God I go to make my peace,
Where Black nor white can follow to betray.
My pent-up heart to Him I will release,
And surely He will show the perfect way of life.
For He will lead me and no man
Can violate or circumvent His plan."

Sometime ago, I had the opportunity to reflect on *"Growing Up In Sparrows Point, MD,"* and my conversion to Catholicism. The Sparrows Point which I described and which I remembered was a quaint, little isolated community located in southeast Baltimore County. It was composed of blue-collar industrial workers and their families. It was a segregated African American community located immediately adjacent to a segregated white community. Homes were either wooden or brick structures and either detached or semi-detached and rented only to Bethlehem Steel Company employees through a rental office. It was a company town!

Three social institutions played a prominent role in integrating community life – the family, the school and the church.

I think active church participation played a major role in the social life of the Sparrows Point community. Most of the church-sponsored activities occurred in two Protestant churches, known in the local parlance as the Baptist church and the Methodist church. The one Catholic parish was primarily white dominated; and during my formative years, only one African American family held active membership in the Catholic Church.

The social values and beliefs of a small town were antecedent to my Catholic conversion which occurred in the mid 1970s. Since then, I have served in the following manner at St. Mary's in Govans: history committee, adult education committee, evangelization committee and a three-year term on the parish council. In addition, I was with the Little Rock Bible Study group for more than five years.

It should be noted that I regularly attended Mass on Sunday with my family prior to my conversion.

My spiritual journey continues. And I am reminded of those now famous words of William E. Henley's from his poem "Invictus":

"It matters not how strait the gate,
How charged with punishment the scroll,
I am the master of my fate:
I am the captain of my soul."

MELVILLE W. PUGH, JR.

Drum Major for Justice

"You ought to believe something in life, believe that thing so fervently that you will stand up with it till the end of your days ... We have a power, a power as old as the insights of Jesus of Nazareth and as modern as the techniques of Mahatma Gandhi."

These words were uttered by a man who was born January 15, 1929, who graduated from Morehouse College June 1948, who delivered the famous "I have a Dream" speech August 28, 1963, who received the Nobel Peace Prize December, 1964 and who was shot and killed in Memphis, April 4, 1968. I am speaking for Dr. Martin Luther King, Jr.

Can you imagine the frustration of a person who has been given a task which is impossible to complete? And further to have the task made more difficult by the addition of more baggage and barriers.

If you can picture this in your mind, and if you can imagine how you might feel, then you begin to see what something called prejudice and discrimination can do. It can take a person of normal abilities who has a chance to contribute to society and culture and live a life with dignity and weigh him down with such penalties that "making it" becomes an almost impossible task.

Martin Luther King saw the negative consequences of society for African American life and culture. He saw the crippling effect on personality and lack of fairness. He became aware what keeps a racial minority group from becoming all that they can be.

If a potential doctor never graduates from medical school, the world has lost. If a potential engineer does not go to school, the bridges of the future may never be built. If a teacher, professor, priest or an artist remains only a potential, the world is less. We all lose out. We all suffer.

This was the truth that became evident to "the drum major for justice." Dr. King was a man who had first-hand knowledge of the horrors that could be wrought by. He saw the suffering and limitations imposed upon a people by virtue of nothing more than the color of their skin, especially limitations in the following behavioral categories: social, economic, political, education, housing and justice.

If anyone had reason to hate it was Martin Luther King. He was, however, a man of God and a man of peace who chose to fight and hate with the most devastating weapon of all ... love.

In John 13:34-35, we read "I give you a new commandment: love one another. As I have loved you, so you also should love one another. This is how all will know that you are my disciples, if you have love for one another." With love as his guide he fought for justice with fervor and conviction that comes from the knowledge that your cause is just and that, with perseverance, hate can be overcome.

Although his life ended in an act of hate, crushed by an assassin's bullet, the love he taught by example of his life continued after him and continues even today. It is a love for all human kind, unhindered by race or creed. It is a love that realizes that every man and woman's freedom is a part of our individual freedoms and that an injustice done to my brother or sister is an injustice done to me and to all humankind.

His was a love for freedom that places him in the ranks of the greatest of Americans. His was a love that teaches us to care for the members of our family, the family of humankind. His was a love that inspires us to be the best of which we are capable of becoming in every way.

Therefore, let us honor this special man by keeping the precepts of love and brotherhood foremost in our lives both in January and throughout the months and years ahead.

And let us accept the challenge of a new and creative leadership. M. J. Brook offers the following tribute:

"The fire within him always raged to break the shackling chains,
And fiercely was the struggle waged in hopes of grasping gains.
Bold Martin Luther King held high the rights he sought to win.
He preached it's wrong to judge one by the color of his skin."

CHARLES G. TILDON, JR.

Dr. King's Dream Today

When reflecting on God's greatest gift to the world, his Son, Jesus Christ, hopefully, we will be inspired by his example and remember that we need to redirect our lives. Hopefully, our leaders will be inspired to bring peace and justice to the world. Hopefully, our church will vigorously face the many opportunities to carry out the plan that Jesus shared with us through his life and the Gospels that left with us a blueprint for living and for salvation.

As we celebrate the life of one of God's messengers, Dr. Martin Luther King Jr., we should review his life, his work and his vision. We will be inspired by his commitment to end injustice, inequity, inconsistency and inhuman treatment.

I was fortunate enough to have attended Morehouse College with Martin L. King, Jr. He was an intelligent, quiet and studious student. We knew he planned to be a minister. I doubt, however, that few of his schoolmates would have predicted the impact that he would have on the course of history in this country and the world.

We yearn for some insight as we search for ways to realize "the dream" and honor King's memory. Perhaps we should be asking ourselves some soul-searching questions that would lead us to an understanding of his dream, its relevance today and ways to achieve it. What was Martin's dream? How did he express it? What can we do to achieve it?

Scientists and historians have reviewed his writings, speeches and other works, as well as chronicles of his life, to answer these questions. The answers will undoubtedly be shaped by those who are doing the reviews.

133

I believe that all reviews will lead to Dr. King's understanding that Jesus left us with a prescription for a world where hate has no place and where love is the only true path to peace and justice.

As we look constantly for ways to share God's love with each other, we hope that we can use Dr. King's legacy as a guide to eliminate racism, remove stereotypes, force change, understand the roots of poverty and destroy those roots.

We sincerely hope that the majority population will recognize that shared power is not only morally right but that it is in the self-interest of all people. A powerless people is a hopeless people. Hopeless people become desperate people. Desperate people become irrational and therefore a people whose behavior is counter-productive for all.

We believe that the faith that Dr. King expressed in so many ways should be shared with all as we work to make this country and this world a place where freedom and equality are a reality. Yes, that faith that Dr. King expressed gives us hope.

His life is an example for us. His words are instructions for us. His sincere, inspiring leadership is a reminder of what is expected of us.

His death is a warning for us to be ever aware of the forces of evil that would attempt to thwart our efforts to develop a just society. His memory must serve to keep us vigilant, determined and committed to bringing about social, economic and political reform.

In short, his memory must be the stimulant that causes us to continue to demand that America and the world must change. We must become a world that keeps hope alive – hope for peace and justice.

Dr. King expressed it best in the last paragraph of an essay – "A Testament of Hope": "A voice out of Bethlehem 2,000 years ago said that all men are equal. It said right would triumph. Jesus of Nazareth wrote no books; he owned no property to endow him with influence. He had no friends in the courts of the powerful. But he changed the course of mankind with only the poor and the despised.

"Naïve and unsophisticated though we may be, the poor and despised of today will revolutionize the cra ... We will fight for human justice, brotherhood, secure peace and abundance for all. When we have won these – in a spirit of unshakable nonviolence – then, in luminous splendor, the Christian era will truly begin."

James Chaney

Malcolm X and Dr. Martin Luther King, Jr. are two men who helped form the attitudes and social behavior of African Americans. They subscribed to different methods and philosophies but the objective of both was the same: enhance the quality of life for African Americans.

The civil rights movement swept across the southern United States during the 1950s and the 1960s. Its impetus was begun December 1, 1955, when Rosa Parks, a Black woman, was arrested for refusing to give up her seat on a public bus to a white man in Montgomery, Ala.

The civil rights movement was the most profound and significant social movement in the United States in the 20th century. Sara Bullard's 1993 book, *"Free At Last,"* records some of the important events in this chapter of American history. Civil rights activists and organizations were challenged to create new strategies and effective methods to bring about the full rights, duties and rewards of citizenship for African Americans.

Freedom Summer (1964) was a campaign in the deep South to register African Americans to vote. The Freedom Summer campaign was organized by a coalition called the Mississippi Council of Federated Organizations (COFO). It was led by the Congress of Racial Equality (CORE) and included the NAACP and the Student Nonviolent Coordinating Committee (SNCC).

Three young adult volunteers for the Mississippi Summer Project met in the Meridian CORE office in June 1964 and became a team to set-up Freedom schools in northeast Mississippi. They were James

135

Chaney (1943-1964), Andrew Goodman (1943-1964) and Michael Schwerner (1939-1964).

Chaney, an African American, was slightly built but considered athletic. He was shy in public but a hot dog at home. Chaney faced problems at the Catholic School for Negroes in 1959 when he was 16. He and a group of friends were suspended for wearing buttons criticizing the local chapter of the NAACP for its unresponsiveness to racial issues. He was expelled a year later for a similar incident and went to work with his father as a plasterer. During this time his travels to different job sites on segregated buses throughout the segregated south exposed him to the Freedom Riders.

Freedom Summer's most infamous act of violence was the murder of these three civil rights workers: James Chaney, a Black volunteer and his white co-workers, Andrew Goodman and Michael Schwerner on June 21, 1964. These three civil rights workers were investigating a church bombing near Philadelphia, Miss., and were arrested that afternoon and held for several hours on alleged traffic violations After their release from jail, they were never again seen alive.

Six weeks later their badly decomposed bodies were discovered under a nearby dirt dam. Chaney had been savagely beaten and Goodman and Schwerner had died from single gunshot wounds to the chest. These acts of violence made media headlines over America and the world and provoked an outpouring of national support for the civil rights movement. However, Black volunteers realized that because two of the victims were white, these murders were attracting much more attention than any previous attacks in which the victims were all Black.

Freedom Summer left a positive legacy. It brought national attention to the subject of Black disenfranchisement and it eventually led to the 1965 Voting Rights Act. African Americans now had a new consciousness and a new confidence in political action.

James Earl Chaney experienced a number of failures and disappointments as a teenager and young adult. But he seemed to have found his niche in the civil rights movement. According to William Huie, Chaney "outside of the movement was a nobody facing a lifetime of being a 'boy' helper to a white painter, plumber or carpenter. But inside the movement he was somebody. People would listen to him and he had something to contribute." The following verse still resonates in mind: "Deep in my heart, I do believe, we shall overcome someday."

Strong Black Women

Necessary change and progress as well as the building of faith and institutions have been molded by great women and men. But I just have to sing the praise of strong Black Catholic women during the month of March, dedicated to women.

If you take a stroll through Black Catholic history in the United States, you may just come to the conclusion that "Black women can do anything." Stretching back to biblical times, we find the Queen of Sheba, "Black, beautiful and strong" along with the Nubian queen mother "Kandake" whose story is connected to the "Ethiopian Eunuch" in Acts of the Apostles.

It took a special attitude and style for a Black woman to break the chains of racism, religious intolerance and sexism in the early 1800s.

Mother Mary Elizabeth Lange, O.S.P., was touched by God. By 1818, Mother Lange was educating Black children in her home during an era when it was against the law for Blacks to gather, no less to learn to read and write.

In 1829 Mother Lange founded the Oblate Sisters of Providence, the first religious order of women of African descent. Mother Lange and the Oblate Sisters of Providence were assistants in the Underground Railroad and nurses during the worse cholera epidemic (1832) in Baltimore. Other religious orders were recognized for their service during this epidemic but not the Oblates.

In spite of indifference, they kept on doing the will of God, opening an orphanage and pushing for educational excellence among people of color. These women still stand among us – teaching, catechizing,

137

witnessing to the providence of God.

In New Orleans, we discover the story of Henriette Delille and Juliette Gaudin who ministered to Blacks. Henriette Delille founded in 1842 the second Black religious congregation in the United States – Sisters of the Holy Family. Delille and Gaudin joined by Josephine Charles bought a house in the French Quarter which served as a hospice. They also distributed food and clothing to the needy. In 1853 yellow fever struck New Orleans. The sisters nursed many of the ill at great cost in physical hardship to themselves.

Out of Savannah, Georgia, came Mother Mathilda Beasley who opened a convent and orphanage by 1891. In the 1850s, Mathilda married Abram Beasley, who was a free Black man who owned a restaurant, general store and land.

Upon her husband's death Mother Beasley gave land to build a church and began a community of Franciscan Sisters of Georgia later named the Missionary Franciscan Sisters of the Immaculate Conception. Eventually, this order would leave Savannah and travel to New York to become the Franciscan Handmaids of the Most Pure Heart of Mary. Today, these women minister in Harlem.

Two distinguished Black Catholic women of today are Dr. Lena Edwards and Dr. Beverly A. Carroll.

Dr. Edwards, an obstetrician, practiced her faith through her profession. Noted as a "determined no-nonsense woman," she was a firm believer that the good physician must be concerned about the total welfare of the patients. She had a love for St. Francis of Assisi. She used her savings to help build a maternity hospital for migrant workers.

From her teenage years up until the present, Dr. Beverly A. Carroll has worked for the church. She is the first executive director of the Secretariat for African American Catholics at the National Conference of Catholic Bishops.

Dr. Carroll serves as a voice for Black Catholics at the conference and is an activist within the Black community. Her genius in establishing networks, combating racism, facilitating the formation of resources and her work in encouraging leaders in their ministry of evangelization has won her acclaim both here and in South Africa.

Black Catholic women, just keep coming! They strengthen their work through faith.

Holding On

Rita Neale and Sister Elaine Frederick, O.S.P., graciously shared some of the incidents, experiences and people who helped shape their relationship with God. Their words of wisdom are passed on to help strengthen others in their walk with Christ.

Mrs. Neale said because she prayed and believed that God was going to bring her through her illnesses, she was drawn closer to him by faith and trust. Her reliance on and relationship with God was further strengthened while raising 11 children. She later realized after the death of her newborn daughter, that God was preparing her for another loss, the death of her seventh child.

Mrs. Neale never questioned God because she knew He had a reason. With that knowledge, she held on. During adversity, her constant seeking out of Scripture, reliance on faith and desire for a closer walk with Christ sustained her.

People instrumental in helping shape her relationship with God included her parents, grandmother, husband's (Deacon Joseph Neale) family, and the Oblate Sisters of Providence. By demonstrated faith, both parents helped keep her close to God. Her grandmother read the Bible to her by lamplight. Deacon Neale's family impacted her by being very spiritual and close-knit and the Oblate Sisters instilled faith and confidence.

Because of her father's inability to continue working due to a hearing impairment, she had to stop attending St. Frances Academy. Yet, she remembers how supportive the Oblates were. A letter written to her by Sister Mary of Good Counsel encouraged her to be strong and to continue on.

"That letter carried me a long way." Mrs. Neale said. She subsequently attended institutions of higher learning.

Mrs. Neale emphasized that in order to strengthen your relationship with Christ, you must get as close to him as possible.

Sister Elaine Frederick was born into a family of African Americans whose faith blossomed and flourished from its "rootedness" in the Catholic heritage of St. Mary's County. Spending summers in southern Maryland, she witnessed discriminatory treatment of Blacks from white members of the parish. While she saw Black Catholics having to sit behind white parishioners and receive the sacraments after them, she learned that personal dignity and worth as human beings are God given and not dependent upon what other races think.

Grandparents, parents, and the Oblate Sisters of Providence influenced her relationship with God. Her grandmother was educated, talented and active in the parish. Yet, during a service for veneration of the cross, she was asked to step aside and instead allow a white parishioner to go ahead of her. She exited the church without performing this act of devotion, but later confronted the pastor about his humiliating discriminatory action.

Through her grandmother, Sister Elaine learned that developing one's natural gifts and helping others to do likewise are a mighty way of giving glory and service to God.

Through attendance at all church services and serving as officers on parish organizations, her parents demonstrated faith and service to God by teaching that faith has to be nurtured and practiced. She learned that if we give God his due, he will take care of us in all ways.

The Oblates influenced Sister Elaine by their example as religious women. Through witness of them while at St. Frances, Sister Elaine began to consider that God was calling her to serve him as an Oblate. The Sisters she knew on mission influenced her by the witness of their faithfulness to prayer, their pioneering spirit and their quiet willingness to minister to others.

Sister Elaine knows "providence provides" and advises that when you are called upon to perform duties for which you feel insufficiently prepared, be obedient. She says, "Think of Mother Lange and the early Oblates who all suffered, endured in faith and found the strength to carry on."

Holding On 2

Father Joseph C. Verrett, S.S.J., has a rich and diverse background that has prepared him for the role of elder in the African American Catholic community.

Born Joseph Casimir Verrett, Jr. on January 17, 1930, to Stella (Smith) and Joseph C. Verrett in New Orleans, Louisiana, Father Verrett has been a Josephite priest for 48 years.

His various assignments include service as a counselor and administrator at St. Augustine High School in New Orleans and 24 years serving people with alcohol and other drug addictions.

Numerous priests served as role models for Father Verrett throughout his formative years. Father Thomas Slater, S.S.J., impressed on him the dignity of the priesthood. He affectionately recalls the day he received his First Communion from his pastor, Father Edward Murphy, S.S.J.

Father Verrett also credits the "God fearing" women in his life who modeled great faith, fidelity to duty and personal sacrifice. His mother Stella, a no-nonsense person, served as a domestic with the same family for 50 years. She attended Mass daily at St. Joan of Arc and was the reason Joseph could be counted on as an early morning altar server. She also repeated often the lessons she had learned from her early years in a Catholic school in Plaquemines, Louisiana, from Sister Gertrude, a Marianite Sister of the Holy Cross.

Long before the days of day care centers or Head Start programs, Father Verrett often accompanied his mother to work where he received his first lessons. While his mother cooked and cleaned, her employer taught him to read and write.

Father Verrett benefited from the attention and care of many women religious. His formal academic development began with seven years of grade school under the tutelage of Sisters of the Holy Family. Sr. Raymond, Sr. Gilbert and Sr. Demetria, to name a few, modeled the values of commitment and dedication. Father Verrett believes growing up in an environment surrounded by Catholicism provided fertile soil in which his relationship with God continues to grow.

A good student, Father Verrett built upon this solid educational foundation. A life long learner, Father Verrett earned a bachelor's degree in education and English from Loyola College in New Orleans and a graduate degree from Xavier in Guidance Counseling and Administration. He later studied theology in Rome at the University of St. Thomas Aquinas. After returning to the United States he completed a degree in Canon Law at Catholic University.

After 11 years as a priest, at the age of 36, Father Verrett entered an alcohol treatment program. This experience sensitized him to the problems that people face on a day-to-day basis. He also discovered that he could teach people and help them become effective as a counselor. To better prepare himself for his new ministry, Father Verrett returned to the academic world and earned a Doctorate in Clinical Psychology. His experience in counseling was rewarding and humbling, forcing him to accept "you don't win them all."

His sister Mary Jacqueline Verrett shared Father Verrett's thirst for knowledge and desire to serve. He refers to her as the "smart one" in the family. At a time when most women were mixing foods in the kitchen, Jackie earned a Ph.D. in biochemistry at Fordham University and conducted research for the Food and Drug Administration.

Mary Ann West Smith, Father Verrett's maternal grandmother is a tremendous source of inspiration for him. Born 1871 in Americus, Georgia, of a freed slave and Native American Indian, at 70 years of age she returned to school to learn to read and write. Father Verrett baptized his grandmother as a Catholic when she was 85, just three weeks prior to officiating at her funeral.

Father Verrett encourages people who are seeking to deepen their relationship with God to look for opportunities to help someone. He believes that often people are not walking with Christ because they are focusing on "how they are walking".

Father Verrett retired from the Tuerk House Drug Treatment Center in 1996 after eight years as director. He continues to serve as a consultant.

Righteous Footprints

As I travel to various parishes, I am always awestruck of the abiding faith, fortitude and perseverance of our elders. The testimony of such elders always brings a sense of direction and wisdom to those yearning to strengthen their relationship with God.

Walking fast but always ready to stop to help and listen to anyone is Deacon John Briscoe, an elder of St. Peter Claver church. A carpenter by profession (doesn't that sound familiar), Deacon Briscoe has a special way of entering into people's lives and hearts. "People are where one can find Jesus" says Deacon Briscoe, "so I spend time with Jesus through people."

Deacon Briscoe's father, Alexander was a Catholic and his mother, Marie was a member of the Pentecostal Church. As a child, Deacon Briscoe remembers going from church to church, listening to sermons and being inspired by the Word of God. These experiences marked Deacon Briscoe for life.

Thirty six years ago, Esther Williams, a member of St. Peter Claver brought John Briscoe to her church. "I was going to Immaculate Conception or other churches at that time, not really settling in" says Deacon Briscoe. "St. Peter Claver became home for me."

When approached to consider becoming a deacon, he heard rumors that folks were saying, "out of all the people Father Harfmann, S.S.J., could have asked, why Briscoe?"As the rumors prevailed, he became more intrigued with the story of Samuel's call in the Old Testament. In scripture, Samuel was called four times before finally realizing that it was God not Eli who was calling him.

Deacon Briscoe said, like Samuel, he received four callings by four people to serve as deacon of the Church – Deacons Americus Roy and Phillip Harcum, Father John Harfmann, S.S.J. and Charles Mercer – now Deacon Mercer. Deacon Briscoe also notes that it took four years for him to answer God's call to the diaconate. On September 21, 2003, at St. Peter Claver church, Deacon Briscoe celebrated 25 years as a deacon.

Always with a song in her heart and a word of encouragement spilling from her lips is Vera Gaines, elder, parishioner and Minister of Music at St. Veronica church. At the age of four, Ms. Gaines, her mother and six siblings entered into the Catholic Church.

Her mother was inspired and influenced by a St. Francis Xavier parishioner, Mrs. Anna Jolley, who was a neighbor from Rutland Avenue. "There was so much warmth received through the family of ministers at St. Francis – The Mission Helpers, The Oblate Sisters of Providence and of course, The Josephites. Father Daniel Cassidy, S.S.J. was a great influence encouraging Vera to strengthen her skills as a pianist and organist as well as serving as a sort of spiritual guide.

Devout people always seemed to surround Vera. "I want to be like them" she said. "Individuals who exemplified spirituality can show you how to grow spiritually. I grew to love Jesus and the ways to stay in close contact with Jesus. I did not want to miss any opportunity to draw close to God. The rituals of the church were strongly appealing. My mother attended novenas and eventually while I was in the eighth grade, I began playing the organ at novenas, sodality and Holy Name Masses. Beginning in 1950, I went with Father Cassidy, S.S.J., to the mission churches in Turner Station and taught Sunday school. In 1955, while playing the organ at St. Veronica's, I taught Sunday school between Masses. I love to pray and to be surrounded by those who want to take a closer walk with Jesus."

Today, Vera Gaines continues to teach and evangelize. She encourages the young and the old to surround themselves with people who can show you how to grow spiritually. "The social and material attractions of the world are overwhelming our youth, this is why we must continually educate and to lay down righteous footprints of spirituality for them to follow," says Ms. Gaines.

BARRY F. WILLIAMS

Called to Serve

When Christ becomes your focus, everything you do is Christ inspired. This is the story of Deacon Americus Roy, a man inspired by Christ, a man called to serve.

Deacon Roy was ordained the first modern permanent deacon in the United States on June 12, 1971. After attending the Josephite Seminary in Washington, D.C., for five years, he was accorded all the powers of a priest minus the ability to say Mass. He has officiated at baptisms, weddings and funerals and has delivered numerous homilies in the churches where he was assigned. His first church after becoming a permanent deacon was St. Ambrose, where he served for 12 years. Following St. Ambrose, he was assigned to St. Pius V. After a short stint at St. Cecelia's, then St. Gregory's, he returned to St. Pius V.

Deacon Roy was not born into the Catholic faith. As a youngster growing up in Baltimore, he was active socially and athletically in the community. He became involved in the activities of St. Francis Xavier in East Baltimore and came under the guidance of a charismatic priest, Father Cassidy, who was then assigned to St. Francis Xavier.

Father Cassidy so influenced Americus that at age 17, he became a Roman Catholic and was re-christened and confirmed in the faith.

Deacon Roy credits Father Cassidy and his own father with influencing him to respond to a higher calling. He said that his father was a man who always gave himself to other people and it was his father's example that he followed. As a married man, he was unable to become a priest. However, in 1966, he embarked on a mission of theological study and became ordained as a deacon at the Cathedral of

Mary Our Queen in Baltimore.

He has served the eastern and western communities of Baltimore City. He was one of the founding members of Baltimoreans United In Leadership Development (B.U.I.L.D.) and was active in the Baltimore Ministerial Alliance.

Archbishop William D. Borders recalls the strong ministry that Deacon Roy rendered at the correctional facilities in the Maryland region, stating "He taught me a lot about outreach and prison ministry."

His first wife Doris and he were extremely involved in each of the church communities to which he was sent. After Doris died in 1996, he met and married Betty Brooks on November 27, 1999. Betty had been the minister of music at St. Gregory's when she met Americus. Together, they have combined to have a large blended family of 14 children, 35 grandchildren and 15 great grandchildren.

Deacon Roy has become a much-loved church elder who is currently residing at the Gilchrist Hospice Care Center. In spite of his illness, he remains a faithful, devoted servant of the Lord who seldom complains of pain.

God chose Deacon Roy to be one of his servants and Deacon Roy answered with his life.

Free for Christmas

A renowned African American Roman Catholic author and journalist, Lerone Bennett, Jr., wrote the book *"Wade in the Water: Great Moments in Black History."* In this book, the historical retelling of Harriet Ross Tubman's raid referred to as "Free for Christmas" is considered a Christmas classic. This famous telling of the Christmas Eve raid, which has appeared many times in Ebony magazine, reminds us of the spirit of Christmas in the eyes and heart of Harriet Tubman.

Tubman, a legendary figure of the Underground Railroad, was born into slavery in 1820 in Dorchester County, Maryland, and made her escape to freedom in Philadelphia at the age of 25. Although free, Harriet felt that it was her mission to free other slaves and returned 19 times to southern states helping guide more than 300 slaves to escape to the North to freedom, including members of her family. The slaves called her "Moses," because just like the Moses, who led the Israelites from slavery in Biblical times, she went south to lead her people to freedom.

One can only believe that Harriet's source of strength came from her strong faith in God as deliverer and protector of the weak, and that he would aid her efforts in leading slaves to freedom. Harriet knew that God was always on her side.

By Christmas 1854, Harriet had returned to Maryland five times to lead more slaves to freedom. She returned during the Christmas season of 1854 to rescue a group of slaves who included three of her brothers, Benjamin, Robert and Henry, who were in danger.

Just how did Harriet know that her brothers were in danger? She had a premonition that something was about to happen to them. And just what was going to happen? Her brothers were in danger of being sold further south, thus separating them from their families. Harriet knew that she had to act fast and was encouraged by her strong belief to act.

Yes, she wanted her brothers free for Christmas and sang the words of this calling song for rescue.

"Jesus, Jesus will go with you, He will lead you to His throne: He who died has gone before you, Trod the winepress all alone."

Since slaves were not permitted to talk openly with each other, their source of communication was often singing spirituals. Thus, the words of this calling song for rescue were sung by slaves and moved quickly across the Maryland countryside of Cambridge on Christmas Eve.

Slave masters heard the slaves singing but paid no attention to the true meaning of the words. However, this song served as a code alerting those who knew that the woman known as Moses was in the area and preparing to follow through on her mission of freeing slaves. They knew that they had to assist Harriet in the rescue mission. Each word of the song meant something to those who were helping to ensure that this group of slaves' escaped.

Harriet quickly and quietly moved through the familiar wooded grounds near the plantations with the group of slaves. Taking refuge in a series of hiding places such as other slaves' homes and wagons along the way, the group journeyed north.

Harriet was successful in freeing the group including her brothers. They were free for Christmas.

Juneteenth

Two and one half years after the Emancipation Proclamation was issued and two months after the signing of the surrender by Generals Grant and Lee at Appomattox Courthouse, Virginia, April 9, 1865, people of color who were enslaved in Texas finally gained their freedom. They were the last to be freed.

It was on June 19, 1865, that Union General Gordon Granger arrived in Galveston, Texas with Federal troops to inform the slave-owners to release their slaves from bondage. He read from the executive order "The people of Texas are informed that in accordance with the Emancipation Proclamation from the Executive of the United States that all slaves are Free."

With this announcement the newly freed slave broke into spontaneous celebration. In the beginning it was celebrated mostly by rural Blacks, who felt that the celebration exemplified their freedom and liberty. Some held a prayer vigil on the site where the document was delivered.

After several years of celebration, people spoke of it in the vernacular, "Juneteenth." The word June was linked with the date – the nineteenth – and it became known and called Juneteenth. African Americans worked all year in preparation to enjoy and observe this holiday. Some of the celebrations lasted a week. There were parades, dances, dinners, picnics, speeches, beauty contests, religious programs and other activities.

Juneteenth was an outstanding African American holiday in the Southwest, especially, Texas, where it became an official State holiday in 1980. It was known in some places as African American

149

Emancipation Day. There were several years when it looked as if the Juneteenth holiday was on its demise. The Civil Rights struggle had over shadowed the observance of Juneteenth and the celebration was not as vigorous as in previous years.

After this lull, emphasis was focused on the holiday and a renewed interest was generated. People began again to talk about Juneteenth, articles appeared in the newspaper concerning the African American Holiday and politicians petition their legislators to make Juneteenth an official holiday. Even Maryland pushed for legislation to honor Juneteenth Day in 2000. There are over 200 cities in the United States where homage is paid during Juneteenth week to the freeing of the slaves.

Many wonder and ask the question why did the slaves remained in bondage after the Emancipation Proclamation, when they were really free. There are several legends that have been kept alive through the generations. It is said that the messenger sent by the Union authorities was murdered.

Another reason was that the Federal troops waited for the slave-owners to harvest the cotton and sugar cane crop before sending a messenger to Texas. The slave-owners were aware of the Emancipation but slavery was intact and Texas wanted the system to continue. The owners kept the slaves isolated and confined to the plantations, so they were not aware of their freedom, although they heard rumors that freedom was coming.

Still another reason was that the Civil War courier could not be spared from combat duty. The War was raging and other means of communications were impossible.

In later years, the focus of the commemoration of Juneteenth embraced education, community pride, cultural enrichment and self respect, in addition to socialization. Today the Emancipation Proclamation is revered and respected, just as it was in 1865 when the slaves of Texas first heard of their freedom.

Overcoming Racism

The historic pastoral document, "What We Have Seen and Heard," presented the vision and challenges of evangelization for African Americans. This document reports that "racism within our church and society remains the major impediment to evangelization."

Professor of moral theology Father Bryan Massingale, at a U.S. bishops' workshop, goes on to say, "struggling against the radical evil (racism) and healing the wounds it causes deserve a higher profile and priority than is now apparent."

Bishops from across the United States, including the late Bishop P. Francis Murphy, issued statements on racism as documented in a recent publication, "Love Thy Neighbor as Thy Self". In December, 2000, Cardinal William H. Keeler also drew attention to this radical evil.

Making the healing of racism a high priority calls for the execution and implementation of many strategies including increasing diverse ethnic personnel within diocesan staffs and school faculties, fair distribution of resources and encouraging inculturation.

One cannot discuss the challenges of evangelization without the mention of the decrease in clergy and lack of lay leadership. Both of these issues greatly impact evangelization in the Black community.

With the decrease of clergy and dwindling church resources, a significant number of parishes across the United States have closed or have been restructured. Since parishes and the services they render become an outlet for evangelization, their closure presents a real challenge.

Traditionally, religious communities have provided the primary source of leadership for pastoring in the Black community. This option is now threatened as religious communities are faced with their own limitation of resources.

Some dioceses have opted to train seminarians and potential deacons for the specific ministry in the African American community as a solution. The influx of African pastoral agents has been experienced. Yet one questions whether this influx is a long-range answer to the clergy dilemma. A serious dialogue needs to be held with Black Catholic communities to discuss this clergy crisis.

The ambiguity of cultural acceptance, a limitation resulting from racism and the posturing of a "missionary mentality" of Blacks has led to a lack of lay leadership. In recent studies conducted by the National Pastoral Life Center, African American Catholics (generally speaking) are not enrolled in formation or lay leadership programs. The numbers are low, very low.

African Americans are either overlooked, are not recruited or program policies prohibit enrollment. Usually programs lack Black faculty and have not factored culture into the educational experience.

The report continues to say that there is less than 1 percent African American enrollment in leadership development. Prompt attention is warranted in this area, or our efforts of evangelization will die.

Through the "Greater Task Leadership Campaign" spearheaded by Bishop Gordon D. Bennett, S.J., urban vicar, and the archdiocesan Board of African American Catholic Ministries, there have been some strides in addressing inculturation within leadership programs as well as recruiting potential pastoral leaders. Here again, structures and minds of people must change to advance this paradigm shift within the church.

While there remain challenges, there is also hope. Operation Faith Lift teams in the 18 predominantly African American parishes continue to provide evangelization outreach internally and externally.

On the vigil of Pentecost, June 2, our parishes will once again go out and pray on each corner within the church boundaries and claim once again our communities for Christ.

Here, Black Catholic laity have responded to their baptismal call as described in the Decree on the Apostolate of the Laity from the Second Vatican Council, "Incorporated into Christ's Mystical Body through baptism and strengthened by the power of the Holy Spirit through confirmation, they are assigned to the apostolate by the Lord himself."

Appropriate Solutions

The ugly face of racism continues to raise its head, and the Vatican continues to address it. In 1988 the Pontifical Council for Justice and Peace said, "Today racism has not disappeared. There are even troubling new manifestations of it here and there in various forms."

Could those new manifestations include inequity of resources, inappropriate requirements sanctioned for people of color which do not apply to those of the dominant culture, an immature dismantling of affirmative action or a silence when a voice and just action is warranted?

Yet, the voice of the Vatican is clear.

Recently, the Vatican released a new edition of the document, "The Church and Racism."

The original text is printed in its entirety prefaced with a 15-page introduction prepared as a contribution to the United Nations' sponsored conference on racism.

An article written by John Thavis from Catholic News Service is worth quoting. According to Mr. Thavis, the Vatican document indirectly touched upon the controversial question of financial compensation to descendants of slaves: "The document said that from a legal point of view, all persons have a right to equitable reparation if personally and directly they have suffered material or moral injury." (Indeed, the enslavement of Africans in America has caused personal physical and moral injury.)

Mr. Thavis continues his discussion of the Vatican document by sharing other insights on reparation: "Ideally, reparation should erase all the consequences of the injustice. When it is not possible, some form of equivalent compensation should be made ... Reparation has implications in relations between nations, for example, the obligation of giving substantial help to developing countries."

He reports that, "The Vatican expressed qualified support for affirmative action policies, which aim to advance the position of racial or ethnic groups that have been discriminated against in the past – for example, in creating special employment, education or financial opportunities. The document said that, on one hand, there was a real risk that these policies could crystallize differences in society, favor recruitment on the basis of race rather than competence and compromise freedom of choice. But it also noted the arguments of supporters, who say that sometimes it is not enough to recognize equality in society, it must be created."

The Vatican said that, in the end, such policies are legitimate as long as they are temporary and do not end up indefinitely maintaining different rights for different groups."

Mr. Thavis writes that the Vatican document "praised the efforts of countries to establish the truth about past practices of racial discrimination, and it noted that the church also recently has examined its own collective conscience on the issue, asking forgiveness for Christians' involvement in slavery and other practices. But it said the root cause of intolerance lies in the human heart, which can only be reached through education and a process of reconciliation."

The Holy Father continues to lift his voice and draw attention to the sinfulness of racism. "Racism must be opposed by the culture of reciprocal acceptance, recognizing in every man and woman a brother or sister with whom we walk in solidarity and peace. Therefore, there must be a vast work of education in the values that highlight the dignity of the person and safeguard his fundamental rights. The church intends to continue with her efforts in this area and requests all believers to make their own responsible contribution of conversion of heart, sensitization and formation."

The Vatican has spoken once again on this serious and sinful issue. Let us, in turn, work just as hard on this justice issue and resolve racism in our church and in society.

Red Summer of 1919

A dreadful wave of lynching and anti-Negro violence permeated the very fiber of America during the year 1919. Lynching was so pervasive that James Weldon Johnson labeled it the "Red Summer" of 1919. During the "Red Summer," 76 Blacks were reported lynched and 26 race riots took place. One of the worst riots took place in the nation's capital, almost within sight of the White House. Six Blacks were killed and 100 wounded.

This inhumane treatment was so blatant that civic and religious organizations began to speak out against lawless groups. One of the main opponents of lynching was the Federated Black Catholics under the guidance of Thomas Wyatt Turner. Turner was a supporter of civil rights and a devout Catholic. Born in Charles County, Maryland, Turner was a graduate of Howard University. Before he accepted the teaching position at Howard, he was the secretary of Baltimore's NAACP.

In September 1919, after the fervor of the "Red Summer" had abated, the U.S. bishops had a meeting on the campus of Catholic University in Washington, D.C. A committee of 15 eventually became the Federated Colored Catholics. They submitted a statement to the bishops requesting an increase in Black priest vocations and to halt racism in the Catholic Church. They also requested that the church be more vocal against the lynching of Negroes.

The bishops did not respond directly, but emphasized the need for more education to better the condition of the Negro. This appeased the committee somewhat and they felt that they made some progress.

However, Marcellus Dorsey, the brother of Father John Dorsey,

S.S.J., was not satisfied with the progress of eradicating racism within the church. He was a promoter for young Black men who had a vocation to the priesthood. He accused the hierarchy of trying to dodge the issue of racism as it pertained to Black seminarians.

Unfortunately, research on the views of Black Catholics concerning the "Red Summer" is limited. In fact, during the peak period of lynching, the church barely said a word against it.

Two ministers in Duluth, Minnesota, begged and prayed for the life of a potential victim. The cries of anguish and pity were ignored and the man was burned at the stake.

Despite the vicious crimes committed against colored folks, they persevered. They never surrendered their courage and pride. Blacks responded to the lynching by leaving the area.

The exodus of Blacks caused labor concerns, especially at cotton picking time. Their exit depopulated some counties before the whites realized that their labor force had vanished. As a result of this, some white and local officials called for a halt to the lynching of Negroes.

At the time that Negroes were migrating north and west, 15,000 people marched in silence down 125th Street in Harlem, New York, in protest against lynching. The Afro American, the Amsterdam News and several other newspapers, including the NAACP and Crisis Magazine, published news for the colored community. Congress tried to get an anti-lynching bill passed but southern senators, who filibustered the bill, defeated them.

The "Red Summer" did not reach Baltimore and the members of St. Francis church did not vocalize against lynching, or if they did, the documents have not been located.

Father N. R. Denis was pastor during "Red Summer." There was a vacant house across the street from the priest house that had been occupied by the Christian Brothers for the School of the Cathedral. The house was renovated and used as St. Francis School. An elementary school opened in 1920 led by the Franciscan nuns who had formerly been the Mill Hill sisters. A printing press was set up in the basement of the priest house and the art of printing was taught.

Father Denis attended to the religious needs of the church and the community. After his stay at St. Francis Xavier, he became pastor of Mother of Mercy, Forth Worth, Texas, where the congregation progressed, in spite of the harassment of the Ku Klux Klan.

GLENDORA C. HUGHES

Mis-Education

In a 1961 executive order, President John F. Kennedy was the first to officially use the phrase "affirmative action." President Lyndon Johnson pushed it as a remedy to discrimination and connected it to federal contracts. Republican president, President Richard Nixon, saw affirmative action as a legitimate strategy to address race problems.

Affirmative action is clearly not a "liberal social engineering" experiment, nor a formal national policy but a strategy embraced by several presidents seeking parity in education, employment and federal contracts for those who do not fit a white male profile. It is an outreach plan suggesting a variety of tactics such as encouraging publication of job openings in the minority media, expanding college admissions to include a diverse student population, and developing relevant training programs that target minority communities.

The intent of affirmative action is to create a level playing field. Contrary to the myth that qualified Whites are being replaced by unqualified Blacks, affirmative action takes into consideration the un-level playing field for "qualified Blacks."

The false image of qualified Whites losing opportunities to unqualified Blacks is the main source of tension. This myth has promoted the inaccurate claim that discrimination is a thing of the past that requires no special intervention. The reality is that racism and discrimination still exist. Affirmative action is an attempt to make inclusive the traditional pool of candidates which historically have been composed of white males.

Affirmative action has been labeled many things: "Reverse discrimination," "racial preferences," "color blind law," "race neutral

157

policies." The manipulation of language and misconceptions attempts to shade the truth that affirmative action does not provide unqualified minorities special rights or privileges.

Opponents of affirmative action have been provided by the media a wide forum to fill up with sound bites attacking affirmative action regardless of veracity. Incredibly, many Americans have concluded that all is well with race relations, thus opponents, including Blacks who benefited from affirmative action consider it ripe for attack.

Fear of being negatively labeled is not without basis and has its foundation in the following stated false perception:

A 1993 report by the Committee for Racial Justice and the Center for Political and Economical Studies noted that Caucasian people perceive another Caucasian as competent until proven incompetent but perceive an African American person as incompetent until proven competent. Often African Americans are presumed to have limited expertise and to have been hired preferentially.

A person hired or admitted under an affirmative action plan must still do the work to retain the job or earn the degree. They must compete with all of the participants for advancement and grades. However, the minority candidate always has the pressure and burden of proving themselves because of the above stated presumption of incompetency or not being considered qualified.

William G. Bowen, former president of Princeton University and Derek Bok, former president of Harvard University, affirm the truth about affirmative action's success in admissions policies.

In their book *"The Shape of the River"*, Bowen and Bok provide empirical evidence on how race-sensitive admissions policies actually work. The book separates the facts from the fiction by revealing that colleges seeking a diverse student population have done so without sacrificing quality. Individuals who benefited from the policies have gone on to excel in school and make significant contributions.

Affirmative action is not the destructive force in our society as its critics would have us believe. It attempts to provide minorities with the opportunity to start the race at the starting line and not 50 yards back because of their race or sex. When white males still dominate over 90 percent of the senior management positions in Fortune 1000 companies, it can hardly be said that affirmative action has unfairly put them at a disadvantage. Civil rights is still the unfinished business of America.

GLENDORA C. HUGHES

Removing the Elephant

At the National Black Catholic Congress IX, many African American Catholics came together to worship not as a minority community but as family to a church we would be planning to improve. We came together to celebrate being both Black and Catholic and to leave Congress IX with a pastoral plan of action for eight principles that need ministering from the church, one of which is "racism."

The topic of racism reminds me of the elephant in the room that no one wants to talk about much less acknowledge. We know the elephant is there. It gets in our way, if not dominates the entire room. However, we just don't want to overcome our fear and address the question of how to move the elephant because it is just too hard. So, we ignore it and hope that maybe it will go away without tearing the house down when leaving. Go figure!

But God did not give us a spirit of fear and more than 200 brothers and sisters at Congress IX courageously signed up not only to discuss racism in the Catholic Church but also to produce an action plan for one year, three years and five years, reach consensus and do so in 40 minutes.

Were we looking for a miracle? Yes, we were and God delivered. Egos, anger, frustrations and personal agendas were checked at the doors as God's people went to work and produced workable solutions to be carried out nationally "on one accord."

The people of God agreed that the first step to addressing the sin of racism in the church, should begin with meaningful dialogue between the bishops and parish leadership about the impact racism has had socially, economically, educationally and politically on the minority communities.

In three years, the consensus was that we should include other ethnic groups in this dialogue to develop strategies to eliminate racism from our parishes and dioceses. And finally, within five years, have in place a strategy to increase Black leadership on diocesan boards and other church institutions.

Clearly, these are very wise and doable action items to move the elephant, but it will take the commitment of all members of the Body of Christ in Baltimore to overcome this sin and leave the house (church) standing.

Racism is not just a Black Catholic community problem; it is a Catholic Church problem. Thus, we must move from monologues about racism to dialogues leading to meaningful solutions. And no, waiting and ignoring the issue is not an option because the elephant is moving around tearing up the interior of the house.

Dr. Martin Luther King said in his "Letter From a Birmingham Jail," "Shallow understanding from people of good will is more frustrating than absolute misunderstanding from people of ill will. Lukewarm acceptance is much more bewildering than outright rejection."

For too long this has been the African American Catholic experience in the church: "shallow understanding" and "lukewarm acceptance."

Racism prevents the people of the church from being truly holy. And the participants of Congress IX have said we are willing to tackle this obstacle to holiness and here is the plan.

Minds and Hearts

Historians have long reported the precarious position regarding race matters in Maryland. The state, often referred to as the place of the "Mason-Dixon" line, is a converging point between northern and southern culture. Baltimore, once noted for its neighborhoods of ethnic diversity, still seems rather slow in its push forward in racial healing. So what's needed?

I grew up Catholic and remember well that one of the steps toward reconciliation is a process called "examination of conscience." In this process one overcomes avoidance, uncovers what is done consciously and unconsciously and becomes aware of the problem at hand. This brings people out of denial and initiates a road toward action to resolve the issue and promote healing.

A personal as well as public examination of conscience is the first step toward racial healing. Overcoming polite avoidance, recognizing racism and raising awareness is the result of such an examination of conscience. Open and honest dialogue among church, business and government leaders is integral in the healing of this infectious wound.

The second step toward racial healing in Baltimore recognizes the moral impact that these leaders have. Their support in eradicating racism is warranted. Thousands of people are influenced through the church and faith communities. Through church institutions and agencies lives are changed.

The business community shapes public opinion through the media, services rendered and resource people. In some ways, business leaders have the attention of the people.

The political community puts together laws, policies and actions to improve the quality of life of citizens within a democratic society. The church, business and political communities have the resources and influence to affect institutional change. They can set the stage for re-orienting people and systems to be open to everyone, regardless of race.

Could our leaders use their voices and influence to address racism and the evil impact it has on every persons' well being? These institutions can lead the way in dismantling racial profiling, patterns of stereotyping and the ignorance that dominates thoughts and actions.

At the same time that church, business and political leaders are lifting their voices to appeal racism and re-orientate people's thinking and action, they could also promote and implement policies. In achieving this goal, internal structures may need to change.

Staffing to be more inclusive, creating policies that formulate an environment that does not tolerate racist systems or economics and partnering with other institutions that are skilled in overcoming personal and institutional racism become a must.

To attack subtle and overt racism calls for many strategies. Aggressively seeking inclusivity in the decision-making boards, not tokenism, is another strategy. Securing proper financial resources to attack racism is still another.

Congruent to the above, I must lift up the importance of implementing "affirmative action." In recent times, there has been an unfortunate distortion of what this means and its impact. This topic deserves to be discussed in its own article.

There will be many who will be surprised that racism exists within their church, their business, their political party or system. Bigotry is not a surprise but a reminder of the work that needs to be done. The church, business and political communities must accept a posture that says, "I'm willing to do the hard work." It will be hard work to change attitudes and structures. It's tough to change minds and systems.

Dr. Martin Luther King Jr. gives us some wisdom: "Let us consider the need for a tough mind, characterized by incisive thinking, realistic appraisal and decisive judgment ... The tough minded individual is astute and discerning ... with a strong, austere quality that makes for firmness of purpose and solidness of commitment." This wisdom comes from Dr. King's speech, "A Tough Mind and A Tender Heart." May we and our institutions have tough minds and tender hearts to eradicate racism, thus promoting racial healing.

Overcoming Challenges

"Within the history of every Christian community there comes a time when it reaches adulthood. This maturity brings with it the duty, the privilege and the joy to share with others the rich experience of the Word of Life." These words are the opening statement of the document "What We Have Seen and Heard: A Pastoral Letter on Evangelization from the Black Bishops."

This pastoral letter, issued in 1984, serves as a vision for enhancing evangelization within the Black community. Now, 17 years later, after experiencing National Black Catholic Congresses, the issuing of several papal and episcopal documents and exploring this topic with Black Catholics, many questions surface. One in particular is about the challenges that face Black Catholics as they evangelize.

Pope Paul VI encouraged an integration and celebration of cultural diversity in the Apostolic Exhortation "Evangelii Nuntiandi" (Dec. 8, 1975). Proclaiming the Gospel includes "incorporating into its common life all the different characteristics of the people of the world – aspirations, ways of praying, of loving, of looking at life and the world".

Pope John Paul II has championed the theme of a "new evangelization," one which factors culture into the ministry, "bringing the power of the Gospel into the very heart of culture and cultures."

These are strong statements celebrated in the African American community. Oftentimes we fear that the strong tenets of Black culture and characteristics of Black spirituality are not valued within the church.

Over the years there have been many celebrations as well as the formulation of policies and programs for leadership development,

163

evangelization and catechetical formation void of cultural diversity. This raises the question whether there is ambiguity within the church surrounding the concept of and implementation of inculturation.

Has the church really bought into affirming and celebrating what and who it really is – a universal church? This ambiguity becomes a challenge for African Americans and our mission to evangelize.

Lack of inclusivity within high levels of the church presents yet another challenge. The "African American Fact Sheet" issued by the Secretariat for African American Catholics indicates that there are 13 African American bishops – seven of whom are ordinaries; four African Americans who serve as heads of religious communities; four African American professors who teach at Catholic universities and one African American Catholic superintendent of schools.

Very few African Americans serve the diocesan church in leadership positions in its central service workings. These are power positions. Thus, decisions are made, policies formulated, resources distributed with little or no input from the Black community. One cannot authentically serve the church family if they are not at the table.

Overcoming subtle and overt racism on several levels within the church structure is yet another challenge. Sadly, there are still places and corridors of the church where the inclusion of our culture and our people is not welcomed.

Acknowledging the pervasiveness of this problem, addressing the lingering injury of racism and correcting policies and attitudes that persist is a step forward in overcoming racism. Reconciliation occurs, too, when one identifies and corrects the impact that racism has placed on the fair distribution of human and economic resources within the church.

In doing so, one pushes for racial and ethnic diversity across the board – in diocesan positions, pastoral positions, celebrations, consultations and at the board level.

"Evangelization means not only preaching but witnessing; not only conversion but renewal; not only entry into the community but the building up of the community; not only hearing the Word but sharing it," said the bishops in "What We Have Seen and Heard."

The above discussion lifts some of the challenges that African Americans face in their ministry of evangelization. There are other issues worthy to be articulated. At the same time, there is great energy and spiritual renewal among Black Catholics of Baltimore to teach, preach and witness, to share within the community and build it up.

Leadership and Pastoral Ministry

"Upon this rock I will build"

Any institution that wants to survive longer than a generation places great investment in the formation of leaders. Leaders who are anchored in faith, fully cognizant of their purpose and role, are the arches that raise up pastoral ministry. These men and women, youth and elders, hear Jesus calling them and saying to them, "upon this rock I will build my Church."

As Black Catholics we find our freedom and fulfillment in Jesus and in His Church. Our unique gift of Blackness and grace-filled experiences enable us to enrich the body of Christ. This section of the book discusses how we have enriched the church through conversations exploring our leadership and pastoral dreams and desires. It shares presentations on leadership in our church, its decision-making processes in national, diocesan and parish arenas as well as the various dynamics of parish ministry including evangelization and youth ministry.

CHARLES G. TILDON, JR.

A Collective Push

The church – the Archdiocese of Baltimore – is directed by the Gospel to spread the "good news" of salvation to all God's people. The African American citizens of Baltimore City present us with a welcome challenge to carry out this mission of evangelization. To be effective, we must recognize the obstacles.

It is well documented that the language, mores, habits and practices of any group create the climate for effective communication. Families and communities look for leadership from people who look, act and think like them; persons whose experiences are similar.

Today, partnerships and equal participation have replaced paternalism and authoritarian leadership. The evolution of consultative bodies, such as parish councils, give credence to the value of this change. The need for diverse representation among the clergy, deacons and religious has been well established.

However, in the Archdiocese of Baltimore we have not done well in attracting African Americans to serve as priests, deacons or religious. I believe we must recognize this fact and find creative ways to correct this dilemma.

The demographics of our city offer opportunity to share our faith with an African American population. To do so, we need role models. We need persons whose experiences and sensitivities fit the African American population, "crying out" for God's saving grace.

It is difficult to overcome the impact of our history, one that excluded African American participation in church leadership. Yet examples of developing leadership against the odds are evident in the African

American response to Catholicism.

Leadership exhibited by African American Catholics in this archdiocese is no oxymoron. Out of Baltimore came the first order of Black religious women, the Oblate Sisters of Providence led by Mother Elizabeth Lange, O.S.P. Out of Baltimore came the first Black priest ordained in the United States, Father Charles Uncles, S.S.J., and the first deacon nationally ordained (in recent times), Deacon Americus Roy.

Out of Baltimore comes the first executive director of the Secretariat for African American Catholics at the United States Conference of Catholic Bishops, Dr. Beverly A. Carroll. Out of Baltimore came the first executive director of the National Black Catholic Congress, Therese Wilson Favors, as well as former executive director, Dr. Hilbert Stanley. Still, out of Baltimore, comes only three Black priests.

Our future in the African American community depends on our willingness to boldly investigate opportunities to increase the presence of African American leaders. Catholic men and women can be motivated to act as leaders, prepared to share the "good news" if we reach out creatively to them, affirming that their talents and skills are both needed and wanted.

Black Catholic men have been identified by their pastoral leaders and parish communities to serve in the role of the diaconate and were denied participation for various reasons.

Can the special needs and interests of the African American community serve as a basis for reviewing our diaconate program? It is clear that the placement of Black deacons in our communities fosters evangelization on various levels.

I recommend that the archbishop convene a special group of African Americans to review the data, study the impact and develop special programs designed to address the problem.

Surely, other dioceses have recognized the problem. Have they had any success? Are there creative ways to attract young men and women to vocations? Can we look carefully at church doctrine, dogma, biblical history and worldwide practices to find models to use lay leaders – men and women?

In short we can maintain the status quo and fail in our challenge to evangelize by denying the powerful role of indigenous leadership, or we can use our collective wisdom inspired by grace.

Dr. Hilbert T. Stanley

Proclaiming

On September 9, 1984, on the Feast of St. Peter Claver, the ten Black bishops of the United States issued a most significant Pastoral Letter on Evangelization entitled *"What We Have Seen and Heard."* This pastoral letter became 16 years of age on September 9, 2000.

In 1984, the Black bishops of the United States joyfully affirmed after decades of being ministered to by generous missionary activities that the Black Catholic Community in the American Church had come of age. This was a time to celebrate this maturity, which "brings with it the duty, the privilege and the joy to share with others the rich experience of the "Word of Life". Always conscious of the need to hear the Word and ever ready to listen to its proclamation, the mature Christian community feels the irresistible urge to speak that Word."

As we reflect on our faith as Black Catholics, during the month of September, it is a most appropriate time to demonstrate our duty, our privilege and our joy as we share with others the rich experience of the "Word of Life."

In order to share, we need to revisit the pastoral letter, so that we might rekindle that joy which the Black Bishops referenced when they again called to our attention the joy experienced by the Ethiopian eunuch in Acts 8:39. We raise the question "Do we demonstrate our witness to our risen Lord and to those with whom we come in contact?" Sixteen years ago, the bishops wrote to us with the teaching that each of us is called to a special task by the Holy Spirit to work on evangelization.

With the convening of the Sixth National Black Catholic Congress in just three short years after the publication of the pastoral letter "What We

Have Seen and Heard," the Black bishops and the major organizations representing the laity, clergy, and communities of religious men and women focused on evangelization in the Black community. Taking a great deal of its direction from the inspiration offered by the pastoral letter, the Congress rekindled that joy spoken about in Acts 8:39 among large numbers of African Americans and the wider Catholic Church community.

How effective are we today in sharing the gifts that Blacks bring to the wider Catholic Church? The pastoral letter highlights "The Gifts We Share." These gifts include:

- our Black culture and values: informed by our faith,
- our African American spirituality based in sacred scripture",
- our gift of freedom as is affirmed in John 8:32 As Jesus said ("You will know the truth and the truth will set you free."),
- our gift of reconciliation,
- our gift of family including the extended family,
- and our reality of answering the call as Black Catholics to serve as a bridge with our brothers and sister of other Christian communities as well as followers of non-Christian religions.

The pastoral letter goes on to highlight "The Call of God to His People." An important part of this document is the section, which issues a call and focuses on the responsibility that we have as Black Americans and Black Catholics to reclaim our roots and shoulder the responsibility of being both Black and Catholic. This responsibility includes proclaiming our Faith and taking an active part in building up the Church – to evangelize.

Those of us who need to revisit the pastoral letter, are encouraged to obtain a copy which should be a part of our mandatory reading list.

(St. Anthony Messenger Press, 1615 Republic Street, Cincinnati, Ohio 45210) 1-800-448-0488 or www.AmericanCatholic.org

Call to Leadership

In a spirit-filled and festive atmosphere September 9 that included the harmonizing voices of the men's choir, 15 sisters and brothers were warmly welcomed at historic St. Francis Xavier (the oldest Black Catholic church in the United States). They answered publicly the Lord's call to service and took up their mantle of leadership in a new capacity as board members of the Office of African American Catholic Ministries.

The new board members are Franklin Collins of St. Joseph's Passionist Monastery; Eric Davis and Darron Woodus of St. Cecilia; Roberta Epps and Brenda Rigby from St. Gregory the Great; Nina Harper and Glendora Hughes of St. Francis Xavier; Father Raymond Harris, chaplain and director of campus ministry at Mount St. Mary's College and Seminary in Emmitsburg; Gloria Herndon and Joann Logan of New All Saints; Arlene Fisher from St. Pius V; Ella Johnson and Marie Washington of St. Veronica; and Gary Pulliam and Tully Sullivan of Immaculate Conception.

Equally as important was the recognition of former board members who provided six years of un-daunting service and support to the office. They included outgoing board president Carl Stokes from St. Francis Xavier; Charles Blake of St. Edward; Ellen Dutton of St. Peter Claver; Michele Jameson from St. John the Evangelist in Columbia; Sister Rita Michelle Proctor, O.S.P., vice principal of Cardinal Shehan School; and Idell Pugh of St. Mary of the Assumption in Govans.

The liturgy, presided over by Bishop Gordon D. Bennett, S.J., and concelebrated by Father Alfred Dean, pastor of St. Francis Xavier, and Father Raymond Harris, was a combination of joy, humor and seriousness.

Bishop Bennett preached a very inspiring homily about the path to holiness. Referencing the spirit and stamina of many of our African American ancestors and saints, he told the congregation that in order to lead we must seek holiness, and from holiness we will discern the path that God wants us to take.

Following Communion, Therese Wilson Favors, director, provided a brief history of the office and an overview of its work, which included a special acknowledgement of the outgoing board. Bishop Bennett, joined by the youth of St. Francis Xavier, said a special prayer of thanksgiving over the former members recognizing their dedication and leadership to the archdiocese. Formal installation of new members occurred.

Bishop Bennett led the congregation in the litany of the saints followed by a prayer response from the board. Current and former members were presented with a copy of the Good News Bible – African American Jubilee Edition. New members also received a stole made of kente cloth, a woven fabric from the Ashanti people of Ghana. Produced for more than 2,000 years, kente is woven in a fashion to convey ideas from one culture to another. Leadership in the Black community is very much like kente cloth in that our leaders have become invaluable vehicles to spread ideas and to serve as liberators.

In conclusion and as a sign of appreciation, present and former board members presented an Ashanti stool to Bishop Bennett. This stool is reserved for authority figures such as the chief or queen. Bishop Bennett's leadership, commitment and advocacy have fostered the creation and success of the Greater Leadership Task Campaign, Operation Faith Lift and this Africentric column.

The archdiocesan Office of African American Catholic Ministries, established in 1989, has as its principal responsibility the promotion of evangelization and leadership development within the African American community and to share with the people of this archdiocese the richness of the African American experience and culture.

The board is an advisory body, appointed by Cardinal William H. Keeler, to generate ideas and establish and monitor goals that promote the office's mission. The board plays a vital role in bringing diverse experiences, special expertise and perspectives to the office's overall direction.

The installation was an historic event forever engrained in our fabric.

The Ninth Congress

A ny institution, movement or organization which wants to survive beyond a generation, places great emphasis and enormous energy on the identification, formation and affirmation of its leaders. Thus is the focus of the ninth National Black Catholic Congress in Chicago Aug. 29 - Sept. 1. Not only is the focus on the identification and affirmation of leaders in the Black community but also the encouragement "to work in one accord" in seeking strategies that will build up the church and its people.

The National Black Catholic Congress is one of the oldest institutions in the Black Catholic community. Through the vision of Daniel Rudd, the Congress movement has been instrumental in addressing the issues and concerns of the Black community. This vision laid a firm foundation and direction for evangelization efforts. Black Catholics will stand together committed to our church to pray and work at Congress IX. Leaders from all over the United States will seek strategies that will transform the spiritual and material condition of our people.

The National Black Catholic Congress Board of Trustees met in 2000 to identify the theme for Congress IX: Black Catholic Leadership. Eight areas to support this agenda were also selected: spirituality, parish life, youth and young adults, Catholic education, social justice, racism, Africa and HIV/AIDS.

Each diocese was given an opportunity last February to make recommendations for action in each of the eight areas. These action plans from the dioceses formed The Plan of Action. At Congress IX participants will be engaged first, in a consensus making process to prioritize which actions should be implemented and then a majority rule process will determine the final selection.

The Archdiocese of Baltimore will have approximately 65 participants at the Congress. Bishop Gordon D. Bennett, S.J., will lead the delegation with a particular hope of supporting leadership within the Black Catholic community while implementing The Pastoral Plan of Action.

Of the 16 predominantly African American parishes in Baltimore, there are three full-time African American lay ministers. The same 16 parishes employ six part-time ministers to religious education and/or youth ministry programs. Fourteen Oblate Sisters of Providence serve in parish religious education programs and/or as teachers in our Catholic schools.

There are 17 African American permanent deacons in the archdiocese. Of this number, all but one are assigned to predominantly Black parishes. Six parishes do not have a deacon on staff. Of the 17, six are retired, three are in their 70s, three in their 60s, four in their 50s and one in his 40s. We have one African American in the formation program of the permanent diaconate and two African American Catholics enrolled at the Ecumenical Institute at St. Mary's Seminary. There are two African American priests (diocesan) and one African priest serving this archdiocese. There is one African American brother in service here.

Certainly there is a concern to increase leadership here in Baltimore. Vocations to religious life and to the priesthood warrant our attention now. Additionally, we need to promote professional leaders to ensure a future.

Black Catholics want a future in the church and the future begins now! That is why the Board of African American Catholic Ministries instituted a program three years ago titled "The Greater Task Leadership Campaign." The program raises awareness, identifies potential leaders and investigates formation opportunities for leadership development.

The national vision of "leadership in one accord" is a gift to us as we consider our situation here at home. As we stand on the shoulders of our ancestors who made their mark in 1889 at the first Congress of Colored Catholics, we echo the spirit of the past and announce a new day of unity and leadership. This is one cause that requires all our help – so that we can ensure a future !

A New Day

This year we witnessed a historic paradigm shift in pastoral leadership here in the Archdiocese of Baltimore. Several men and women were appointed as pastoral life directors for parishes. With the appointment of these parish life directors, the dawning of a new day of pastoral leadership has come.

This new leadership surrounds us, but does not include us – yet! Have we not seen the handwriting on the wall? Have we seriously faced the realities of an aging clergy, limited clergy and few vocations? Have we, the laity, crafted a plan to insure a future for our parishes by encouraging leadership and securing viable avenues of support and training of our own? (Any institution that seeks to have a future, always places great support and resources in securing, attracting and maintaining new leadership.)

Are we ready, willing and able to step up to the plate when needed for our parishes? A new day has come and this new day has provided opportunity for us to go places where this generation has not gone before.

Of course, we have spirited individuals within our parishes with the genius and faith that is required to lead and to lead successfully. Now is the time to harness the commitment by making plans to walk into this new day – prepared!

We also have a precedence in serving in this capacity that dates back to 1909 when an African American man and woman led a parish and attracted many to the Lord through the Catholic Church.

Lincoln Vallé, born in 1854, was a comrade of Daniel Rudd, initiator of the first Black Catholic congresses (1889-1894). Mr. Vallé was also a parishioner at St. Monica Church in Chicago at the time of Father Augustine Tolton (first Black priest in the United States, ordained in Rome in 1889). In fact, Vallé was a boarder in the home of Martha Tolton, mother of Father Augustine.

In 1908, Lincoln Vallé married Julia Yoular. The couple moved to Milwaukee with the avowed purpose of preaching to the Blacks in Milwaukee. On their arrival they visited Archbishop Sebastian G. Messmer requesting his approval to conduct lectures on the Catholic religion in the Black community. Archbishop Messmer encouraged the Vallés in the work of evangelization. Together, Lincoln and Julia walked into history, a new day for Milwaukee.

Eventually the Vallés purchased a building to promote evangelization. The building was dedicated to St. Benedict the Moor, the patron saint of African American Catholics. From the beginning there were converts. The baptismal register of the first Black parish in Milwaukee, led by a lay Black man and woman, shows "the first 30 or so people asked the Vallés to serve as their sponsors." Archbishop Messmer said of Lincoln Vallé, "He was a true lay apostle."

The Capuchin Friars celebrated Mass at St. Benedict and eventually took over the parish. They questioned the Vallés' role and the relationship between them began to deteriorate. By 1912, the Vallés had no more connection with St. Benedict. Lincoln considered himself a professional, while the friars thought Lincoln as more of a "janitor" and his wife a "maid."

Undeniably, there are some tragic elements of this story but it does reaffirm the important role of indigenous leaders to serve their own people. The Vallés were successful leaders in attracting and maintaining their people to the Lord through the Catholic Church. They continued serving as evangelists, publishing a Black Catholic monthly newsletter titled "The Catholic Truth."

We, too, must take the initiative and a proactive stance in joining the newly formed circle of parish life directors. Let's take a long hard look around us and identify who is ready, willing and able. Let's make the plans and move the paper work and get the training because in this case, history needs to repeat itself. Pope John Paul II affirmed Black Catholic leadership in the summer of 1987, saying, "The church needs you!" A new day has come and the need is even greater now.

Leadership and Service

Every great institution of sustaining power and innovative progress attributes its success to the vision and dedication of its leaders. Our parishes are institutions of sustaining power where we find a rich legacy of African American Catholic leaders diligently leading and serving.

They prayerfully go about their tasks with determination, vigor and faith. These leaders continue to carry forth consistently God's word, will and vision and are dedicated to uplifting his people to live life more abundantly. They are deeply rooted in their strong faith and in God's word – they are phenomenal.

Jesus knew of the importance and power of the right leaders for the right ministry. He spent time searching for the 12 disciples, watching them, teaching them, challenging them, walking with them, praying with them and sharing with them.

We see many hearts and hands doing the work of the Lord in parishes and communities. Our parishioners are praising God, witnessing to God's mercy and kindness and reaching out to those who need help the most.

Our pastors are leading and guiding congregations of various sizes, ministries and compositions. Our children, youth and adults are discovering deeper relationships with God and the Christian community and are inspired to lead and serve.

On any given day you see African American adults utilizing their leadership qualities through their commitment to their parishes and in the implementation of parish missions. These are individuals who can translate intentions into reality by leading a specific ministry, program,

177

initiative or effort and continue to encourage others within the parishes to participate.

These individuals are the glue that keeps our parishes alive and consistently reach out to our communities to serve. They have made and continue to make long-standing or significant contributions of time, talent and treasure to their parishes – they are phenomenal.

Our adult leaders are inspiring children and youth to take more active roles as leaders and in service within the church and in the community. Children and youth are taking leadership roles and are utilizing their skills, time and talents as well as resources toward the accomplishment of parish goals and initiatives.

They are following in the footsteps of their priests, deacons, parents, elders, teachers and lay leaders. Our youth exhibit Christian witness to others, lead and serve in their parishes and communities and help in implementing the mission of their parishes – they are phenomenal.

Today, our African American Catholic leaders are like Mother Mary Elizabeth Lange, founder of the Oblate Sisters of Providence, who was a phenomenal woman. She was phenomenal in her love for her people and her church. She was phenomenal in her vision to see where others of her time could not see. She was phenomenal in her compassion, courage and steadfastness. It is good that we take an example from her, for our God still calls the service and leadership of phenomenal men, women and youth.

We must affirm those in our midst who are phenomenal and consistently serve, lead and act as anchors in our African American Catholic community. Celebrating those who quietly make a difference while serving and leading is important to individual men, women and youth who, although often not given outward recognition, are vital to the life of our parishes.

SISTER MAGDALA MARIE GILBERT, O.S.P.

Black Catholic Studies

Nestled in the bayous of New Orleans is the Institute for Black Catholic Studies at Xavier University. Unique from its inception, it is a powerhouse of intellectual and transforming energy. The leaders within the Black Catholic community founded the institute to train leadership for clergy, religious and laity in and for the Black Catholic community.

The institute affirms Gospel values as well as the teachings and traditions of the Catholic Church as seen through Black minds, Black eyes and heard through Black ears. As a result, Blacks for the first time were able to see themselves as God sees them and not through the lens of other cultures.

Development of Black leadership continues to be a central focus for the institute. However, clergy, religious and laity of other cultures who work in predominantly Black parishes or Black-related institutions are encouraged to participate. They have found the institute to be a source of insight and inspiration in their ministry in the African American tradition.

Baltimore boasts of both graduates and professors from the institute. Graduates with Baltimore connections include Kathleen Dorsey Bellow, Sister Magdala Marie Gilbert, O.S.P., Sister Clarice Proctor, O.S.P., Sister Barbara Spears, S.N.J.M., Brother Martin de Porres Smith, C.Ss.R., Cheryl Weems and Beverly White. Currently there are four Baltimoreans in study at the institute.

Baltimoreans who have served as professors at the institute include Dr. Beverly A. Carroll, Therese Wilson Favors and Father Donald A. Sterling, Ph.D.

The Institute for Black Catholic Studies was the vision of Father Thaddeus Posey born from an urgency to do something to assist Black people to name and claim their Black Catholic heritage. In 1977, Father Posey brought before the boards of The National Black Clergy Caucus and the National Black Sisters' Conference a proposal to sponsor and implement a symposium on Black Catholic theology. From Oct. 12-15, 1978, a group of Black Catholic theologians, women and men, met in Baltimore at the Motherhouse of the Oblate Sisters of Providence.

The symposium called for the establishment of an Institute for Black Catholic Studies where African American men and women could learn about themselves, their culture, their Blackness and their Catholicity from an Africentric modality.

Here Black women and men could face the truth about issues that often were considered precarious and difficult to discuss. The challenging issue of racism within the church and wider society is discussed and a search for solutions formulated. In order for healing to take place, oral histories and storytelling is shared. The story of slavery and overcoming must be told to encourage a continuous journey.

Xavier University, founded by the Sisters of the Blessed Sacrament (whose foundress is St. Katharine Drexel) was chosen as the site for the institute. It seemed the appropriate site since it is the only Black Catholic university in the United States.

The Institute for Black Catholic Studies began in 1980. The first classes were held in the Office of Campus Ministry. Originally, the institute was primarily for those studying for a master's degree in theology. Today, the institute also includes certification and enrichment programs in catechesis, youth ministry and leadership.

The institute is unique not only in its formational structure but also in its attitude of inclusiveness. All of its members as well as faculty are responsible for taking part in religious, social, cultural and recreational activities. Liturgies are lively, rich in Black culture and symbolism and are a vital segment of the institute.

The Institute for Black Catholic Studies has come a long way since its origin. The three week program, beginning in June and ending in July, is rather intense but worth the time and effort. According to Sister Eva Regina Martin, S.S.F., director of the institute, "It is a non-stop academic and spiritual experience year round because people are taking what they have learned during the summer and applying it in their ministries."

FATHER RAYMOND L. HARRIS, JR.

Encouraging Vocations

Almost seven years ago, I was the first African American to be ordained an archdiocesan priest in 20 years. I hope that we will not have to wait another generation for this to happen again. The smaller numbers of young adults preparing for the priesthood and consecrated religious life are a concern for the entire church.

Signs of hope in many parts of the country, including our archdiocese, may be tempered by concerns about whether this will match the numbers of those ministers who have retired or have been called from labor to eternal reward.

In my regular reading of Catholic, Eastern Orthodox and mainline Protestant news services, I have learned that these concerns are not exclusive to the Catholic Church in the United States.

We cannot ignore the additional fact that African American candidates for the priesthood and religious life were not generally accepted into our church institutions until well into the 20th century. These tragic choices influenced by racism have reaped unfortunate consequences for Catholic evangelization in the African American community.

One positive note over the past three decades has been the rise of the permanent diaconate and professional lay ministry.

An increase in vocations to the priesthood, consecrated religious life, the permanent diaconate and professional lay ministry among the many cultures of the church should be the concern of the whole church.

Our primary motivation should come from the firm conviction that God is still calling people to these ministries. Developing a program to recruit, retain and support African American candidates for these ministries is a major plank of the National Black Catholic Pastoral Plan. To achieve this goal, several strategies are suggested for implementation.

First, when I was one of two African American archdiocesan seminarians, the Vocation Office developed culturally sensitive vocation material to reach out to our community. These attempts should continue in a sustained campaign.

Second, our seminaries and houses of formation should include in their curricula an understanding of the diverse cultures of the church in America. This is in keeping with Pope John Paul II's understanding that we should see North and South America as one America.

Third, we need to continue to affirm that ministry in our predominately African American parishes is a valued ministry with opportunities for spiritual growth.

Fourth, parishes should sponsor "vocation awareness days" and make concerted efforts to educate parishioners (particularly families) about their role in promoting vocations.

The most important thing that we must do is to pray. This was a command of our Lord. "The harvest is abundant, but the laborers are few, so ask the master of the harvest to send out laborers for his harvest."

Every Christian is called to labor in this harvest. Those who have received a divine call to serve in the aforementioned ministries have special and very necessary roles that build up the church.

We should be ready to allow God to answer our prayers through us. We need to encourage those who may have the qualities to serve to consider if God is calling them. They should believe that where God guides, God will provide.

The encouragement that I received from my family, parish priests and fellow parishioners of St. Joseph's Passionist Monastery in Baltimore to consider the priesthood is the reason I am a priest today.

God is still calling people to the ordained, vowed and professional lay ministries of the church for the building up of the community of faith. We cannot be complacent about how the situation exists now. Let us be inspired by the firm conviction that God can do more than we can imagine when we take the risk to cooperate with him.

Black Sisters Conference

The National Black Sisters' Conference (NBSC) began on Aug. 17, 1968, in Pittsburgh at Carlow College under the able leadership and vision of Sister Martin De Porres Gray, a Sister of Mercy, and a small group of African American women religious. They came together to build bonds of unity, support, camaraderie, and prayer time together.

The majority of these women were in predominately white congregations. Their desire was to find a welcoming space to be with other Black women religious, where they could "walk the walk" and talk the talk" without fear of being put down or criticized.

The founding of NBSC would give them a forum to be able to speak out their frustration to other Black women religious in the same situation. It was not easy trying to cope in a different culture and be accepted for who they were as children of God. They needed a place to, "let their hair down," as it were, an expression used in the Black community for people to be who they are without any pretense.

The new conference allowed the Sisters to be able to cope with seemingly hopeless situations in congregations where some of the white Sisters were not respectful of Black people or their African heritage.

One might ask, "Why would these women subject themselves to such racism and discrimination? Why not enter one of the three Black orders, namely the Oblate Sisters of Providence in Baltimore, the Holy Family Sisters in New Orleans or the Handmaids of Mary in Harlem?"

The answer is simple. Each congregation has its own charism, apostolic works and prayer style. God calls each of us to that congregation which suits us as individuals, where we are to work

183

out our salvific calling. After prayerful discernment, Black Catholic women, have the option and the right to choose which congregation the Lord deems best for them.

In the secular world, one enters a career or profession that one feels called to. So it is with the religious life. It is sad that conditions warranted that this had to happen, but then, God in his providence knew that through all the pain something good would spring forth. God is always on time. One might say that the finger of God was and is in this wonderful Spirit-filled, Christ-filled conference.

Changing times have forced congregations to deal with racism and discrimination in their membership through community forums and other forms of communication. With that issue somewhat behind them, NBSC shifted its focus to the Black Catholic community, looking at how it could impact the larger African American Catholic community. As a result of inner discernment, NBSC formulated various programs to cope with some of the racism and discrimination that was alive and well also in our African American parishes.

The conference was and is about us as a Black people, also seeking and finding our roots in the Bible. The conference began to forge a new path in catechetics, called cathechesis, from the Black Perspective. The Imani program at the Institute of Black Catholic Studies at Xavier University, in New Orleans, La., was an off-shoot of a book sponsored by the National Black Sisters Conference called, "Tell It Like It Is: A Black Catholic Perspective on Christian Education," edited by Sister Eva Marie Lumas, S.S.S.

Although Sister Martin de Porres Gray is no longer with the conference, the thrust of her vision lives on.

Who could have imagined the huge impact that would be made on the Black Catholic community in that small beginning in Pittsburgh in 1968? NBSC has not only impacted the African American Catholic community in the United States but has also made its influence felt in other parts of the world as well.

Thank a Deacon

"There are persons whose lives are so much like that of Christ's, who have so much genuine Christianity in them, that we cannot come in contact with them, we cannot even steal a glance at their faces, without being made stronger or better."

– Booker T. Washington

The "Treasure Chest" is getting empty and no one seems to care.

Since 1971, the urban churches of Baltimore, especially the African American parishes have enjoyed the gentle and loving presence of deacons. Thirty-three years later, we are in danger of losing one of our most prized resources. Why? No one has the time or maybe the interest to pick up the gift of service. Maybe we are all so busy that we don't have the time. I think I need to stop making up excuses for the men who cannot and will not hear the call of God.

Let me fantasize about a time without deacons for the urban church. A time we will not have an intermediary to help us in the Catholic Church. No tireless, peaceful presence that could help us to abate the storms of life, a friendly smile, a needed hug, or a timely "God bless you."

How soon do we forget those good old days when we celebrated one of our own for taking that step of faith to serve his sisters and brothers? However, those times have happened and we have been blessed by the presence of deacons. However, those treasures are fading away and somehow it seems to be all right. Don't you know that there are still churches in the archdiocese that have never had a deacon?

I would imagine that you could say that this is a self-serving article because I took the walk, however I want to testify that if it wasn't for those deacons before me, I would not have answered the call. I was inspired to answer by a deacon. He never asked me, but his behavior and walk helped me to hear the soft and gentle voice of God calling out to me. Another deacon who gave me his blessings further confirmed my walk. My urgency is that we cannot wait until the well is dry. We need role models and commitments now.

I feel the loss of my brother deacons. When I look, there is no one at the plate, no one in the on-deck. It is empty. Are we going to let the legacy of African American deacons in Baltimore City die? Are we going to continue to sit on the sidelines and hope someone will step up to the plate? If not now, when? If not you, who? We have the unique opportunity to serve God in ways that will help all as well as ourselves.

I can hear the echoes of our deacons who have crossed over urging us to continue to work the vineyards of Baltimore. The crop is plenty but the workers are few. If you are Catholic today, then thank a deacon. I can see Deacon Roy smiling and telling you, "God has a plan for you," and Deacon Smith, the gentle giant who only wanted to be a good servant to God's people. Deacon Neale, who made music where there was no music, and Deacon Wilson smiling and telling you, "God loves you."

Those are memories we cannot let fade. There are only a few deacons left, and then what? Only you can answer that question. Let us as a people and church pray that God sends us more of his wonderful gift, deacons. Sisters, you can help in these efforts. Wives, share this article with your husband and sons, and sisters, read this to your brothers, girlfriends to your boyfriends. Just share this and the article by sister Favors with someone. Men, if you are wondering, give me a call at St. Bernardine or call the Office of Clergy Personnel 410-547-5427.

Knights of Peter Claver

In the early 1900s, southern Black Catholics were not afforded the opportunity to be members of fraternal organizations such as the Knights of Columbus, the Catholic Daughters nor the Knights of St. John.

Racial integration was frowned upon and simply was not tolerated in these Catholic organizations.

As a result, in 1909, four Josephite priests (two Black and two white) and three Black layman founded the first Black Catholic fraternal organization, the Knights of Peter Claver.

The purpose of this organization was to provide Black men with fraternal support and life insurance benefits. Today, there are more than 100,000 African American Catholic men, women and children in 56 dioceses across the United States who are members of this noble order, dedicating service to God, the church and the community.

The Knights of Peter Claver organization chose Peter Claver as their patron saint because of his commitment to the slaves. During his life he ministered to the slaves and cared for them as if he were caring for Jesus himself.

At the age of 13, Peter Claver decided to become a priest and by the time he made his final profession as a Jesuit priest at the age of 42, Peter Claver was known as "Peter Claver, slave of the slaves."

The Knights of Peter Claver is a family organization consisting of the Knights, the Ladies Auxiliary, Junior Daughters and Junior Knights divisions.

Their main objective is to be staunch supporters of the clergy of the Catholic Church, to participate in the spiritual and corporal works of mercy by assisting parish and community activities, develop youth, encourage lay apostolic and Catholic action, support worthwhile causes financially and provide social and intellectual fellowship for its members and their families.

In Baltimore there are more than 200 active members in the Knights of Peter Claver. Council and Court 62 have been in existence working for the Baltimore community for more than 70 years.

The Ladies assist families in need throughout Baltimore City and contribute monetarily to the retired priests and nuns in the archdiocese. The Knights provide food and clothing for needy families and volunteers at St. Edward Church soup kitchen.

The Gift of Hope Center is a home for patients with the AIDS virus and is supported by the Ladies of Courts 62 and 323. Members provide supplies and toiletries for the nuns and prepare home-cooked meals for the residents.

Court 323 also supports the Mother Mary Elizabeth Lange Center with clothing for young girls and host an annual cookout for the Oblate Sisters of Providence, donating toiletries for the nuns in the infirmary while Council 323 operates and volunteers in the Share Program at St. Francis Xavier Church.

Court 331 prepares an annual dinner for about 150 homeless men and supports the Thelma March Scholarship Foundation financially.

The Meritorious fourth-degree assembly is a division of the Knights of Peter Claver for members who provide exemplary work in the church and community. Their primary focus is on the education and development of youth.

In addition to the local projects, the Knights and Ladies of Peter Claver in Baltimore provide monetary support to their national projects which includes: a Sickle Cell Anemia program for victims with the disease and institutions that provide research in this area; a strong vocational program to encourage vocations in the African American community for the ordained, religious and lay ministry; a social justice fund to promote and provide for humanitarian causes; and the Tree of Life Foundation which aides the relief and cure of persons with Alzheimer's disease.

These are just a few of the charitable projects the Knights and Ladies of Peter Claver are involved in the Baltimore community. Many of the members are very active in lay ministries and are committed to rendering service to God, the church and community.

THERESE WILSON FAVORS AND SISTER M. REGINALD GERDES, O.S.P.

Collecting for Missions

A s early as the Second Plenary Council, American bishops voiced a plea for a national effort to evangelize the Black and native population of the United States. However, it was the Third Plenary Council of Baltimore in 1884 that put into motion the establishment of a permanent Commission for Catholic Missions among Black and Native Americans.

"A special collection shall be taken up in every diocese of this country each year ... and the proceeds thereof shall be sent to the commission ... to be expended by the commission in the interest of the missions among the Blacks and native Americans."

This commission, authorized by the prelates at the Third Plenary Council was mentioned in the "Acta et Decreta," title 8 "Of Zeal for Souls." Formally organized by our own Cardinal James Gibbons in 1886, this commission was his pride and joy until his death in 1921. The commission is headed by a board of three archbishops from the following archdioceses: Baltimore, New York and Philadelphia.

Today, the executive director, Monsignor Paul Lentz, has held this position for 25 years. Monsignor Lentz's predecessor, Father Tennelly, S.S., served in this same capacity for 50 years. The administrative office is in Washington, D.C., on land given to the commission by St. Katharine Drexel, who founded a religious community, the Sisters of the Blessed Sacrament to serve Black and native Americans.

In the annual report of 1935, Father Tennelly reported "a hardiness in the missions," citing the work of Sister M. Baptista, O.S.P., in Leavenworth, Kan., and the Josephites in Wilmington, Del.

Sister Baptista served as superior of a Boy's Home and School in Kansas, sharing the faith and building the church in Leavenworth. The Josephites reported that on their arrival in Wilmington, there were seven Black Catholics to be found. Seven years later, 400 Black men and women were active in the Catholic Church of the diocese.

Because of the funds collected and distributed by the commission, schools were opened, churches were built and maintained, programs of religious education were embellished and missionaries were sent to Black and Indian communities across the United States.

In 1935, the commission reported 238,894 Black Catholics. In 1988, the Josephites reported a count of 1.3 million Black Catholics. Today, the official number is two million Black Catholics including immigrants from both the Caribbean and Africa.

In the early days of the commission, the four Black parishes in Baltimore, under the direction of the Josephites (St. Francis Xavier, St. Peter Claver, St. Monica and St. Pius) were recipients of substantial financial assistance for the ministry of evangelization and education. By 1970 and up until the present almost every Black parish in Baltimore has received some benefits from the commission. The Office of African American Catholic Ministries is also a recipient of this collection.

The National Black and Indian Mission Collection is the oldest national collection of the Catholic Church in the United States.

BISHOP GORDON D. BENNETT, S.J.

Operation Faith Lift

In many of our African American parishes this weekend, a familiar and extraordinarily important event will take place. Teams of believers, under the auspices of "Operation Faith Lift," will be inviting neighbors and family members to celebrate the birthday of the church and "to taste the goodness of the Lord" at their neighboring Catholic church. Operation Faith Lift teams and other Black Catholics will also bring the Gospel of Jesus Christ from the eucharistic table in the church into the community through our presence at the African–American Heritage Festival at Camden Yards. These contemporary apostles will make a connection with people, a necessary part of the faithful following of Jesus.

Lest we unconsciously devalue this effort either by taking it for granted or by ignoring its enormous potential, I wanted to equate what these men and women are doing with the celebration the church marks this weekend: Pentecost Sunday, the primal experience of the foundation of our church, and the church's capital feast day.

On this weekend the church celebrates what it considers to be its birthday. And just as our own birth into the world is preceded by a very real life for some time in our mother's womb, so the church experienced a kind of preparatory life for some time before the events of Pentecost Sunday. This preparatory life spanned the covenant God made with Abraham, the Exodus with Moses, the prophets, and lastly, the life, death and resurrection of Jesus. All these events in our history as the people of God prepared us for the event we remember this weekend. And all these events happened "in the fullness of time," that is, as God ordered them, just as he orders our own birth.

The Scriptures record that the experience of the church's birth and its effect upon the world was marked by an extraordinary passion, a zeal for the life in God that the Gospel promises. And it was marked also by, not only wonder and awe on the part of the hearers of the proclamation, but by indescribable joy on the part of the disciples-become-apostles, the joy that is the gift of the Holy Spirit of God. That gift of joy had made the frightened, confused, sluggish inhabitants of that Upper Room bold, clear-minded and enthusiastic.

When we read that account in the Acts of the Apostles, it may seem that, as we celebrate the birthday of the church, our experience bears no resemblance to the outpouring of joy, of wonder and awe, which accompanied the actual event of the church's birth, no resemblance to the recognition that, because of the gift of the Holy Spirit to each and every one of the baptized, our preparation time as a people is completed, and our new life as a church has begun.

Where is our joy today? Where is our passion today? Where is our wonder and awe at the "wonderful things" God has done in our midst today? How are we using the gifts the Holy Spirit has given to us to build up the holiness of the church and to spread the good news of the forgiveness of sin to everyone without exception?

This seems to me to be the real significance of Operation Faith Lift and of its witness to all of us: disciples on fire with the love of God, grateful for his mercy, who have heard the call of Jesus and who are responding, with all our hearts and despite our limits, to his command: "Teach all nations, baptizing them in the name of the Father, and of the Son, and of the Holy Spirit."

And so, on this birthday of our church, as we see or hear about or even, hopefully, participate in the activity of Operation Faith Lift, let us allow ourselves to be more deeply and more personally drawn into the great mystery of God's plan.

Operation Faith Lift 2

B lack Catholic churches in the city play an integral role of providing Christian witness, social outreach and unlimited hope for the village and the villagers. In these parishes you will find evangelizers rolling away the stones that block blessings (in the neighborhood and family) and sharing the good news of Jesus Christ.

These evangelizers going door to door, sharing sacred Scripture and sacred music. This initiative, Operation Faith Lift, is serious in its evangelization mission of enhancing people's happiness by encouraging them to take a closer walk with Jesus.

Operation Faith Lift originated last year with 17 parishes sharing the word of God – distributing spiritual reading and New Testaments in 17 neighborhoods. More than 600 Black Catholics and their pastors visited neighborhoods from the westside to the eastside, north and south of Baltimore including Cherry Hill, Walbrook Junction, Druid Heights, Edmondson Village, Liberty Heights, Greenmount, Rosemont, Waverly, Govans, the Pennsylvania Avenue corridor, Sandtown-Winchester, Park Heights, Woodbourne, Poppleton, Pigtown, Fulton Avenue, Johns Hopkins Hospital area and the Oliver and Caroline streets corridor.

Three hundred prayer warriors positioned themselves in prayer at our parishes, praying for the intercession of the Holy Spirit. It was a glorious day, and other follow-up initiatives have been pursued.

A 1990 Gallup Poll explored what attracts and maintains African Americans to a specific Christian church. Its findings reveal five strategies.

For the most part, African Americans are attracted to and remain in a church if they experience good teaching, good environment, good music, good preaching and good leaders.

This research provides direction to Operation Faith Lift organizers. Last year good leadership was illustrated through the organization of street evangelists and promotion of parishioners toward involvement. This year our leaders explored how we could share our "good sacred music" with our neighbors.

In this effort an invitation to "take a closer walk with Jesus" and an invitation to fellowship with Catholics in their neighborhood has been extended.

Choirs were invited to tape two renditions. Our pastors or designated greeters have added a message of welcome/invitation to visit our Catholic worshipping communities to the two musical selections.

Now, parishes distribute tapes (good sacred music) to neighbors inviting them to worship Jesus through our Catholic faith.

In these same parishes and Catholic schools, catechists are organizing resources and preparing themselves to "keep on teaching." For the past 12 years Black Catholic catechetical leaders of Baltimore have created resources and workshop experiences that "factor culture" into the catechetical process.

Evangelists and catechists are on mission so that the word of God may run and be glorified. We are convinced that when connected to God's word, our people find strength for the journey.

Dr. Robert Hill, noted African American sociologist, said that "African Americans with strong religious orientation have higher social and economic attainment than those with little religious commitment." When we join in the mission to share God's Word and promote the mission of Jesus we help to strengthen our people. Let us then, be serious, focused and prayed up so that we fulfill our baptismal promises.

Taking Back

There is a mission afoot in Black Catholic parishes of Baltimore to "take back what the enemy has stolen" from us. Since 9–11 people have examined their lives and made sweeping changes in attitude and in lifestyle. This change in lifestyle (or the hope to make a change) has caught the attention of leaders of evangelization in our own "Operation Faith Lift" campaign.

Operation Faith Lift reaches out to inactive Catholics during Advent. The theme of "taking back what the enemy has stolen" was designated to emphasize that a certain presence and joy has been stolen from our parishes when those who used to be with us are no longer witnessing the word or surrounding the eucharistic table. This "taking back" requires systematic evangelization strategies and fervent prayer.

During the weeks of Advent, parishioners are asked to identify individuals or families who once were enrolled in parishes. Names are submitted on cards and placed near the altar. Parishioners are encouraged to pray for inactive Catholics during the week and at intercessory prayer at Mass.

This phase of the outreach is titled "pray them back for a comeback." Pastors and evangelization team leaders are encouraged to call and write each family.

Of particular interest for outreach are families who buried loved ones, newly baptized (who have been inactive) and those who have family members sent into military action. In this telephone and writing campaign, evangelization team leaders will invite families to come back home for Christmas and experience "soul food" for the journey.

Realizing that prayer changes things, and a personal touch of outreach makes all the difference in the world, Operation Faith Lift leaders anticipate a "comeback" of inactive Catholics. These same evangelization leaders realize that the next phase in the "comeback" is to "keep them back."

A New Testament (courtesy of The American Bible Society) will be given as a Christmas gift to all who attend Christmas Mass with the invitation to engage in a "Winter Soul Stir." The "Winter Soul Stir" (stop as the world turns – winter solstice) will be an opportunity for families to engage in a family centered Bible reflection.

This "Winter Soul Stir" is just one opportunity planned in the "keep them back" phase. (The Office of African American Catholic Ministries was awarded 5,000 copies of the Jubilee New Testament (CEV) for Operation Faith Lift from The American Bible Society.)

We hope that Operation Faith Lift and its initiatives is what the Black bishops of the United States refer to in "What We Have Seen And Heard" (a pastoral letter on evangelization) as "a significant sign among many other signs that the Black Catholic community in the American Church has now come of age."

Our history tells us that throughout the ages, God has sent powerful evangelists among us so that the word may run and be glorified. We get inspired by the striking work of Black Catholic laity such as Lincoln and Julia Vallé.

In 1908 the Vallés moved to Milwaukee with "the avowed purpose of preaching to Blacks in Milwaukee." On their arrival, the Vallés visited Archbishop Sebastian G. Messmer and asked for his approval to conduct lectures on the Catholic religion in the Black community.

Archbishop Messmer encouraged the Vallés. They purchased a building and opened a center for evangelization dedicated to St. Benedict the Moor. Eventually a parish grew from the center under the patron of St. Benedict. The baptismal register indicates that during the first year, Lincoln and Julia Vallé acted as sponsors for the first 30 or so people.

So, during Advent, let us be avowed in our baptismal promise of evangelizing and "take back what the enemy has stolen."

In Spite of the Challenges

It's been tough in 2002! The child abuse scandal, violence of children, has been overwhelming. Standing in the midst of the storm as the media reports daily "a church in crisis" has warranted our prayers and steadfast faith. Children gunned down on our streets, as they play in front of their homes, became a far too often occurrence. Mothers and fathers were prematurely forced to be childless as they buried their children. This should warrant our prayers, attention and steadfast search for solutions to address such violence.

Revisiting the horror of 9–11 in the wake of its anniversary stirred up mixed emotions and raised new questions putting us all on our knees in prayer and supplication for peace and solace. Our nation is at war, contemplating expanding its theatre of war with another nation whose people are ravaged by poverty and injustice. It's been a tough summer!

Some have characterized these incidences as warnings of the approach of "the final days". Others say it is a test of faith. I'm not so sure why these actions have occurred and how they will play out in this universal cosmic flow of life, but one thing I am certain of is that our reaction to these actions must be deeply rooted in our relationship with God.

We must turn to God and live the truth of the message given to us from St. Paul as he ministered to the church in Corinth, "Keep alert, stand firm in your faith, be courageous, be strong. Let all you do be done in love."

In times like these, we must "keep the faith" and recognize that our true peace and happiness comes in knowing Jesus for ourselves. Great things can happen to us when we know God! As disciples of Christ, we are compelled to share this relationship with Jesus with others ... so that they may have life; and have it abundantly! Our task is to evangelize inspite of ... "for there is nothing that can separate us from the love of God."

Parishes in the Black community continued to evangelize inspite of challenges and grief. Operation Faith Lift members came together to pray together and to plot out street outreach efforts. Black Catholics were on the move, visiting neighbors, holding street festivals, feeding the hungry, sponsoring vacation Bible schools and preaching through word and action.

The National Black Catholic Congress held in Chicago was also an evangelizing event of great momentum. It gave movement, structure and focus to our evangelization efforts in spite of the challenges set before us. Covered in prayer, steeped in hope, lanced with dedication, our people developed a Plan of Action to strengthen our evangelization efforts. The Congress stressed the importance in working in the vineyard of the Lord in one accord. Our success lies in our willingness to be steadfast in faith and united in action.

Inspite of the challenges, we must press forward in our evangelization efforts. Transformation for the good always happens if what we do is done in love. God has placed some opportunities in front of us. The situations and conditions of this summer tell us that there is no time to waste. Let us bring the good news of the Gospel to our people! Let us bring the love of Jesus through Operation Faith Lift to our people. Let us bring the hope of the Black Catholic Congress to our people and to our church!

It Takes a Church

Make no doubt about it, Baltimore is a city of churches. Drive down any major thoroughfare for about a mile and one will probably pass at least six to seven churches.

I remember once when I was leading a religious education session with children on the streets of Reservoir Hill and somehow our discussion led to that ultimate question, "Is God real?" The children were quick to share evidence of God's reality. One comment particularly made an indelible mark on me: "He's got to be real, look at all the buildings named after him and established for worship of him."

Yet challenges loom around this same city where churches abound. These edifices are indeed symbols that God is real and that those who are in covenant with God are on mission to "transform the world." This transformation ministry is an awesome mission to behold. It is the very mission that was given by Jesus to the Apostles and is now given to us. Being on mission to be transformers can become a sign of God's reality, love and compassion.

In the book "*It Takes a Church to Raise a Village*," author Dr. Marva Mitchell discusses the plight of many American cities that many churches call home. Dr. Mitchell leads the reader to a sharp observation: too many churches have become self-centered and self-serving. Knowing the depth of depravation that many cities endure – poverty, deterioration, crime and a breakdown of systems (education, health, housing, etc.) – what will it take to raise up the village? Government alone is unable.

Thus, Dr. Mitchell concludes, "it takes a church to raise the village."

She continues, "If the church is to raise the village, it must come out from behind its walls to impact the village through a display of the love of Christ and a demonstration of the power of Christ. Inside of our walled fortresses we have carried out our religious exercises ... while the village lies in ruin around us. The church must rise up and take responsibility for the village. We must turn to our Lord for a new empowerment and a fresh filling of his love. It is the church who must establish integrity and biblical standards. The church possesses the wisdom and power to raise the village and set a new course for the future."

What does this mean for us? First, let's take responsibility and examine our social justice agenda to define/explore what we do, what we don't do and what we could do as it impacts the village. This is the direction given to us in our Catholic social teachings and in "The Pastoral Plan of Action" from the National Black Catholic Congress.

Although there is much being done through our parishes and through organizations such as Catholic Charities, St. Vincent de Paul, Baltimoreans United In Leadership Development (BUILD) and Beyond the Boundaries, let's "go out into the deep" and be enthusiastic and directed in our efforts of legislative advocacy. Let's get to know what the Catholic Campaign for Human Development does and what could we do in partnership with them in this opportunity for community empowerment. Let's unite with other churches to find solutions to address education, housing, poverty and crime.

Dr. Mitchell's book provides an occasion for reflection: "The church has been given the greatest opportunity since the writing of the Book of Acts to significantly alter the state of the village. Our tools for renovation are the love of Christ, the truth of the gospel, and the power of the Spirit."

City Evangelization

In my role as a public servant, I saw firsthand the needs of the city and was able to assess frequently the impact of the Catholic Church in affecting change and improving the quality of life of city residents. The church serves as a ready bridge to the community, offering spiritual, educational, social and human resources.

Our city Catholic parishes, compared to the ever-growing and expanding suburban parishes, are small yet significant. Their impact on the community is invaluable. These small "outlets of evangelization" touch lives and maintain a Catholic presence in communities where hope does not always spring eternal.

These ready bridges, significant parishes, can do even more with proper resources and steady support to stabilize them in the community. They are needed, each one of them, for there are many who are un-churched who walk the streets of Baltimore searching for a blessing. Do we recognize the bountiful harvest for the Lord that sits right before our eyes?

What makes inner-city Catholic schools so inviting to so many Black non-Catholic parents, teachers and students? What gives many non-Catholic city dwellers the sense that Catholic pastors are very accessible to them regardless of the residents' own faith or lack thereof? Stated very simply, Catholic schools educate well, and Catholic pastors are accessible because they live in the neighborhoods where they serve.

In fact, in many working class and low-income neighborhoods where there is little faith in institutions, corporations or government Catholic churches and schools stand as beacons, ports in very stormy social conditions.

And yet, on Sundays, many of these churches see very few of its neighbors or students in the pews. Though the citizens and their children avail themselves of the schools and daily fish to eat, there is often no long-term relationship established or outreach of evangelization. The small parish needs more support from the diocesan church to aggressively evangelize.

Can we steady the bridge at our schools and parishes by insuring their existence by adding additional resource people to serve as staff to simply evangelize and help students, families and neighbors to make the "spiritual and emotional" connection with our churches and the Catholic faith? The bridges at our schools and within our parishes need greater support and greater resources to establish such connections.

For what seems to be futile ground for the expansion of the faith community, (our schools and the neighborhoods surrounding our churches) is often ignored. Although the daily works performed by our neighborhood parishes are often counted as the works of the church, the greatest work could be in the gift of faith.

The recent successful efforts of Operation Faith Lift confirms for me that the bountiful harvest for the Lord has been seen by many African American Catholics and their pastors and pastoral administrators. Efforts such as this need repetition and resources to massage "spiritual relationships" with neighbors.

Trained lay leaders are needed in our parishes, especially those where there is only one priest as staff, serving the myriad needs of the faith and neighborhood communities. African American deacons and leaders who can serve in a full-time capacity have been proven invaluable in this evangelization development and process.

All of this, in my opinion, steadies the ready bridges from the church to the community. Many thousands of souls ought to be encouraged to come into the fullness of the Catholic Church. To our faithful leadership, I say, do not let this harvest pass and make the investment in our city parishes. Our impoverished communities should be lifted by faith and by works.

JOANN T. LOGAN

A Vital Lifeline

Have you have ever stopped to think what your parish will be like in the next five to 10 years? Have you ever considered that your parish may not exist? With the critical shortage of vocations, especially in the African American community, the issue of lay leadership and the quality of parish life are two issues that require immediate attention if the urban church not only in Baltimore, but across the country as well, is to survive.

I was part of a delegation of 70 that traveled from Baltimore to the National Black Catholic Congress in Chicago, where we joined with over 3,000 Black Catholics in prayer, fellowship and dialogue to discern God's will for the formation of a comprehensive Pastoral Plan of Action for evangelization and leadership in the African American community. Congress IX, titled Black Catholic Leadership in the 21st Century: Solidarity In Action, was a spirit-filled, invigorating and self-renewing experience, of which the design of the Pastoral Plan of Action was the highlight.

I have been involved in discussions regarding parish life and would like to share thoughts concerning that.

For Catholics of African descent in America, the parish remains the central place where the faith community gathers and worships. The composition of parishes to which Black Catholics belong varies greatly. In some, we are the majority of the parish membership. In others, we are part of a diverse multicultural and multiethnic faith community.

Whether our numbers are large or small, in whatever parish setting we find ourselves, Black Catholics must assume greater responsibility for the welfare of the parish communities to which we belong; and the church must provide the resources and opportunities for us to contribute and develop our talents for the good of the entire church.

Parishes and dioceses are called upon to nurture Black Catholics in programs of lay ministry and leadership. In this way, we will be empowered to assume increasing responsibility for the welfare of the church – a responsibility that is ours by virtue of baptism.

Because many Black people are not Catholic, parishes need to be places that celebrate both Black cultural heritage and our instinctive Catholic tradition. Our parishes should be encouraged to develop sacramental and ritual practices that are both authentically Black and truly Catholic. Black people are often victims of discrimination and injustice in society; our parishes should make a clear connection between Sunday worship and our responsibility to society, and encourage further development of programs of social charity and outreach to the poor.

Additionally, our people often live and worship in areas ravaged by violence and economic distress; our parishes should be places of hope in the midst of despair.

In increments of one, three and five years, action steps were identified at Congress IX for implementation to improve parish life in the African American Catholic community. Within a year, parishes should identify the gifts and talents of parishioners and develop plans to affirm them on the parish level. Within three years to nurture growth, parishes should identify and/or begin the formation of formal leadership programs for various roles of parish lay leadership. And within five years to establish roots using newsletters, the Internet, resource clearinghouses, or other networking techniques, develop parish-to-parish sharing initiatives that promote maintaining and strengthening Black Catholic parishes in the community.

While it is realized that many parishes are already loving and nurturing places for African American lay leadership and growth, others are not, and more needs to be done if churches, especially in the urban community, are to survive. In addition, it is essential that we continue to pray for vocations from our community – priests, nuns, deacons and brothers are in desperate need. Further, African Americans in greater numbers should undertake formal studies to fulfill roles as parish administrators, directors of religious education, youth ministers, catechists, directors of music, etc.

The survival of our parishes depends in large part on us. How are you preparing to ensure your parish's continued vitality and growth?

Reclaiming Our Spirit

The African American family has been a source of strength throughout history in the African American community.

I was raised in a traditional family. I had a father who was employed and lived in the home, a mother who took care of the family and was not employed outside of the home and siblings, each with his or her own set of contributions to the family unit.

A block and a half away, my grandparents lived in the same house where my father was raised. One block in the other direction, my uncle lived with his wife and two daughters.

As a child, I thought this was the way of all families. It was a safe and nurturing existence. I felt that I was loved, and I knew there were people who cared about me. I was not dependent upon television for validation (there were no positive images of African Americans on television when I was young) because my family affirmed my existence.

The church played a major role in my life. My family strictly adhered to the tenets of Catholicism, and my mother made sure we were observant.

The members of my parish became part of my extended family, and each Sunday I looked forward to seeing various members of my larger "family."

The church provided me with a healthy social outlet. Growing up, I spent many hours with our youth group, which provided me with an opportunity to grow with other Catholic youths of similar backgrounds.

Religious orientation and affiliation has always been a strength of the African American community. Dr. Robert Hill's research found that African American families who attend church on a regular basis tended to have a higher education, income and produced children who encountered success in both work and in the educational scene.

Yet clearly, in many parts the African American community, there has been a departure from these religious and life values. Church attendance among youth in urban areas is way down from 30 years ago.

The leading cause of death for African American males between the ages of 15-24 is murder. (One out of 21 will be murdered before the age of 25.) Sixty percent of African American children live in a single family. Forty percent of African American males under the age of 25 are currently a part of the penal system.

One out of five African American families live in poverty. The public schools struggle to educate students with scant resources. The spirituality of African Americans seems to be at an all-time low. Yet it is the spirituality that so often defined us as a people.

African American spirituality is grounded in connectedness, not just to the supreme force of God but to the community. What is most meaningful in life is ultimately relations, our obligations to other humans and to a Supreme Being. This is the essence of our spirituality. It profoundly influences our lives.

This spirituality is rooted in our African past. Our African ancestors lived constantly with the idea of "spirit" working in all nature and in their lives. It is what guided them and sustained them in times of struggle.

This same "spirit" has sustained African Americans throughout the tumultuous times of the 19th and 20th centuries. Without the "spirit" to sustain us, we are left with empty, bereft lives, hence the negative influences (drugs, gangs, etc.) that have occupied too many in our community, particularly our youth. In the absence of the spirit, it is only natural to want to fill the void.

As a people, we must reclaim our spirit. We must reach out and within our community and share the considerable resources that are contained therein. We cannot afford to leave any segment out. We must help direct our spiritual values to rebuild our families and through them, our communities.

If there was any one lesson to be learned from the events that began September 11, it is that people need to have a sense of connection. Let's use the "spirit" to connect with all parts of our community to develop and build our extended family. If we are to survive as a people, it is required of us all.

SISTER MAGDALA MARIE GILBERT, O.S.P

Catechists are Extraordinary

In each of our parishes and schools there stands among us some extraordinary people who are active in an extraordinary ministry. These are catechists on mission to teach the word of God, instruct the tenets of the church and familiarize children, youth and adults in the power of God for their lives.

Catechists are a special group of women and men; ordinary folks doing something extraordinary in their lives and in the life of the church. They are salt and light for the church. These are the people Jesus is talking about in Matthew 5:13-14 in his discourse on the mountain.

Catechists could rightly be called the backbone of the church. This can be said about catechists not only in Baltimore, but throughout the world, especially in developing countries.

Catechists are usually people who have full time jobs; although there are many who are retired and desire to give something back and so they serve. The most amazing aspect of these wonderful people is that they recognize and appreciate the power of God in their lives, thus they serve as teachers; testifying to God's goodness, mercy and compassion. They teach, because they can not help themselves. "They love the Lord."

In their service, they sacrifice time from family as they prepare lessons, meet students and parents and undergo training and enrichment. Yet in some parishes or schools not much thought or thanks are given to catechists. Oftentimes they are the invisible people. When some catechists leave the ministry, little or no notice is taken of his or her departure. Most catechists minister for 20, 30 or more years, all for the love of Jesus.

Many catechists use their own resources to fulfill their mission and often times in some of our parishes, classrooms are makeshift. These spirit–filled people are creative and dedicated.

Catechetical Sunday is an opportunity to bring attention to the ministry of catechesis and to the extraordinary people who serve in this ministry. Things are happening to make this Catechetical Sunday a celebration of the ministry and the ministers.

Nationally, a Black Catholic Catechetical Network has been formed to link catechetical leaders together. A newsletter has been composed, sharing resources that "factor culture into the catechetical process."

In the Archdiocese of Baltimore credit has to be given to the archdiocesan Catechist Formation Program and personnel who have been supportive of cultural awareness. Leading this inculturation process and dialogue is Therese Wilson Favors and the members of the Na'imah Outreach who have been in the forefront in bringing an Africentric perspective to catechesis through the "Keep on Teaching" resources and workshops as well as the newly formed "Walk In The Light" seminar. These resources are right on target for those who teach in the African American community and are instrumental toward the development of an effective culturally sensitive catechetical process.

Through the Office of African American Catholic Ministries, other cultures have become aware that Blacks have a Catholic heritage and culture that they can be proud of and are willing to share this knowledge with our brothers and sisters in Christ.

Let's recognize the extraordinary catechetical ministry and the extraordinary people of this ministry. Let's send out gestures of appreciation to these extraordinary folks. For those who teach, "keep on teaching" so that the Word of God may run and be glorified.

DR. KENNETH M. DEAN, JR.

Black Church Music

The Black music expression on the North American continent began with the spiritual, the language of which was borrowed from the dominant society and rearranged to meet the religious needs of the Black community.

The Catholic Church enjoys a rich tradition of music (like Gregorian chant, plain song, stirring hymns and anthems both traditional and contemporary) which the Black community has embraced. The Black community sings the great master works, written by famous European composers, with the richness, warmth, depth, power and conviction that only we as former slaves can bring to the tradition.

However, one additional contribution is ours and ours alone and that is gospel music – the good news proclaimed with elements of blues and jazz.

It all began with slaves chanting in the fields, which was the basic means of communication with each other. Chanting was, also, a means of signaling each other to meet in the brush arbors or down by the river to worship God.

There were three major forms of religion: witchcraft and voodoo, Islam and Christianity. Witchcraft, the religion of the Africans, contained pageantry, dancing and singing.

As the centuries evolved, one is still able to see evidence of these three aforementioned elements in the current worship experience today in the Black church community.

One of the original ways of singing was to "line a hymn." What this means is to have the worship leader sing a line of a hymn and have the congregation repeat it until the entire hymn had been sung.

During these early days reading and writing was illegal for slaves, so this was the method used to teach the hymns.

As we come forward in our tradition, from the brush arbors and riverbanks into the wooden-frame churches, we see the "Ring Shout."

White preachers and plantation owners did not allow dancing and shouting. The slaves were told that dancing and shouting would lead them to hell.

In order to maintain their cultural expression with their God, within the context of the white man's rules, the "Ring Shout" was born.

Forming a circle, they practiced the "Ring Shout" and moving in rhythm to the steady beat of a drum, by shuffling your feet without picking them up off the floor, the "Ring Shout" evolved. They also sang and shouted while this was taking place.

If you were to come into New All Saints, Liberty Heights, for a typical liturgy, you would see and hear evidence of this tradition.

As we come forward we have seen a steady evolution of the music to include the chant, the spiritual, the hymn, (traditional and contemporary) and gospel music (classic through contemporary – to include Thomas Dorsey, The Ward Singers, James Cleveland, Walter Hawkins, Andrae Crouch and Kirk Franklin).

We also present in our liturgy the European genre (the Latin Gregorian chant, psalm chant, baroque, classical and contemporary). All of this is performed in the style and fervor of the Black experience.

In order to perform all these types of music, the instruments in the Black church are much more demanding. We use the traditional pipe organ, piano, the Hammond B-3, percussion, strings and brass in order to support this wide range of music.

This is just a brief account of some of the aspects that accompany music that is performed in the Black church experience.

DARRON C. WOODUS

Young Adult Speaks

There comes a time in life when you are called to serve the Lord. Can you recognize your call?

I almost missed mine. My pastor, Father Sylvester Peterka (pastor of St. Cecilia and Immaculate Conception, Baltimore), asked me to lunch one day.

We ate and talked about a lot of things: sports, music, family, life, etc. I thought I had done something wrong. We never talked about church or God. At this point I was a little confused as to the reason for our lunch.

A few weeks later, he invited me to a meeting to organize young adults in our parish. I was not excited at all and kept thinking, "all people do is meet and talk but produce little or no work."

I went to the meeting, and my life was changed. I caught the spirit of other young adults – "we can make a difference and God is calling us right now, right here to be his witnesses."

St. Cecilia established its young adult group in 1997. The group consisted of six members. We have grown to 20. Our goal is to continuously seek improvement in ourselves; to grow spiritually; to be instruments of God's faith; and to be consistently responsible for what we speak and how we act. We also strive to provide the highest level of service to our parish elders and youth.

Our group meets once a month. We have Bible study every Monday evening and many service projects and fund-raisers. The group felt it was important to help support the parish financially. With that in mind, we sponsor baked goods and candy sales, a parish T-shirt and sweatshirt promotion and trips.

The young adults coordinate the Thanksgiving and Christmas basket campaign in which food baskets are packed for community families in need. The youth are important to us as well; we always give support to youth ministers because it truly takes a village to raise our children.

We desire to become even more involved in the operation of parish activities and liturgies. Our members are active in the Mass choir, as lectors and as members of the Parish and Pastoral Council, Beyond the Boundaries, the 2001 Archdiocese of Baltimore Young Adult Conference and Greater Task Leadership Campaign, just to name a few.

St. Cecilia's young adult ministry named itself NMESIS meaning no more excuses – share in the spirit of Christ. We have come to the realization, as disciples of Jesus, a need to teach and lead our peer group to Christ. To do this, we seek to deepen our understanding of our Catholic faith and the Scriptures which guide our living and strengthens us.

This experience has confirmed the fact that young adults want to be involved. We have been inspired by God's revelation in Scripture. Our study and reflection has greatly impacted our ministry, our life decisions and our need to be real witnesses to the hope of Jesus. What we read and understand from the Bible has marked our way of life.

As young adults we are searching for "something," and that "something" is a connection and oneness with Christ. We are hungry for the truth. We seek more answers, more information, more about our God and our church teachings.

We know that information and inspiration is power. The more we confirm for ourselves that we are believers with a mission, the more committed we become in making the sacrifices needed to see and receive the big picture, eternal life.

Young adult ministry is a wonder-filled ministry.

To Be Read

S ummertime often ushers in time to catch up on some reading. May I suggest two items for your reading list? My first selection offers hope for racial healing, and the second takes one on a walk back in history to reaffirm the strength of the Black family.

Meet some of the bishops of the United States as they speak out against racism in the newly released document titled, "Love Thy Neighbor As Thyself." The Committee on African American Catholics at the U.S. Conference of Catholic Bishops documented statements and research pursued by Catholic bishops from 1997 to June 2000.

In 1998 Bishop Curtis J. Guillory, S.V.D., addressed the U.S. Catholic Conference. The topic was "A Dialogue on Racism." Something needed to be said about the brutal killing of James Byrd in Jasper. Something needed to be said about the blatant incidents of racism that receive media attention and quick condemnation by people of faith and good will.

Something needed to be said about the two percent of people of color placed in decision-making positions in dioceses and archdioceses. Something needed to be said about the 140 Web sites pushing racial hatred. The lifting up of Bishop Guillory's voice encouraged other bishops to speak up and speak out through homilies, remarks, press releases and statements.

A rallying cry covered the nation. The voice of our own Bishop P. Francis Murphy spoke of our local initiative, Beyond the Boundaries, and its thrust to encourage racial healing "as a way to reflect and discern what our responsibilities are and to address the moral issues of regionalism."

Cardinal Francis George of Chicago said, "The sin of racism challenges all of us to conversion, for it reveals that we have not yet enveloped ourselves fully in God's love." Thirty other bishops shared sentiments. To obtain a copy of this book, call the U.S. Conference of Catholic Bishops at 800-235-8722.

Meet Lifee, Mor, Abbey, Mema, Ben, Preacher Brattle and so many more in J. California Cooper's novel, *"The Wake of the Wind."* Some of the characters in this story may put you in the mind of your own ancestors and elders who risked much to protect and maintain the family. Their story also affirms the simple tradition (among Africans who were once enslaved) that "you make family where you find family."

"The Wake of the Wind" is a compelling story of capture, enslavement, quasi-freedom after the Emancipation Proclamation, migration, the quest for knowledge and education and plain old overcoming; succeeding against evil odds.

This folktale is woven in such an enchanting manner that places you inside the Freeman family and their circle of love. Lifee and Mor are descendants of Suwaibu and Kola, who were herdsmen from Africa, captured by slave merchants in 1764. Suwaibu and Kola crossed the Atlantic together, but upon arrival in the states were separated. Generations later, their blood meets again through Lifee and Mor Freeman.

Lifee knows not her mother or her father. She longs for family, the kind of family found deep within her own longings and needs. Mor is introduced as a man who tries hard not to love because family separation is too hard to bear. Together, they become family and make family among enslaved people forced on a Texas plantation.

In this story you will conjure up faces from your own family, and you will hear voices from your own kin.

We all have stories that speak of our value of family life and the support rendered in our own "circles of love."

These "two to be read" are provocative. Treat yourself to some inspiration.

Outreach– Community, School, Parish

"I come that I may serve"

There is an African proverb that says, "It takes many hands to put the roof onto a hut." Intentionally, the church actively builds relationships and strengthens the community through the services it renders. Our call to evangelize is a call to meet the full spectrum of needs in the community. We yearn to faithfully answer this call because we continue to hear Jesus say, "I have come to give you life and give it to the full." To accomplish this mission, "it takes many hands" of service.

As people of God, we are called to minister and to address the various and sundry needs of the community and our brothers and sisters. Our church must be an active agent in the community, combating those challenges that oppress and demoralize. At the same time, we must offer hope by activating our love through action.

This section discusses outreach in the community, school and parish.

SISTER GWYNETTE PROCTOR, S.N.D.

Who is my Neighbor

We have an opportunity to step back and take a long look at our life choices. The Gospel of St. Matthew speaks of the challenge before us:

"And one of them, a lawyer, in an attempt to trip him up, asked, 'Teacher, which commandment of the law is the greatest?' Jesus said to him: 'You shall love the Lord your God with your whole heart with your whole soul and with your whole mind. This is the greatest and the first commandment. The second is like it. You shall love your neighbor as yourself. On these two commandments the whole law is based."

The challenge in Matthew's Gospel holds great potential both individually and communally. There are questions that beg our attention though let's ask ourselves, who is my neighbor? What price am I willing to pay to lift all to their rightful place of dignity? What will have to change in my life to really embrace all as my neighbor? To consider some of the challenges we face, let's glimpse briefly at the conditions in our communities today.

There are those who would have us believe that it is acceptable that some in communities will experience the privilege of race while others will continue to be victimized by racial injustice. There are those who would have us believe that:

- Diversity is a problem
- Blacks and whites should go their separate ways
- The poor and homeless are lazy
- The rich deserve to get richer
- Violence against women is an inalienable right of men

As people of goodwill what is our response to these conditions? It will fall to us to fashion just and fair solutions. And yet, far too often, we fall short of reaching our full potential.

"You shall love your neighbor as yourself."

Catholic Charities' Christopher Place is an employment academy with a residential component that supports addiction recovery. The program houses some 44 formerly homeless men and offers job readiness training, employment placement, addiction recovery education, adult basic education classes, healthy relationships/parenting classes and opportunities to develop sound financial practices.

We invite men to embrace a radical change in the attitudes and behaviors that have resulted in homelessness and unemployment. Currently, we are experiencing a 100 percent employment and housing placement rate, and as its director, I have witnessed both the worst in the human condition and the best.

I am privileged to walk a sacred journey with the poor and homeless people of our city; those traditionally deemed society's throwaways. I am privileged to witness the generosity of supporters, people who genuinely wish to share their wealth and human resources with those less fortunate.

"You shall love your neighbor as yourself."

Broken, tired and used up, men come to Christopher Place seeking a different way of life. Most know that to continue living as they are may cost them their lives. At Christopher Place, they encounter a dedicated staff of professional men and women and a core of generous volunteers and supporters.

What I have seen time after time is that when given a meaningful chance to reclaim life, our academy members strive for and achieve new heights of accomplishments. When people of goodwill come together to embrace all in our human family as "neighbor," we are able to transform our community. It will require that we set aside judgments and reclaim our tradition of caring for and about all in our "extended family."

Let us take to heart the words of Dr. Martin Luther King Jr.: "Everybody can be great because anybody can serve. You don't have to have a college degree to serve. You don't have to make your subject and verb agree to serve. You only need a heart full of grace and a soul generated by love."

DANISE JONES DORSEY

Between the Sundays

During the Advent season, a time when Catholics prepare themselves to celebrate the anniversary of the birth of Christ, we are reminded Christ took on a human nature in order to be an example for each of us.

Providence dictated that Jesus would be born into a working poor family. It was not an accident that when Jesus was born his family was homeless.

Jesus desires that all who follow him understand the special affinity he has for the widow, orphan, poor and the oppressed. In fact, Jesus' very first sermon says, "The spirit of the Lord is on me because he has anointed me to preach good news to the poor. He has sent me to proclaim freedom for the prisoners and recovery of sight for the blind, to release the oppressed to proclaim the year of the Lord's favor."

In Matthew 25 Jesus reiterates how important the poor and the vulnerable are to him when he outlines the judgment criteria that he will use on Judgment Day: "For I was hungry, and you gave me something to eat. I was thirsty, and you gave me something to drink. I was a stranger, and you invited me in. I needed clothes, and you clothed me. I was sick, and you looked after me. I was in prison, and you came to visit me."

In Matthew 35, Jesus said, "I tell you the truth. Whatever you did for the least of these brothers of mine, you did for me."

Jesus' poignant declaration begs the question, "How do we, as Catholics, live out the meaning of Jesus' words?"

The modern Catholic Church provides a framework for living out

Jesus' prophetic word in a body of thought known as Catholic social teaching. Beginning with Pope Leo XIII's *"Rerum Novarum"* published in 1891 to Pope John Paul II's *"Centesimus Annus"* 1991, Catholics have been called to enter into a right relationship with God through the poor and the vulnerable.

Modern Catholic social teaching spans a little more than 100 years. Catholic social teaching discusses the dignity of the human being, the dignity of work and the need for each of us to create options for the poor and the vulnerable.

Hence, Catholics understand that being Christian is a way of life. Catholics understand that our church's social teaching calls us to live out charity and justice.

What can we do between the Sundays?

There are many opportunities to provide direct service to the poor and vulnerable through programs at our parishes. There are opportunities to staff soup kitchens, food pantries and clothing banks. There are opportunities to volunteer for programming sponsored by Catholic Charities. There are opportunities to empower poor and vulnerable people through support of programs that are sponsored by the Catholic Campaign for Human Development.

There are opportunities to advocate for state resources for the poor and vulnerable through Welfare Advocates. A statewide coalition, Welfare Advocates' goal is to advance public policy that moves Maryland families out of poverty. There are opportunities to advocate for national policy that insures the dignity of work (i.e., Reauthorization of Welfare Reform in 2002) and full funding of the Workforce Investment Act (WIA) that provides sufficient funding to move families out of poverty.

Previously mentioned activities require a daily commitment to the work and perseverance in response to the challenge.

A Christian is called to witness God's word between the Sundays. We understand that Christ calls us to love our neighbor on and between the Sundays! In fact, Christians understand witnessing God's word is not an option. We are compelled to live out the Gospel between the Sundays.

Mantle of Service

On Ash Wednesday I was intensely aware of the 50-plus years I had embraced this affirmation of my God-centered origin and mortality. An image of dust flitted through my mind and with it one of Christ washing it away from the feet of his apostles. With that single act he established an unmitigated degree of selflessness, service and responsibility. Humbled once again, the Lenten season began for me with the reminder that we are made to serve; to serve God and one another. As a friend says, "Our rent is due."

In a complex world of war, depravity, poverty and greed, he compels us to move beyond the ordinary. We are urged to conform each action and interaction to one, which builds up the body of Christ and empowers others to embrace his teachings. We must shake the dust from our hands, hearts, bodies and mind as we seek to remove it from the feet of others.

Lent is a time for us to shake the dust from our complacency; a period to reflect and act on our indifference. We are asked to recall and remember that, being made in his image and likeness, we are to assume the mantle of service. As we embrace the call to fast, pray and repent during these 40 days, we must not lose sight of our purpose in doing so. At each station of the cross we are challenged to accept God's transforming grace; that unearned blessing which draws us to an abiding love and service to him as well as our fellow man.

Cloaked in our servant garment we may assume many roles. Often it is our position or membership in a parish ministry. Sometimes we measure it by the number of hours we spend at the church, degree of responsibility we assume or leadership position we fill. Frequently, we accept ascribed parish roles and consider it enough. For many the mantle of service is not evident. It is an inherent manifestation of their abiding faith, love and devotion to God that is lived daily.

Each of us is called to don the cloak, pick up our basin and perform the cleansing ritual. In so doing, we perform not only a service but enter more fully into communion with our Lord. It is an embarkation on the path of blessing that transforms not only the lives of others but allows God to transform us. Whether it be anonymous acts of kindness and consideration, prayer intercessor, parish council president or supportive co-worker, we must heed his call to serve.

As a child, I was surrounded by holy men and women. I did not know them as such then. They seemed to be somewhat meddlesome, often dull and frequently the unofficial Roman Catholic police force. They moved furniture and organ from store to community building to old garage each weekend. They laundered, starched and ironed altar linens. Tired hands picked flowers from gardens to grace the Lord's table, braided hair and tied ribbons, pressed Sunday clothes, recited the rosary, made wings for May procession angels and slipped pennies and dimes into the poor box. Sometimes they repaired our pastor's shoes and darned his socks. With love, faith and joy their service transformed our lives, our church, and our community. They knew that their rent was due and paid with fervor, devotion and anonymity. They wore the mantle.

As we continue this journey, let us cloak ourselves in the cloth of service, the holy garment that can transform the world. Perhaps then we will truly become the holy women and men of God.

A Dirty Mess

It was in 1999 that I first heard about the 250 workers at Baltimore's largest industrial laundry. Trials of unimaginable measure had befallen the men and women who worked at Up-To-Date Laundry as they tried to organize a union.

Laundry work is hot, dirty and extremely dangerous. They handle the soiled and bloodstained linen from our community's major hospitals, often times facing the threat of needle sticks from contaminated syringes left in the dirty linen. Workers faced constant abuse by management, sexual harassment and racial discrimination in addition to the horrendous conditions in the facility.

They organized themselves for change. Most employees at Up-To-Date Laundry are Latino and African American women. Workers with up to 30 years' seniority make as little as $5.50 per hour. It has been noted that African Americans are paid a lower starting wage.

I was struck by the injustice then, and my desire to support the brave Up-To-Date workers grew. Guillermina Rivera, a woman who worked at Up-To-Date for almost two years, developed a serious lung and heart infection from the hazards of her job. The company did not provide Guillermina with a light-duty job. Guillermina does not have health insurance.

Two government agencies investigated Up-To-Date and found sufficient evidence, after almost two years of fact-finding, to issue complaints against the company and its owners for violations of labor law and discrimination against workers based on race. The Maryland Commission on Human Relations is poised to issue the final finding

223

of fact on their sexual harassment complaints by young Latino female workers.

Up-To-Date is a disgrace to our community. Some hospitals and agencies have agreed to stop doing business with Up-To-Date when their contracts expire if conditions do not change. Employers should use their position to encourage leadership and inspire growth, but instead these employers have chosen to deny workers even the most basic rights and perpetuate an atmosphere of severe racial intolerance and sexual predatory actions, as described in the commission's reports.

I listened to workers tell their stories of struggle and hope. I was moved by the resilience, bravery and dedication of the workers. The workers needed support. We are people who believe in justice.

During my life-long residency in Baltimore I have involved myself in the politics of this town as a member of the City Council and as an activist. Baltimore has never seen such madness where employers subject their workers to such mass abuse.

How can a business be run this way? How can we turn our backs on this corporate misconduct? I believe that we should join hands in prayer and work together to end the abuses suffered by the Up-To-Date workers. If not, this could occur again in our city, and there could be no end to the injustice.

Catholic social teaching identifies protecting human rights and dignity as crucial to building a just society. Our teaching supports the rights of workers, "by working, we participate in God's act of creation. Work contributes to human dignity and to feelings of self–work. Work can uphold the dignity of the human person in a variety of ways. The church sees work as a duty. Therefore, it should allow people to live in dignity. According to modern church social teaching, the rights of workers include the following:

- Productive work
- Living wages
- Ownership of private property
- Unionization and organizing of workers

Many of these issues were resolved last week. It was about time to stop such madness!

Stigma

B lack Catholics united nationwide at the 9th National Black Catholic Congress to build a strong agenda on Leadership for the 21st Century. One area where Black Catholic leadership is severely needed is in speaking out against the stigma and discrimination associated with HIV/AIDS.

The keynote speaker for the HIV/AIDS workshop at the Congress was Joseph C. Gaithe, Jr., M.D., F.A.C.P., who is the chief of Infectious Diseases at Park Plaza Hospital in Houston, Texas. He indicated we have a very serious situation.

If you recall the famous line in "Apollo 13," "Houston, we have a problem!" We could surely say to Africans, African Americans, and those from the Caribbean, we have a problem.

We have a problem when African Americans are roughly 12 percent of the population, but make up more that 54 percent of the 40,000 new HIV cases diagnosed annually.

We have a problem when 60 percent of African Americans who tested positive with the virus didn't even know they had it.

We have a problem when the face of AIDS in the Black community is becoming a woman's issue. In 1998, African American women constituted 64 percent of new female AIDS cases.

We have a problem when the number one killer of African American men is HIV/AIDS and we have a problem when Black children represent almost two-thirds (62 percent) of all reported pediatric AIDS cases.

The National Black Catholic Congress challenged the participants to go home and break the silence about this disease. Unless we eliminate the stigma and shame associated with this epidemic, we can't provide education or get people into treatment.

The Pastoral Plan of Action (from the Congress) on HIV/ AIDS exhorts us to be on task within a year to provide educational opportunities for parish staffs, schools, parishioners and the local community, with emphasis on parenting, education and HIV/AIDS awareness for youth. The plan continues to direct efforts within three years to develop a Black Catholic fund to support HIV/AIDS ministries in the United States and Africa. Within five years the plan encourages us to establish comprehensive parish-based youth programs that address the dissemination of information, behavior modification and follow-up for HIV/AIDS related issues.

World AIDS Day is December 1. This is a day that the entire world community recognizes the impact of AIDS and its effect on the global family. World AIDS Day is also a day that the world joins hands and hearts to address the pain, the stigma and the great loss of so many lives. World AIDS Day is a time for us as Black Catholics to unite with the international community in addressing AIDS. It is also a time for us to witness by our words and action, the compassion of Jesus and to pray as a people of faith and hope for the healing of HIV/AIDS.

As we respond to this challenge, we are reminded of the words from Scripture: "There is a real opportunity here for great and worthwhile work (1 Cor. 16:9) ... He helps us in all our troubles, so that we are able to help others who have all kinds of troubles, using the same help that we ourselves have received from God" (2 Cor. 1:4).

As we gather to ask the Lord's blessings, families are requested to ask God's blessings for the healing of AIDS. Gather as a family and pass the plate to help fund a local AIDS program in your neighborhood. Ask your parish to print the HIV/AIDS prayer in your Sunday bulletin. Parishes that already have health committees should consider hosting an education program after the Masses on this weekend.

FATHER DONALD A. STERLING, D. MIN.

We are Stewards

When you think of "the church," what images come to mind? What do you consider to be the purpose of the church? How do you see the liturgy and sacraments fitting into your images of the church and your understandings of its purpose?

The church is not ours. We may have the title and deed to the physical edifice, but Christ and Christ alone has the title and deed to the spiritual body, which is the living church. It was he and he alone who said, "Upon this rock I will build my church."

The church does not have a mission. The mission has a church. God's business or the mission of God is to be "goodness everywhere." Evangelization is God's goodness literally brought down to earth.

Evangelization is a job description of Jesus. Jesus the word of God dwelt amongst us. Let's face it; Jesus was an itinerant whose life was spent encountering people. He proclaimed God's mighty deeds by talking and eating with them, and attending to their needs and concerns.

Discipleship is what the followers of Jesus do. Discipleship is a job description of Christians – those baptized with the very same Spirit as Jesus and called to continue the work of Jesus, which is the work of God. To be disciples, we must faithfully evangelize: proclaim the truth about Jesus and his promises; witness – put our faith, hope and love-in-action; dialogue – encounter others as equal partners in the venture of life; and liberate – free others from inhumane and undignified burdens, humiliation, oppressions, addictions, etc. The church is called to be faithful to its promise to Christ.

The parish does not have a mission; the mission has parishes. Parishes are one of the instruments of God's mission. God is the creator; we are the creatures. God speaks and creation occurs. God calls and humanity responds. It is our glory to be called by God and to be able to respond.

As the Body of Christ, we must be an inviting community. When Jesus ministered, he was inclusive in his invitation to join in the work of establishing the kingdom. We must be a community committed to liberation. After all, the purpose of God's grace is to free us from those things that bind us so that we might live with real God-given dignity and respect. God's liberating love has the power to free us from sin and death.

We cannot accept a complacent Christianity that lets us feel that we have fulfilled our commitment to God by simply attending the church. We cannot come to Mass thinking more about what we can get out of church than thanking God for the blessings already bestowed upon us.

We must be consciously "convicted" by the Holy Spirit. The Holy Spirit must guide and inform our politics, our decisions, our relationships and our entire life. We must be open to the love of God in order to bring the love of God. Don't panic, God's grace is sufficient! God is awesome. However, remember, "faith without works is dead."

We must be reconciled to God and to one another. Each of us must enter into a faithful trust relationship with God and one another. We will not make it to heaven by ourselves. We must not expect of one another what only God can do. We are all sinners. Each of us constantly stands in the need of prayer and forgiveness. We are not in a position to judge who is or who is not worthy of God's generosity.

Let us value prayerful worship. Let us share with those who wish to serve. Yes, we celebrate the past. However, let us anticipate the future. God has great things prepared for those who love, trust and serve God. After all, God's Spirit is in front of us, behind us and beside us.

War on Drugs

After 22 years of serving as a substance abuse counselor, one gains insight and wisdom about addiction struggles and recovery. Recovery from addiction is a dynamic process when the individual works on reclaiming all facets of their lives.

Some come into treatment so empty that recovery is not an option. Many feel they have nothing or no one to return to, having been addicted from an early age. In these cases, the individual is devoid of many of the basic life experiences, and treatment becomes a time for discovery. Despite a poverty of experiences, many come with a longing for God.

While the government may view the remedy of the drug epidemic with a war on drugs, the addicted see themselves engaged in a war in which spiritual growth and religious devotion is central to rehabilitation.

As people of faith, engaged in a myriad of social services, I am convinced that we can win this war on drugs if we mix an alchemy of faith and action to gain victory with the addicted and the community at large.

Over the years, I've discovered that many of the recovering addicts are so racked with guilt and shame that they feel that God can never forgive them. They fear that their recovery and quest for sobriety will be an empty victory.

They have a difficult time identifying why they feel that way: "Why can't I get it right?" They sometimes call it a hole in their soul. I try to patch up that hole with activities and suggestions.

However, those efforts only brought about large degrees of frustration for the individual and for me. I felt less than inadequate. I cared and tried to do my best. I searched for the emptiness that the clients were talking about and denied my own emptiness. What was missing in my treatment services?

I was at a presentation where a medical doctor talked about this walk with God, and he wasn't complete if he left his faith out of his work.

I was trained to separate faith from my practice. I don't know how many times I had to keep my mouth and spirit shut down. The light bulb came on, and I knew what was missing.

I started listening to the recovering individual with new ears; ears embellished with the voice of God. My task became easier. I could hear their yearning for a forgiving God, a gentle God and someone to help my clients back from a living hell. Once I started taking God to work with me, my load became lighter.

When you lead the recovering individual back to God, they can achieve wholeness. God's grace is sufficient through the storm and is able to calm the tempestuous waters.

The church has a vital role in reclaiming our sons, daughters, brothers, sisters, mothers and fathers. The church can be a very active partner with treatment programs opening wide their doors to welcome and journey with the addicted.

Many of those recovering have so many fears of returning to church because of the anxiety of unacceptance from churchgoers. They find it difficult to tolerate the stares of unforgiving people.

They are not given opportunities to testify about how "they got over" with the grace of God. We lose so many Catholic brothers and sisters to other denominations because we are not there sojourning with those who seek recovery.

We can win this war on drugs if we intentionally help "suit–up" those undergoing spiritual warfare. We, as church, can use our resources and help those who need an armor of faith and a quiver of hope.

We can win this war by opening wide the doors of the church and resourcing special ministries for the addicted. Some of our churches offer space for AA or NA, but can we do more? Yes, because we want victory in Jesus for all.

Developing & Expanding

I attended a meeting of the Baltimoreans United In Leadership Development (B.U.I.L.D.) action team. The meeting was held in a "Child First" room at Greenspring Middle School.

I looked at the walls and flat surface of the room and saw evidence of many projects, some quite sophisticated, that reflected the after-school work and activities of the young people enrolled in the Child First program. I reflected on the hours of time these youngsters had used to produce such models of excellence and thought. What a wonderful example of worthwhile use of after-school time to grow, develop and expand.

Next I wondered where these young people would have been and what they would have been doing if B.U.I.L.D., through its Child First Authority, had not made these opportunities available to them. What a shame if our city doesn't make permanent funding available to continue this program. What will happen to our youngsters with nothing special to do with so many idle hours of after-school time?

The Child First Authority is not the only contribution B.U.I.L.D. has made to improving the life of families in Baltimore. The organization has negotiated with local, state and corporate officials to win other benefits for Baltimore citizens.

The College Board Foundation has raised more than $15 million to promote counseling and tuition assistance for young people on their way to college.

B.U.I.L.D. worked with Governor Parris Glendening and the Department of Human Resources to get recognition of college as a viable welfare option in Baltimore. B.U.I.L.D.'s Living Wage Ordinance helped more than 2,000 workers earn $7.40 an hour rather than minimum wage. This has been an example for more than 70 other cities that have won the same or are working on it.

Along with the Enterprise Foundation, this organization has been responsible for almost 1,000 affordable homes for low- and middle-income families in such communities as Reservoir Hill, Sandtown-Winchester and Cherry Hill.

B.U.I.L.D. has diligently spent time in Annapolis during the recent legislative sessions, lobbying for the needs of our citizens for funding for Head Start, parks and playgrounds.

A pilot program for two Fellowship Houses connected to B.U.I.L.D. churches is underway to create programs for people in drug rehabilitation and ex-offenders returning to Baltimore from prisons.

Because of B.U.I.L.D.'s work, the check-cashing industry has been regulated and its outlets required to be licensed. There is a much lower limit on percentage that they can charge for services. Pay-day lenders can no longer charge outrageous interest rates that sometimes went as high as 800 percent. The Attorney General, Banking Commission and other allies worked with B.U.I.L.D. to ensure that lenders charge only 33 percent APR on these small loans to workers who write post-dated checks.

These are some examples of ways in which B.U.I.L.D. members, mostly volunteers, are helping our city.

How does this all come about? B.U.I.L.D. believes in the power of organized people and organized money. We take very seriously the leadership development part of our name. I say, "we," because I have been an active member of B.U.I.L.D. for most of its nearly 25 years. When a church or an organization joins, we claim the members of that church or organization as our members.

With this in mind, our leadership team and experienced members teach others to think through and analyze problems and issues. We evaluate our actions and decide what worked and what didn't. We discuss organizational characteristics and traits and decide where and what needs improvement.

I believe there will always be B.U.I.L.D. with great leadership, willing and ready to do whatever is necessary to make our interracial, multi-cultural and multi-denominational city a better place to live.

MELANIE A. REESE

Impacts

When World AIDS Day approaches my soul becomes restless.

A rich African American Catholic history has been passed down to us, left as a legacy to cherish, embrace and share with others into the future. As I stand on the shoulders of my ancestors, I look to the future and make a pledge to do whatever I can to ensure that our ancestors' efforts were not done in vain. These ancestors were about life, faith, the building up of the church and the protection of their people.

As African American Catholics of today, we, too, must put on the banner of our ancestors and march into the future. This march must recognize the devastating affect of HIV/AIDS on our community.

All of us are affected by HIV/AIDS and it is not curable. New treatment regimens, partnerships with primary care providers, psychosocial professionals, peer educators, support groups and involvement with the faith community enable us to live longer, healthier, productive lives. Yet, HIV/AIDS can be 100 percent preventable.

African Americas are infected and affected by this disease especially here in Baltimore, which ranks 19th in the nation in terms of city size. It is third in new HIV/AIDS incidence cases in the nation. African Americans comprise 83 percent of those living with HIV in Maryland and 79.5 percent of those living with the HIV virus.

African Americans are disproportionately affected by this disease nationally, where 54 percent of the new incidences recorded are African American. There are at least 6,500 who know their HIV status and are not in treatment. We can prevent the spread of this disease through education and down right honesty.

The Ninth National Black Catholic Congress convened August, 2002, in Chicago making HIV/AIDS an issue warranting our attention and follow up. The pastoral plan of action from the Congress encouraged Black Catholics in the United States to engage in efforts to assist in the research, treatment, education and elimination of this disease. We are to provide educational opportunities to parish staffs, schools, parishioners and the local community with emphasis on parenting education and HIV/AIDS awareness for our youth.

One of the World AIDS Day themes was "live and let live." Why can't we do all that we can to help our people survive? We can change human history. We can continue to have a rich cultural and spiritual history if we reach out to our brothers and sisters infected and affected by HIV/AIDS without judgment, with compassion, just as Jesus would. Since we are called to be Jesus to his people on earth, let us get busy with our Father's work.

Join the Office of African American Catholic Ministry and the National African American Catholic Task Force on HIV/AIDS, as we remember those who have lost their battle with HIV/AIDS and those still in the daily struggle with this disease. Your parish has information, prayers and suggestions for follow up for World AIDS Day December 1.

At a forum held at New All Saints Church on World AIDS Day, I followed through with a call from within to reveal my HIV status. I later revealed this to my St. Cecilia church family. A face had to be put on the disease that showed that anyone can be infected and that everyone needed to get involved with their gifts and talents to stop the spread of this disease.

I discovered my status donating blood at the first Martin Luther King Blood Drive in January, 2002. I wanted to save lives with that donation of blood now as well as donate my organs and tissues later when I go home. I save lives now as a peer educator, serving on two hospitals' planning councils, a consumer advisory board member, a public speaker, a recruiter for clinical trials and a recruiter for Christ, sharing the love, mercy, grace and the salvation of Jesus.

HIV/AIDS is 100 percent preventable. Do you know your status? Encourage testing and treatment for addiction, substance use and abuse, domestic violence, mental and emotional illness. We are a mighty chosen people of faith. We can do this.

Entertaining Angels

One of my most precious memories of my grandmother is of my lifting her from the bathtub at Stella Maris and carrying her back to her bed. The awe of that experience has no words.

My grandmother was a strong woman who would walk downtown everyday, and she would not leave the area until she had attended Mass at St. Alphonsus and made her visit to St. Jude Shrine. There she laid many intercessions at the foot of the cross.

While as children we all feared her, there is not a family gathering where we do not speak and laugh intimately about her strict counsel regarding attendance at Mass, cleanliness and dental hygiene.

The other day I went into a restroom and heard an elder crying out in the stall. I called out, but she did not respond. As I came closer, I was embarrassed to note that she was not crying out, but she was praying to God. I could not help but overhear as she screamed, "Lord please help me! They work you all your life as a slave, and when you can't work any longer they throw you out into the pig's pen. Save me Lord!" Nothing could hold back my tears. I could not speak.

Aging in this country has lost something precious. I work with an African American population that has worked all their lives in service for meager wages and have little to show for it. That the poor should become poorer is not a reflection on their lives as much as a reflection of how America chooses to shoulder the responsibility for the "tired and poor."

My interactions with African American elders are a challenging yet rewarding service. Their history, trials, deferred dreams and triumphs of spirit help to put my life into perspective. On the continuum of discrimination, theirs is the greater pain.

Here and now is where reparation begins. The aged African American is vested with a passage that America chooses to forget, and younger African Americans struggle to understand.

Many who age in comfort cry out in loneliness and fail to receive what they expected from material things. I wonder if our African American elderly can find peace in letting go of deferred dreams and all that they were denied because of the color of their skin. I pray that they receive gentle peace as they pass the baton and become affirmed that they built this nation, and we are free.

In 30 years, one in every five Americans will be over age 65. As managed care organizations move away from services, it is vital that there remain a visible structural matrix that role models commitment to our frail and disabled elderly.

I work with colleagues that actualize services to the poor and elderly every day. Senior leadership takes the time to serve a meal, deliver baskets, touch shoulders and advocate for services. In those brief hours on our watch, under our roof, we ease their burden from having to worry about this one thing, on this one day. Moment to moment is an opportunity to affirm their dignity.

My grandmother's nurturing spirit brought me through a turbulent childhood to a committed relationship with Jesus. She never preached racial hatred, only hope. She preached about the goodness of others, the value of family, honest work and to treat others as we wanted to be treated.

I pray that African American elders will be remembered by all of America. That America will take the time to smile at them, open their doors, offer them a meal at their table or just sit and listen to their rich history. And when our Lord bids them come and rest, they will take with them many stories of random acts of kindness.

Thoughts & Prayers

President George W. Bush issued an executive order titled "Agency Responsibilities with Respect to Faith-Based and Community Initiatives."

Related to the above initiative is "Rallying the Armies of Compassion" by President Bush. This document reports that the goal is to energize civil society and rebuild social capital, particularly by uplifting small non-profit organizations, congregations and other faith-based institutions that are lonely outposts of energy, service and vision in poor and declining neighborhoods and rural enclaves.

Our parishes with a history of serving the poor should be responding to President Bush with the summons of "show me the money."

At the same time, President Bush unveiled his $1.6 trillion tax cut program to rejuvenate a sluggish economy. The Democrats raised caution that the actual cost of the tax cut could grow to $2.6 trillion. The president plans to pay for each initiative out of the projected surplus.

Black Catholic parishes serve citizens in declining neighborhoods with a variety of social programs such as drug and alcohol rehabilitation, outreach to those imprisoned and emergency food services. These ministries would be eligible to compete for federal grant dollars. The possibility of receiving new dollars to support these ministries is welcome news.

As grassroots faith-based and community-serving organizations consider competing for these federal dollars, some questions arise.

• One, in order not to violate the separation of church and state as required by the Constitution, how will the religious activity of the

237

ministry be required to change?

• Two, does the ministry have adequate overhead dollars to pay for the staff to operate current programming? Expanded programming?

• Three, does the ministry have the appropriate type and adequate support staff to operate current programming? Expanded programming?

• Four, does the ministry have the appropriate financial resources to sustain the current or expanded programming when the grant ends?

Any responsible faith-based and community-serving organization must face these sobering questions as they consider competing successfully for federal grant dollars.

The answers to these questions are crucial to strategic program planning because it is unclear how they will finance this initiative after federal funds are exhausted. Further, it is unclear how many actual program dollars will be available to faith-based and community-serving organizations because the initiative calls for providing technical assistance to the organizations and encouraging through tax credits donations by private citizens to the organizations.

Catholic Charities and its affiliated agencies are faith-based and community-serving organizations. Catholic Charities has been receiving some public sector dollars for many years to subsidize housing for the elderly and children's welfare programming.

The history of the partnership between Catholic Charities and the government suggests that government will provide some dollars but not all of the dollars needed to operate quality programming. Therefore, grassroots faith-based and community-serving organizations need thoughtfully and prayerfully to consider how they would raise the dollars to sustain services and ministry.

President Bush's faith-based initiative is intriguing. The initiative does encourage new ways to consider partnering to address the social ills of modern American society.

Encouraging is the notion of valuing the proven work of grassroots faith-based and community-serving organizations. It is important and responsible to consider the details of how they will carry out the partnership at the grassroots level and what financial support will be available to operate the program.

Catholic social teaching calls each of us to work to provide option(s) for the poor and vulnerable. The president's initiative could provide a different and creative strategy for fulfilling our obligation.

Not a Day Off

The concept of "the American dream" brings to mind many connotations and a multitude of thoughts.

For some among us, freedom to exercise the American dream of voting resulted in the threat of physical and mental harm. For others, the dream came to fruition through the acquiring of 40 acres and a mule. Others have been locked out of the American dream due to racism and injuries inflicted from the war with poverty.

Racial profiling has found its way into institutions and public offices. Our prisons are full with Black men and women, some of whom did not experience fair trials (like Michael Austin) while others were beat up with the chains of poverty.

Civil rights for all Americans continue to be a challenge, complicated by economics, bigotry and neglect. Travesties of injustice continue to perpetrate in America, and Dr. Martin Luther King's legacy gives each of us some "homework" to complete.

That is why our celebration of Dr. King's birthday should be a day on in promoting equality, justice and a step forward in fulfilling the true "American dream."

From the early days of the civil rights movement, Dr. King required of volunteers much more than what was seen on the surface level. Many participated in dramatic marches and demonstrations. Less noticed activities, such as running errands, typing, writing, organizing mailings and prayer vigils, gained equal attention from Dr. King.

"Every volunteer was required to sign a commitment card to follow 10 commandments" of nonviolence. They included:

- Meditate daily on the teachings and life of Jesus.
- Remember always that the nonviolent movement seeks justice and reconciliation – not victory.
- Walk and talk in the manner of love, for God is love.
- Pray daily to be used by God in order that all men might be free.
- Sacrifice personal wishes in order that all men might be free.
- Observe with both friend and foe the ordinary rules of courtesy.
- Seek to perform regular service for others and for the world.
- Refrain from the violence of fist, tongue or heart.
- Strive to be in good spiritual and bodily health.
- Follow the directions of the movement and of the captain of a demonstration.

Certainly, a relationship with Jesus requires us to "do as Jesus would do." A remembrance of the birth and life of Dr. King requires us to do something to advance freedom and justice for all God's people.

True celebration of Dr. King's birthday is realized when we work for justice – a day on, not a day off. It's a time to write to our public officials in both Annapolis and in Washington to voice our opinion and our expectations of laws, legislation and budgets that support life, justice and freedom.

It is a time for us to tell the story of struggle and victory to our children and grandchildren. It is a time for us to stretch ourselves for the benefit of someone else so that they may have life and the pursuit of happiness.

It is a time to pray for the end of violence in our world and to resolve ourselves to work for justice.

Whatever you do, do it sincerely and with the hope that many will consider the Dr. King holiday as a day on, not a day off! This has the capacity to change human history.

Baltimore Believes

The Baltimore Believe Committee sounded a call to action for all of Baltimore City and the surrounding counties.

The call was for all of us to have the faith to believe that the citizens and the city of Baltimore can overcome all of the maladies that are facing it today and become a municipality that people will be proud to call home.

Baltimore's problem is not an isolated problem; it is a regional problem with tentacles that creep into all branches of the state.

"Faith is the realization of what is hoped for and for evidence of things not seen" according to the Letter to the Hebrews. Faith is what the Baltimore Believe Campaign is asking us all to have.

As we sang in the '60s, "We Shall Overcome," we can sing the same song in the new century. We had a real agenda in the '60s when we wanted to break free from those bonds that were preventing us from reaching our potential as a group and as individuals.

The new campaign calls for us to renew that vigor, spirit, hope and faith to a new level. To believe that, we can make a difference in this city, our home, if we all contribute to rid the city of the blight that is slowly eroding the life of the citizens, the city and the state.

We must believe that we deserve to live in a city where we can visit friends at night. We must believe in a city where the only chalk marks on the streets are those of games that our children are playing.

We must believe in a city where citizens can feel safe going to church at night, and employment is gained for the many who are looking.

There are many skeptics who are saying "What? Another slogan campaign, just like Barbara Bush's 'Just say no?'"

Baltimore Believe is not a slogan campaign. The total foundation of the program is that the people of Baltimore should no longer see themselves as victims during these times of trouble.

The call to believe, to have faith, has been intertwined with all of us throughout history. Noah believed, that's why he built the Ark. Abraham believed, and he has descendents as numerous as the stars. Moses believed and parted the Red Sea.

We are asked to believe to do our part no matter how small because "when spiders unite, they can tie up a lion."

For the urban church, the campaign is a wake-up call for faith in Baltimore to be preached from the pulpit and to incite all of us to action. Our young, our future must prophesy as Ezekiel did in the "Valley of Dry Bones": "Prophesy over these bones: see I will bring spirit in you so that you may come to life."

The call is for all of us to believe that with the guidance of God we can renew this city of "Dry Bones," to put sinews and flesh and skin on the very fabric of the city.

We cannot stop at that stage; we must bring the Spirit to the people. The Spirit that aids us to stand up against the odds that threatens us – the odds that make us feel and act helpless.

The devil is a lie, and we must shine the light of truth on the street corners, in our churches, where we work and in our homes.

The faith and hope that our works will not be in vain, to be brave when we sing, "We Shall Overcome," and soon the song will change to "We Have Overcome."

Baltimore, we have to believe. We have lived through the kidnapping, the arduous Atlantic crossing, slavery, the Civil War, Jim Crow, substance abuse, HIV, murders and all types of tribulations because we did not come this far for God to leave us now. Believe Baltimore because God believes in us.

Baltimore Believes.

CLINTON E. JIGGETTS

One at a Time

Come travel up Park Heights Avenue near Park Circle and witness a miracle in the making. Inspired by our Christian values, God's people have done something new in Park Circle. What was broke, busted and disgusted has now turned into a beautiful village of home ownership. After all, Pope John Paul II has said, "We need to bring the Gospel of life to the heart of every man and woman and make it penetrate every part of society."

The Cottage Avenue Community (CAC) is an innovative program of St. Vincent de Paul of Baltimore (SVDP) located in Southern Park Heights in Northwest Baltimore City. The program was the vision of Sister Charmaine Krohe, S.S.N.D., director of the St. Ambrose Family Outreach Center, who has lived in the community for 32 years.

The CAC Transitional Housing Program is designed to help families make a successful transition from emergency shelters to permanent housing and economic self-sufficiency; the program is open to homeless families who are income-eligible for Section 8 housing.

St. Vincent de Paul of Baltimore renovated 12 formerly vacant and abandoned single family row houses for 15 families. The community consists of eight two-bedroom, apartments and seven three-bedroom row houses on Cottage and Ulman Avenues. A neighborhood setting ensures that the program provides housing on a human scale, residents feel part of a community and they have the opportunity to develop supportive relationships with other families.

The CAC is a two-year comprehensive structure program, providing life skills, parenting, job readiness, and budgeting classes, as well as volunteer service, mentoring, counseling, addiction education, employment and securing permanent housing.

It's a collaboration between the Cottage Avenue Community Program and the St. Ambrose Family Outreach Center to provide supported services, such as GED classes, computer classes, a Head Start program, and a food pantry.

The CAC program began operation in May, 2000; 27 formerly homeless families have participated. Out of the 27 families, 19 have successfully graduated and moved on to permanent housing and self-sufficiency, becoming employed tax-paying citizens.

The program has greatly impacted the Park Heights Community at large with its well-landscaped lawns and well-kept units. Another wonderful effort of St. Vincent de Paul was to purchase the vacant lot at the corner of Park Heights and Ulman Avenue. This lot was a former hang out for drug dealers and undesirables. St. Vincent renovated the lot into a state-of-the-art playground for the use of the Cottage Avenue Community Program families, St. Ambrose Family Outreach Center youth, teen and Head Start children and for other community residents.

The CAC has established a partnership with other landlords, city agencies and the St. Ambrose Housing Aid Center to assist with finding affordable permanent housing for the participants. Many of the graduating participants have relocated in the Park Heights and Reisterstown Road community, as well as other parts of the city.

As the program director, I consider this my personal mission and ministry to serve the community and give back, to lift as many people up to become self-sufficient, viable citizens. Due to reduced and lack of government funding for housing, I think the church and other nonprofit organizations must play a significant role in providing housing to revitalize Baltimore one community at a time.

CHARLES G. TILDON, JR.

Elections

Our country has just experienced a presidential election that has the potential for widening the gap between African Americans and the white population. Reports are widespread about voting irregularities and the disproportionate impact that African Americans experienced as they tried to vote. Nevertheless, we elected a president, one which we must accept. Analysts will debate the "real" winner for years to come.

How do we use our strength, faith, love, survival skills and determination to ensure that our president keeps the clock moving forward? How do we as Catholics use the recent acknowledgement of the church's role in slavery as well as the basic tenants of our church to help our president understand the dangers of developing and supporting policies that will turn back the clock?

Our progress toward equality has been slow. As an institution the church has a wonderful opportunity to be bold and courageous. The church can help our president understand why African Americans voted in record numbers resulting in such a close election. As policies are shaped, it would be well to have persons at the table who understand the impact that those policies could have on African Americans. They must be willing and able to point out clearly the negative impacts, and the new administration must listen. We must be willing to investigate the alleged voting irregularities and make corrections where necessary.

Among the many actions that we must monitor are appointments to all positions – both judicial and administrative. We should offer counsel on these appointments. Church leaders can join African American leaders in seeking the answer to the question – "How will this appointee or this policy affect all of God's children" – especially African Americans.

Our voting system clearly needs to be overhauled. Can we play a role in developing a fair system that provides all citizens the assurance that their vote counts? I am sure we can. It means, however, that we may need to take some risks. We need to follow Jesus' example as he took many unpopular positions.

The church's role as an educator can be the catalyst for providing all of its members with information that may help them understand the importance of casting their votes intelligently.

Parishes can share their knowledge about the power of voting. They can be sure that issues are articulated clearly and that parishioners exercise their rights in support of that which is fair and equitable.

African Americans question whether their vote is in jeopardy. Exit poles and a review of the data show that nine out of 10 African Americans voted for the candidate who did not win. If we follow the political points of view – that to the victor goes the spoils or that one should reward one's friends and punish ones enemies – the African American community should be frightened.

Decisions and actions of our new president should evidence a sensitivity to the depth of the problems we face and begin to address the root causes of those problems. Identification of the problems without searching for and recognizing the cause will only lead to "band-aid" solutions.

Can this administration understand our need to be seen as equals and treated as such? Can this administration understand that various forms of compensation are required if we are to compete as equals in every field of human endeavor? Will this administration recognize the superhuman efforts it has taken for so many Black Americans to join the mainstream?

As we experience the beginning of a new church year and rejoice in the birth of our Lord and Savior, Jesus Christ, there are many examples from his teachings that tell us that we can answer "yes" to the questions that have been raised.

Those teachings also give us many instructions that would lead us to appropriate actions. We must have the courage to exercise the moral imperatives that will influence our president-elect and everyone who would advise him to follow those instructions and examples. Perhaps, then, we can say that this close election gave us the impetus and opportunity to do the right thing and in so doing begin to close the gap.

246

Ex-felons

"Happy are those whose wrongs are forgiven, whose sins are pardoned. Happy is the person whose sin the Lord will not keep account of."

The day started as most days in August begin, full of hope and wonder. The event was a community festival hosted by a community beset with all the ills of this city. A community that was all too familiar with gunshot and the sight of our best and brightest engaged in the evil act of selling poison.

I had ordered several booths and a soundstage from the city's Department of Public Works. When the equipment finally arrived (after many frantic calls from me) they were a full two hours late.

Naturally, all the booths were not there. Furthermore, I was told there would be no additional booths. Of course, being the calm and rational woman I am, I vented.

Adam Sykes was the employee from the Department of Public Works who caught all my wrath. This young man explained calmly that his shift was near an end but that he would go in search of additional booths for us. I did not believe Adam would return. How wrong I was!

Upon Adam's return with the required booths, he and I began to talk. He shared with me his past criminal history and subsequent felony convictions. Adam then said quite emphatically that crime was a thing of the past for him, and he'd learned his lesson. He talked at length about his daily struggle to support his family on $9 an hour. His every other sentence was about the magnificence of our Lord.

Adam then shared a deep, deep hurt he suffered every Election Day –

his loss of voting privileges. He discussed the need of a father showing his children how to live. Adam referred to himself as three-fifths of a man. His question to me was, "how many times do I pay for a crime of the past?"

Standing before me was a man who was a living testimony of the awesomeness of our God. A God who can take a young "hustler" from the street and set him on the right path.

I promised Adam I would call the president of the Board of Election Supervisors for the city. I did call Marvin "Doc" Cheatham, president of the board. We discussed the possibility of holding hearings and collecting testimony from others who have been impacted.

I couldn't wait to speak to Adam to let him know of my progress, but that was not to be. One cold winter morning earlier this year, Adam Sykes, while driving a truck for the Department of Public Works, was killed in a traffic accident.

As I heard the news I wondered how many people had been as fortunate as I to have glimpsed the spirit of this powerfully built young man – this young man who had indeed been redeemed and only wanted to participate as a citizen. I still see the pain and confusion etched across his face and his eyes as he asked, "how many times do I pay for a crime of the past?"

Our faith speaks to us about the power of redemption. We are called by Christ to do the "right thing." A popular Gospel song now fills airwaves with a daily admonishment: "We fall down, but we get up!"

We must address Adam's question. Each legislative session we see the introduction of a bill to address the issue of restoration of voting rights to ex-felons. Each year these bills fail to pass.

Let us, as true Catholics, send a message to our legislators in Annapolis to do the "right thing." Restore voting rights for ex-felons. Do it for Adam who was more than three-fifths of a man.

By and for the People

Being Black in America is a challenge. Being Black and Catholic adds another dimension to the challenge when it comes to addressing the new political realities.

Republican landslides, shifting demographics, civil rights, protection of the unborn and the elderly, immigration laws, welfare reform, racial profiling, capital punishment and budgetary reductions give rise for Black Catholics to lift up their voices and remain involved in the public policy arena.

The presidential election illustrated the enormous value of just one vote. The power of lobbying state legislators and members of Congress can alter a vote and establish new laws. Working and organizing as a mass of people under a well-crafted, justice-based agenda is a powerful advocacy strategy.

Power only speaks to and respects power. Directed and intentional advocacy has always been on the agenda for Black Christians. Today – like never before – it is of utmost importance that Black Catholics act on the principles of Catholic social teaching. We are called to "create options for the poor and vulnerable," support "subsidiarity" and never waiver from "solidarity."

Being Catholic and African American places each of us in a unique position to understand and articulate the plight of "poor and vulnerable people," regardless of race or creed.

We are called to identify "the table" where the story must be told. The table may be the parish pastoral council that is considering a ministry to address the needs of the "poor and vulnerable people." The table could be the diocesan social justice office. The table could be the board of the local Catholic charity that delivers services to the "poor and vulnerable people." "The table" could be local, state or federal government. Wherever "the table," we are called by our faith and compelled by our heritage to participate in the shaping of just policy.

There are 11 basic steps to policy development. We are to:

1. Tell "what we have seen and heard."

2. Draw conclusions concerning the root causes of what we have seen and heard.

3. Offer solutions to the articulated root causes. Solutions should consider immediate responses to the needs of the individual and long-term responses to correcting dysfunctioning or obsolete systems.

4. Identify the appropriate level of government to communicate the proposed policy (subsidiarity).

5. Be prepared to work in partnership with government (solidarity).

6. Identify people, groups and organizations that share your point of view.

7. Meet with influential people (i.e., legislative and administrative staff) to "educate" them.

8. Meet with the decision-makers to shape policy.

9. Be prepared to draft the language of the proposed legislation or rule.

10. Monitor the status of requested policy.

11. Mobilize supporters and impacted constituency to advocate for the requested policy.

Policy development is patient work that requires consistent commitment, but it is work that the church calls each of us to do. Our faith supports the notion of government of, by and for the people!

DANISE JONES DORSEY

War Impacts

As war plans proceed, many of us resurfaced in our spirit that age-old question from Marvin Gaye: *"What's Going On?"*

March 19-20 became memorable days:

• Secretary of Defense Donald Rumsfeld announces in a press conference "the liberation of Iraq has begun."

• Kofi Annan, secretary general of the United Nations, calls for the U.N.'s full participation in the rebuilding of Iraq.

• The national media report the target is the forced removal of Saddam Hussein and his sons from Iraq.

• One hundred Towson University students gather to protest the war because they believe the purpose of U.S. involvement is not securing the world from a madman but securing Iraqi oil for American capitalists.

• The African American community contemplates whether these citizen-soldiers will find a "grateful country" that addresses their needs when they return home and are in need of services.

As Americans plan to protect themselves from domestic terrorist attacks, how do the elderly, working poor and vulnerable families provide for their protection? How do they provide for plastic sheeting, duct tape, bottled water, canned goods, when they must decide between paying the rent, buying food, paying the utilities or buying life–sustaining medicine?

What is the immediate and long term cost of the war with Iraq?

NETWORK, a Catholic social justice lobby, advises in its legislative alert that President George W. Bush's budget request for the Pentagon is $400 billion. However, the Pentagon request does not include an allocation for the war with Iraq.

Further, the president's budget requests drastic tax cuts primarily benefiting the most affluent citizens. The president must pay for a war for which he has not budgeted dollars and the current federal budget is in a deficit spending mode. The Gramm-Rudman Act requires a balanced federal budget and the U.S. congress must decide how to respond to the president's request.

In order to balance the budget in the future, the House version of the budget resolution makes severe cuts in programs that fund education, environmental protection, agriculture and poverty alleviation. Cuts of hundreds of billions of dollars from Medicare, Medicaid and veterans benefits will also have to be made. The Senate plan does not make the deep cuts in Medicare, Medicaid and veterans benefits but freezes funding for key social programs to pay for the tax cuts.

"War! What is it good for? Humph! Absolutely nothing" – Edwin Starr

Before the beginning of hostilities with Iraq, government was finding it difficult to fund programming for poor and vulnerable families. A combination of tax cuts and an economy in recession has the effect of increased demand and few available dollars for government to respond.

Most of the states in the union report budget deficits. California reports a deficit of $34 billion. Maryland has a projected budget deficit of $1.8 billion.

Recently, the local media reported, Bethlehem Steel workers will be losing their pensions and health benefits. These hard-working, tax-paying families are now vulnerable families. How will the citizens of Maryland address their needs?

"I ain't going to study war no more!" – a Negro spiritual

A myriad of variables must be contemplated in deciding whether to go to war. Today's process must be exhaustive and encourage extensive dialogue from the world's people. The decision must include a thorough consideration of the impacts of war on the poor domestically and in the suggested war theatre. No one is exempt from the conversations.

As African American Catholics, we are called to provide leadership in the discussion. Our comments must reflect our heritage as followers of Christ to be peacemakers and our Catholic heritage of social justice.

GWENDOLYN A. LINDSAY

Those Who Suffer

I can remember the facilitator of an HIV/AIDS awareness seminar several years ago saying that the older we get or the longer we stay alive, we will come to know someone in our families, churches, work and communities who is or will be infected with or affected by HIV and/or AIDS.

More that 20 years after the first AIDS case was reported, this statement has become a reality in the African American community, and the statistics reported are alarming. We can't wait to take action to raise awareness in the African American community.

We can't wait because the leading cause of death for African Americans under the age of 55 is now AIDS.

Did you know that African Americans comprise about 13 percent of the population, but according to the federal Centers for Disease Control and Prevention, African Americans account for 45 percent of new AIDS cases and nearly 50 percent of total AIDS deaths?

We can't wait because one in 50 African American men and one in 160 African American women are infected with HIV.

More shocking is that scholars at the Harvard AIDS Institute estimate that by the year 2005, 60 percent of all AIDS cases in the United States will be among African Americans.

The statistics about AIDS and African Americans are chilling when it comes to Maryland. According to statistics from the State of Maryland AIDS Administration, HIV and AIDS cases are 82 percent African American, of which 67 percent are African American males and middle-aged. Seventy-two percent of cases are between 30-49 years old.

In the words of the song, "Whatsoever you do to the least of your brothers, that you do unto me," God is saying that if we turn our backs on our brothers and sisters, we turn our back on him.

We cannot turn our backs. We cannot wait to educate and build awareness about the impact of HIV/AIDS on the African American community. We must pray and encourage outreach in our parishes and communities sharing programs that service the African American HIV/AIDS populations.

Beverly Carroll, executive director of the U.S. Conference of Catholic Bishops' Secretariat for African American Catholics, has formed an AIDS task force to raise awareness in the African American community and to respond with pastoral outreach. This new AIDS task force is working with parishes to educate Catholics in the pews about the impact of HIV/AIDS in our community.

We must become a part of this outreach, support our brothers and sisters and get the word out, be compassionate and pray about this alarming epidemic in our communities.

We cannot be educated about AIDS prevention until we talk about it with ease. If we can talk about it at church, then we can talk about it anywhere.

The Bible consistently affirms that God loves and cares for everyone, without regard of physical or spiritual condition, and we must do the same. Now is the time for us to take action and bring awareness to the devastating impact that HIV/AIDS is having on the African American community.

We cannot wait to reach out and offer understanding to those hit by the disease and to educate those who are at risk. We cannot wait to reflect on God's redemptive love and offer hope and comfort to all who are suffering and hurt. Now is the time – today, right now – for us to take action and bring awareness to the devastating impact that HIV/AIDS is having on our community. Tomorrow may be too late.

Spreading Hope

"Hello, Arnaud. Your mother told me that you are very sick. Tomorrow morning I'll tell our classmates and teachers that you are sick. On Monday we'll come visit you to explain the lessons you've missed. We hope you will get well soon. Your friend, Abdoul."

These simple words from a 10-year-old boy in Burkina Faso to his AIDS-afflicted friend depict a common recurring event in Africa today and reflect in very simply yet profound terms how Africans are supporting each other in solidarity through this terrible crisis.

There are many people like Abdoul in Africa, not only comforting their friends, but many times also caring for siblings because their parents have died. The odds are incredible, but the people of Africa affirm the power of hope.

Here in the United States, hope for healing in Africa is beginning to spread. The U.S. bishops have called Catholics in the United States to be in solidarity with Africa in this time of crisis. And we are responding.

In Denver it is estimated that more than 6,000 people are living with HIV/AIDS. The people in the archdiocese face many other domestic problems as well, yet Denver is reaching out to Africa.

The archdiocese heard the message of Catholic Relief Services' Africa Rising, Hope and Healing campaign – a two-year initiative to raise awareness in the United States of African issues – and wanted to get engaged.

The archdiocesan workers teamed up with a variety of community leaders with interests in HIV/AIDS and/or Africa in order to support their initiative. Together, they devised a plan to raise awareness of the issue and how it is affecting African communities.

This group of service providers included the Denver Mayor's Office of HIV and AIDS, Black Nurses Association, university professors teaching Black and African studies, several prominent African American pastors from other denominations and first generation African immigrants.

They formed a local organization called DAWA, which is Swahili and Arabic for "healing, medicine and ministry, acting as servant or nurse and giving comfort." They used the acronym to stand for Denver and Africa Working against AIDS.

DAWA challenged its members to develop cooperative support opportunities with cities, churches and organizations in Africa around the issue of AIDS and create awareness of these cooperative ventures in local U.S. communities. This also created a safe way for local communities to enter into the discussion of the rise in AIDS-infection rates in Denver, a difficult endeavor due to stigma and fear.

The Denver Mayor's Office is working with cities in South Africa and Kenya and has challenged other mayors, through the National Black Mayors Conference, to get their cities involved in similar cross-border relationships. Other groups are establishing their own connections.

The Denver archdiocesan HIV/AIDS ministry is using the Africa Rising, Hope and Healing campaign and the U.S. bishops' Call to Solidarity with Africa as catalysts to their own action in creating awareness of African issues.

The ministry office in Denver decided to create a cooperative venture through CRS with the HIV/AIDS ministry office in the Diocese of Dar Es Salaam in Tanzania. They have started off small, working in two Black Catholic parishes so far, but the word and the action has already spread wider than they ever imagined.

Working in partnership with communities in Africa, CRS is witnessing change every day, as lives are renewed in spirit and anticipation for a better future. For Arnaud and others, there is greater reason for hope.

Like those in the city of Denver, please join us in bringing to reality the Holy Father's call that "Despite the mainly negative picture which today characterizes numerous parts of Africa and despite the sad situations being experienced in many countries, the church has the duty to affirm vigorously that these difficulties can be overcome."

SHARON H. WINCHESTER

Renewed Commitment

L ast year before Christmas, Radio One, 95.9, began advertising a trip to South Africa in late March. The trip included all the places a tourist would want to visit and the North Sea Jazz Festival was going to be held during the trip. It included five-star hotels, Sun City, Robben Island, Cape Town, Johannesburg, Soweto and a trip to the game reserve.

We also visited the Lesedi Cultural Center and were educated on five different cultures. I went for all that, but what I discovered was much more. The country is beautiful. Cape Town reminded me a little of Boston or San Francisco. Johannesburg definitely reminded me of Manhattan. I was awestruck by the mountains. The view from Table Mountain in the morning was breathtaking. The countryside was so vast that I think I put that on almost all of the postcards I sent.

Of course the hotels were wonderful. Our ride to Sun City took a couple of hours, which allowed us the opportunity to see the countryside. Our last hotel was Caesars in Johannesburg. And yes, I spent the last hours of the trip getting a mineral bath, seaweed wrap and a massage. Even considering all of that, it was the African Americans that made the trip one that I'll remember.

The trip was sponsored by Radio One and both 95.9 and 102.3 took a group. So, there was a group similar to the one from Baltimore coming from D.C. There were nearly 80 people on the trip including the owners of Advantage Travel, who planned the trip.

As we continued on our journey, we truly bonded. We looked after one another. We respected each other's time.

Not only were the people on the trip great individuals, they were conscientious. The group distributed food and monetary gifts to the people of Soweto. They gave school supplies to one of the schools and discussed forming lasting relationship with them.

While we were in Cape Town, one member of the group arranged a trip to visit a township that wasn't part of our itinerary just to get a first hand look at the situation. The township was typical, on one end devastating poverty, on the other end upper class. The group was truly touched by the poverty.

Listening to the statistics on HIV/AIDS caused their hearts pain. South Africans have overt racist labels of Black and colored. The impact of this was seen at the Apartheid museum in Johannesburg.

I was reminded of the poverty that exists here. The statistics of HIV/AIDS in South Africa reminded me of the terrible statistics that exist in Baltimore/Washington. It seems to me worse here because the drugs, doctors, hospitals and educational materials needed to decrease the people infected and affected are available.

I've renewed my commitment to be of some assistance at home. The National Black Catholic Congress has AIDS as one of its initiatives. In this regard, I plan to channel energy infused by this trip to assist my people here. After all, charity begins at home.

SISTER FREDERICKA JACOBS AND ISMAEL MUVINGI

Implement Actions

Attending the National Black Catholic Congress (NBCC) in Chicago was a reassuring and uplifting experience. The presence of the Spirit could be felt throughout and the outcomes from the Congress were inspiring. The Plan of Action called for the implementation of eight principles, one of which focuses on Africa. Others include HIV/ AIDS and social justice.

As was clear during the Congress, the challenges facing Africa, most notably the HIV/ AIDS pandemic, cannot wait to be addressed; they urgently require our involvement. Without argument, America is plagued with its own needs and challenges. However, the enormity of Africa's issues cannot be ignored. Aware of the importance of making Africa a priority, the NBCC has rightly chosen to focus on her most critical matters.

Already the statistics are mind-blowing: Africa, with 10 percent of the world's population, has 70 percent of the world's HIV-positive victims. In many African communities, the HIV prevalence rate among adults is 30 percent; whereas in the United States, the HIV prevalence rate is 0.6 percent. Of the world's AIDS orphans, 95 percent (11.2 million) live in Africa. These are just a few of the staggering statistics on AIDS in Africa but behind the statistics lie the devastation of real, ordinary people like us.

Africans are making heroic efforts to alleviate the problem, but they cannot tackle it alone. African Americans, who have a special bond with Africa, are urged to realize the immediacy in taking the lead in reaching out to their African counterparts as the AIDS pandemic in

Africa moves from a social disaster into a truly destabilizing crisis.

Where do we start? The problem is immense and symptomatic treatment is not sufficient. A deep and long-term commitment is necessary. Such a commitment would involve studying the problem, looking for preventative measures and working towards solutions. For example, low-cost drugs, which make a tremendous difference in reducing suffering and increasing the life expectancy of AIDS victims, are not available to the majority of people in Africa. It must be noted that it is not enough to advocate for access to treatment. Other factors such as poverty, ignorance and social stigma, which can prevent people from seeking AIDS treatment equally, need to be addressed.

It is possible to make a significant contribution to the crisis once we are made aware of its magnitude and complexities. Baltimore parishioners could form working groups in African American parishes, schools and other organizations. Catholic Relief Services (the Baltimore–based international relief and development agency of the United States Catholic Conference of Bishops) through its Africa Campaign can provide the necessary materials and resources in order to help launch these working groups once their respective plans of action are presented.

Dr. Margaret Ogola, a pediatrician in Kenya, gave this stirring appeal at the end of a video, *"Coming to Say Good-bye: Stories of AIDS in Africa"*:

"I have hope that people are good … I have hope that people who share this world with the rest of us will look and see another child starving in the Sudan, or another child dying of HIV in Africa, and one day say, 'No! It's too much. This is enough.' So I have hope."

Africans have hope and we can give meaning to that hope by our response. The National Black Catholic Congress has heard this appeal and at the heart of the organization, they are saying, "Yes, Africa, enough is enough. We can wait no longer!"

Africa Is Waiting

There was a story orally shared with me about how our brothers and sisters from Africa look for us to come back to our homeland. They yearn to see our face and to touch our spirit.

Those who live on the coastlands of Africa travel to the edge of the Atlantic Ocean each Sunday to stand and watch, look and see if any of us from the diaspora are returning to the homeland.

As they stand and watch, look and see, they pray, imagining how it would be if all of us were back home even for just a visit.

As I listen to the news reports of bits and pieces of life on the continent of Africa, I pray and wonder what this gesture of waiting really means.

Is it a gesture of hope seeking encouragement by Africans? Is it a beckoning gesture awaiting our response? How can we in America, in Baltimore, respond at this time and hour? How can we go back home, even if it's just for a visit?

What transformations could occur from such a visit? Is the "visit" restricted to a physical visit? Could it be a mental visit, a social visit, a spiritual visit, a helping visit?

Both the party being visited and the visitor always benefits from such an exchange regardless of the realm of the visit. I know one thing for sure, Africa is waiting for us and our response is warranted.

The U.S. Catholic bishops released a statement in December, 2001, titled, "A Call To Solidarity With Africa." The statement calls attention to the church in Africa as a source of hope for a continent in transition.

It discusses the tremendous challenges facing the African continent. It challenges the United States and the international community to examine their policies and provide urgent assistance for strengthening health care, eliminating poverty and debt, promoting educational development, fostering trade relationships as partners, supporting peacemaking and assisting refugees and displaced people.

Can our visit be one that addresses one or some of the challenges stated above?

"A Call To Solidarity With Africa" reports that Africa is the fastest-growing region in the world, with more than 350 million Christians. The Catholic Church in Africa has more than 116 million members. It is rich in human and material resources, many of which have been stolen and/or co-opted by foreigners.

Corruption and inefficient governments have also ravaged the resources of Africa's peoples, thus diminishing their capacity to address human needs.

HIV/AIDS is the number one killer in Africa. There is an estimated 13 million "AIDS orphans" who face the risk of malnutrition, social displacement, reduced prospects for education and forced conscription into military service.

There are too many more alarmingly sad statistics and painful wounds that Africans carry. Can we make a visit to heal these wounds and place an ointment where our brothers and sisters hurt?

Can we make that visit to Africa? The U.S. Catholic bishops call us to make our visit through prayer, responsible investments that can strengthen Africa's ability to address problems, corporate responsibility in promoting prosperous and just economics, self-education and public advocacy, diocesan and parish twinning.

The U.S. church has designed a specific program, titled "Africa Rising: Hope and Healing," to assist parishes and dioceses with resources to help understand the situation in Africa and support us in our role as an advocate, prayer warrior and activist.

Can we make that visit? The healing would be enhanced by our support, our engagement, our prayer from here and would be an actualization of the solidarity for which the pope and the bishops are calling. Can we make that visit?

If you or your parish is able to help out and make that visit individually or congregationally, contact Catholic Relief Services (410-625-2220) in the program "Africa Rising: Hope and Healing."

BEVERLY C. WHITE

Seeds of Faith

The National Black Catholic Congress held in Chicago was an unforgettable experience that allowed Black Catholics from around the world to celebrate their rich cultural heritage and Catholic faith.

The major focus for the Congress was to address issues and concerns for Black Catholics nationwide.

As a catechist in the Black community, the issue of Catholic education was of great interest to me. The principles state that, "Catholic education continues to be one of the best means of evangelization and social justice in the Black community. Efforts must be made to create and expand religiously sound and academically effective Catholic primary and secondary schools in the Black communities of our nation."

Catholic education began as a way to preserve and protect the faith and culture of the poor and immigrant population in the United States. The availability of Catholic education for our children with identified skills training that was academically sound and religiously-centered was a priority. Further, as Black Catholics, it was crucial to preserve our Black culture and Catholic faith in a society where discrimination and marginalization from society and the church was prevalent.

As a number of Catholic schools in the Black community continues to close their doors to our children, the principle for Catholic education adopted by Congress IX needs to be implemented and supported at the national, diocesan, and local levels. Dr. Rosalind P. Hale, Ed.D., the presenter for the principle on Catholic education, has spent much of her professional career educating students, professionals and community leaders on the importance of support on all levels to expand and/or maintain quality Catholic education in the Black community. Matthew 28:19 keeps us mindful that, "we must teach all peoples."

In solidarity, our discussion group came to a consensus to put into action a plan for growth for one, three, and five years. Within one year we will plant the seed and investigate and develop, on the parish and diocesan level, new and creative ways to provide financial assistance for Black Catholic schools. Within three years we nurture the growth by locating and/or establishing grants and scholarships to support Black educators in their roles as teachers and administrators for religious education programming.

Finally, within five years we will establish roots by recruiting, hiring, and maintaining adequate/competent administration and staff that supports an effective Black Catholic school program.

As Black Catholics, we must maintain viable Catholic schools in the Black community. These schools are needed to provide an education rooted in religious values and academic excellence. It is imperative that we continue the legacy of the school in the Black community as an instrument of Catholic evangelization, so that the church's mission of social and racial justice among Blacks and the urban poor will be visible.

Dr. Antoinette Gabriel Lyles

Needed Education

Catholic schools are essential to our Catholic identity and are an instrument of evangelization. They have demonstrated their ability to provide excellent academic programs, which are faith-based. Students are nurtured in an atmosphere where the story of Jesus is told and retold, where prayer permeates and liturgical celebrations are prominent without apologies. Catholic schools promote a system of values based on the Gospel of Jesus Christ, and live those values within the schools. The schools' names, presence of priests and some religious who continue to choose education as a ministry, are constant reminders of the Catholic faith.

Far beyond faith-based academic curricula, Catholic schools offer an atmosphere of nonviolent conflict resolution and self-respect. This takes place in a structured, personalized, supportive and challenging learning environment. Students learn to become goal-oriented and focused on success. Activities such as computer training, art, music, and sports also contribute to the total development of the student. Students are taught to care about the well-being of others. Therefore, they are engaged in activities in which they share what they have for the sake of others. Some of these activities are Rice Bowl, food drives, visits and gifts to nursing home residents, and volunteering at soup kitchens.

Catholic schools are a proven and needed educational institution in the United States, offering alternatives and opportunities to families who have children waiting for their chance. These schools work to engage the entire family in the educational process and continually strive to be a consistent stabilizing influence in the lives of students.

Therefore, invitations are extended to families and students to special parish Masses, catechumenate, Bible studies, family nights, parish youth group and other youth activities. Invitations are also extended to worship with the church, especially if families do not have a church home to call their own.

Catholic education for African American children began in Baltimore as early as the 1820s with Mother Lange, a free woman of African ancestry, and an educational leader.

Certainly, it is our hope that our Catholic labors are not in vain, but that the community will be better off because we were there and because we cared.

Today, a Catholic school education has been made available to families of all faiths. However, families pay for the education. While there is financial aid, based on demonstrated financial need, no one comes close to a "free ride."

On average, the African American income is still between 60-79 percent of white income, yet parents sacrifice to send their children to Catholic schools.

Special thanks is extended to the archdiocese for the Cardinal Shehan Scholarship Fund, and "Partners in Excellence" programs that support financial aid; and local foundations such as the Knott and France Merrick Foundations who assist with physical need improvements of Catholic schools.

African American families have always viewed education as a high priority. Children are the African American family's greatest treasure and hope. Over the years, they have sought out Catholic-sponsored schools so that their children could receive an education that would serve as a way out of poverty and prepare them for life. African American families have trusted Catholic schools with their children's education.

Education and a spiritual base become crucial to the personal growth and development of African American children as they prepare to live in a global society as competent and contributing members of their communities. Like their forefathers, African American families must continue to be strengthened and renewed by education and a strong spiritual base. One day, another priest or Sister, a Nobel Peace Prize winner, a judge, chief justice, a mayor of Baltimore, a congressman, a U.S. senator, a governor, an ambassador, will have come through our African American Catholic schools and we will all be proud!

Dr. Kirk P. Gaddy

Education

Sprinkled throughout the City of Baltimore and extending into Baltimore County are a number of predominantly Black Catholic schools. These schools, in my opinion, are wellsprings for evangelization and effective education. Catholic schools have potential in attracting African Americans to the church.

History reports that wherever Black Catholics congregated, there stood in the midst of that community a Catholic school. In 1889, during the first Black lay Catholic Congress, a pledge was consummated to advance the development of Catholic education within the Black community. These Black Catholics felt an urgent need to establish schools whereby Catholic attitudes could be transmitted and upheld.

The Black Catholic school stood strong as an agent of hope for future generations as well as a fortress from racial abuse and permeating attitudes of inferiority. The Catholic school in the Black community served as a stronghold for leadership development, social progress and intellectual discernment.

When school concludes, I often review the past year, evaluating the effectiveness of our school's educational process as well as our evangelization outreach to the families we serve.

Looking back, I confirm that Black children grow up in a distinct culture. Black children, therefore, need an educational system that is uniquely conducive to their strengths, abilities, culture and spirituality that incorporates them into the learning process and prayer experience. Failure to recognize the integrity of Africentric thought and educational methodologies can be detrimental to Black students.

Urban Catholic educators gathered at a conference (initiated by Sister Barbara Spears, S.N.J.M., assistant superintendent of Catholic schools and a number of principals with support from the Office of African American Catholic Ministries) to discuss various issues about educating in these times.

Several workshops were given, speaking directly to multiple learning styles, assessment and the impact of culture on cognition. Research done by Albury and Boykin pointed directly to the effectiveness of employing certain methodologies (group learning, emphasis of relational learning activities, affective and cognitive objectives) resulted in Black children achieving higher academic scores on standardized tests.

Research such as this is valuable to teachers and administrators who work vigorously to implement systems and strategies toward the success of our children. Educational insights discussed in the book *"The Education of Black Children and Youth: A Framework for Excellence"* by the late Samuel L. Banks are foundational ambience at St. Katharine School, supporting excellence in education.

In short, to know successful strategies and not implement them would become detrimental to our children, and that is unacceptable at St. Katharine.

Our investment in Black Catholic schools is an investment in educational excellence and evangelization. The pastoral letter, "What We Have Seen and Heard" states, "we are aware of the economic reality, but we are equally aware of the Gospel injunction to teach all peoples." It continues by expressing this thought: "As an important agent for evangelization, the Catholic school must be the concern even of those who have no children in the schools."

The Catholic school signals a spirit of faith and prayerfulness within our communities. Our schools mobilize the faith, encouraging students and faculties, parents and families to deeper spiritual realms. The Black Catholic School serves as a solid reflection of our values and aspirations.

Should we not invite those who do not know Jesus as personal Lord and savior to sojourn to Jesus with us in the Catholic Church?

Let us take note, too, that Mother Mary Elizabeth Lange, O.S.P., began her ministry to "do the will of God" through education. Many came to know Christ through the Oblates ministry in education. There is power and direction in this history lesson. Let us then "be watchful, and strengthen the things which remain."

DR. KIRK P. GADDY

Maximum Potential

Education Week published an article by R.C. Johnston and D. Viaderoi that stated that when 3.4 million kindergarten students entered school in 2000 at the dawn of their educational careers, researchers foresaw a widely different future for them. The researchers were able to predict their success in school, whether they go to college, and how much money they will earn as adults based on economic status (specifically poverty) and parental involvement.

Today, there exists an achievement gap in our educational system that warrants our attention. As an educator, I am concerned with the achievement of all children. However, I am engaged in maximizing the potential of Black learners.

First, there are benefits of small classes for the learner, the teacher, the classroom and parent. Research provided by C. Achiles, C. Jencks and M. Phillips advances that if we keep class size to 15-18 for at least three years and preferably four years that African American children will benefit by participating and being engaged in the learning process.

Teachers will benefit too, because they will be better able to assist in the early diagnosis and remediation of learning difficulties experienced by students. Moreover, teachers will be able to have better classroom management and be able to teach to mastery. Individual attention will be more readily accessible and therefore, teachers will be able to provide immediate reinforcement.

Classrooms will provide better air quality; space and the environment will be conducive to learning. The classroom will be a place of inclusion, community building and positive group dynamics.

Noise level will be held at a minimum and there will exist opportunity for peer interaction.

Parents' interest will increase and they will become strong agents for accountability and responsibility. Parents will really become partners in our schools with smaller classes, especially in the formative years!

Second, J. Hale's book, *"Black Children: Their Roots, Culture and Learning Styles,"* L. Delpit's book, *"Other People's Children,"* and G. Ladson-Billings' book, *"Crossing Over to Canaan,"* are recipes for understanding how culture impacts achievement and the learner's potential for success. These authors suggest that teachers must be trained to teach diverse learners at any given time. Teachers must understand and respect the distinct culture of others.

In 1979, noted researcher Ron Edmonds stated in *"The Effective Schools Project"* that in schools with low achievement, the most negative room in the school is the teacher's lounge. This room is filled with condescending negative comments about students' culture, roots, and learning styles. In longitudinal research of successful urban teachers, Haberman (1995) has identified the attributes of "star" teachers, individuals who are successful with poor, urban students.

Let us be reminded of the profound wisdom of Marva Collins, who stated, "There is no secret … I just deal honestly with children. They know I don't turn my nose down at them. … If everyone in the neighborhood treated these children with the same consistent interest, the children would do for them what they do for me."

Thirdly, lately in the news media there has been a resurgent and push to have single-sex schools especially for African American students in middle and high schools. There exists evidence to support this notion. V. Polite and E. Davis, editors of *"African American Males in School and Society,"* advance that attention should be paid to broader outcomes such as educational attainment, job procurement, and quality of life. I do believe that all-male schools and all-male classrooms could benefit from this type of research rather than the traditional argument that single-sex schools provide less distraction to the student. Moreover, Nancy Arnez (1978) provides startling statistics of the number of African American males assigned to special education classes.

In addition, African American males constitute a disproportionate number of those who are in prison. If single-sex schools and classroom are going to exist, then there will be a need for additional funding. We must realize that it costs less to educate children than to incarcerate them.

Begin Healing

In my professional field (sometimes called ministry by others) I serve as a family support services coordinator in the Circuit Court for the City of Baltimore. Many challenges confront families, one of which is identifying and responding to attention deficit/hyperactivity disorder (ADHD). When approaching the topic, my responsibility is to dispel myths, educate and redirect resources to assist in strengthening individuals and eventually the entire family.

Did you know that ADHD can be found in adults as well as children? ADHD affects 3-5 percent of all children. Perhaps as many as two million American children, at least one in every classroom in the United States, are treated for this disorder.

Did you know that a battery of tests, presented over a sustained period of time, under various environments should be completed before an individual is determined as having ADHD? Do you know the distinct symptoms of inattention, hyperactivity and impulsivity?

The essential feature of attention deficit/hyperactivity is a persistent pattern of inattention and/or hyperactivity-impulsivity that is more severe and frequent than what is typically observed in individuals at a like level of development. Some hyperactive-impulsive or inattentive symptoms that cause impairment must have been present for a number of years. Some impairment from the symptoms must be present in at least two settings (e.g., at home, school or work).

The symptoms of inattention include: often failing to give close attention to details or making careless mistakes in schoolwork, work or other activities, often having difficulty sustaining attention in tasks

271

or play activities, often not seeming to listen when spoken to directly (often does not follow through on instructions and fails to finish schoolwork, chores, or duties – this is not due to oppositional behavior or failure to understand instructions), having difficulty organizing tasks and activities, often avoiding, disliking or reluctantly engaging in tasks that require sustained mental effort, often losing things necessary for tasks or activities, being easily distracted by external activity such as a car horn, and often being forgetful in daily activities.

Symptoms of hyperactivity (six or more, persisting for at least six months to a degree that is maladaptive and inconsistent with developmental level) include: often fidgets with hands or feet or squirms in seat, often leaves seat in classroom or in other situations in which remaining seated is expected, often runs about or climbs excessively in situations in which it is inappropriate, often has difficulty playing or engaging in leisure activities quietly, is often "on the go" or often acts if "driven by a motor" and often talks excessively.

Impulsivity carries the symptoms of often blurting out answers before questions have been completed, often having difficulty awaiting turn and often interrupting or intruding on others. As children mature, symptoms become less conspicuous.

Attention-deficit/hyperactivity disorder must also be distinguished from difficulty in goal-directed behavior in children from inadequate, disorganized or chaotic environments.

Reports from multiple resources are helpful in providing a full spectrum of observations concerning the child's inattention, hyperactivity and capacity for developmentally appropriate self-regulated behavior in various settings.

ADHD is a challenge. One challenge is to differentiate it from other diagnoses such as depression, anxiety, specific situation/stresses (e.g. death in family or moving). It is critical to differentiate from a conduct disorder or oppositional defiance. For example, a child with ADHD doesn't steal or bully other kids nor likes to argue.

Some things to think about: When did the hyperactive-impulse or inattentive symptoms begin? What were the settings, length of time, age at onset? Is the inattentiveness due to a lack of clear instructions? If you believe there is an impairment, then ask questions about treatment options when you consult your doctor or trained professional.

There are alternatives. I might consider putting medication last. Our kids are worth the time that it takes to find out what is going on with them.

Crying Out for Help

Have you heard the cry of our children? What are parents and concerned community members doing to wipe away their tears to assure life and abundant living for our children?

It is said that fruit does not fall far from the tree. Does this mean that the violent community that threatens our children is a direct result of what's going on with the parents? Do parents and family members need more wake-up calls? Our innocent children can no longer play in front of their homes without the threat of being a fatality.

Violence is everybody's business. It tears communities apart and keeps them from working together. Violence can manifest itself in many ways – just like an addiction. A million families each year are ripped apart by domestic violence and child abuse touches over a million children a year. Assaults are more likely to occur between people that know each other than between perfect strangers.

The violent impact of weapons, gangster rap and indifference have become acceptable conditions that we live with. The big picture of "family-hood" in the Black community warrants our attention. Without looking at all aspects, we will only make limited progress.

Can we go back to the days of caring about each other and respecting each other as human beings? The days of people working together and pulling together – having the true sense of a community – strengthened our families. A simple and comfortable start would be to check out those attitudes, values and beliefs that we personally model for our children. (i.e. do you own a firearm? Is it kept in your home? Is there a possibility that someone could get hurt?)

We live in a materialistic society, and the fundamentals of raising a child have taken a lower priority. Yet, our traditional African worldview places child rearing as a sacred and holy duty. Fundamentals like saying "please," "thank you," "excuse me" and "I'm sorry" appear to be vanishing from our vocabulary and actions. If we act now, it won't be too late to retrieve them back into our child-rearing practices.

Respect for each other is an honored value among most of us. What would it be like if we strengthen our efforts to teach our children to respect themselves and draw strength from the icons who heroically paved our way? What would it take for our children to be able to co-exist as one, who will surrender first? What behaviors and attitudes are we modeling for them?

How do parents communicate when there is conflict or do they stop talking all together and hope that the problem will resolve itself? Have our foremothers and forefathers labored long and hard for nothing? Our history is rich with the lessons learned about working together and trusting each other. Are we allowing our kids to be persuaded by the predators of society with false dreams of happiness that has a short shelf life?

I know that the children today are growing up in a world that is faster and the moral fabric of it is deteriorating. Family structures are changing and the challenges are different. So, we must be more creative in resolving those challenges. The answers to the challenges lie deep within our souls, hearts and minds, but we have to dig deep.

Are we leaving the children defenseless in these tumultuous times? Some have fought to take prayer out of the schools. Have we eased prayer from our homes as well? Have we under-estimated the power of forgiveness, love, prayer and religious practices?

Let's talk to our children about the therapeutic value of working, setting attainable goals and being patient. When they are overwhelmed by experiences of terrorism, drive by shootings, scandals and fights, we can teach about anger management, conflict resolution, coping skills, respect and love. That's how we wipe away the tears of our children.

SISTER M. REGINALD GERDES, O.S.P

Celebrate 175 Years

In 1828 Elizabeth Lange met with Father James Joubert to discuss the educational problems of the students in his catechism classes; her life of reaching out to others took a new turn. Directress of her own school in Fells Point, Elizabeth took on the added responsibility of teaching another set of pupils on a non-school day. It meant traveling from Fells Point to Paca Street every Sunday in all kinds of weather. No taxies or busses were in operation then. A carriage was something Elizabeth did not own. Her zeal for God urged her on in this apostolate.

Giving words to what was in her heart, Elizabeth voiced to Father Joubert her desire to make this new venture her life's work, that of dedicating her life to the service of God, making known his words and works to the young. This dream became a reality when Archbishop Whitfield gave permission for the foundation of the first order of African American nuns in the United States. Reaching out to others then became a way of life.

Elizabeth and three companions set up shop at St. Mary's Court. The training for the religious life included starting a school for young ladies. And in a spirit of reaching out, the future Oblate Sisters took in some orphans called "children of the house" to educate, to care for and to evangelize. Later on, a gentleman, whose wife had died, asked the women to care for his two girls. They entered the school as boarders and later one of the young girls entered the convent and became superior general.

In 1832, the cholera epidemic was in high gear. The city officials asked the Oblates to serve the African American poor in the alms house. Father Joubert told him that the Oblates Sisters were teachers not nurses. Yet, every sister volunteered to serve the sick and poor.

The Sunday religion classes for the children expanded to include adults. Various religious organizations were started for the African American population. In turn, the African American population started fund raising organizations to help the sisters financially.

Reaching out also took the form of begging on the streets of Baltimore. With the consent of various archbishops, the sisters solicited funding and food for the children. The practice of soliciting donations continues today. In modern day terms, it is called "development."

In 1830, the sisters took in widows and elderly women thus beginning a tradition that became part of the Oblate motherhouse. Until her death at 102 (a week or so ago) the mother of our Sulpician chaplain, Father John Bowen, S.S., lived with the sisters at 701 Gun Road.

During all wars, abandoned children are numerous. The Civil War was no exception. The Oblate Sisters took in the war orphans and continued the custom of caring for the homeless. The project under the direction of Father Peter Miller, S.J., later became St. Frances Orphan Asylum. Today, on the Chase Street property, Oblates sponsor the Mother Mary Lange House for Young Ladies.

When the sisters moved from Richmond Street to Chase Street a new ministry of serving the poor began. Food lines began at the side gate of the convent. Later on, these lines included requests for clothing as well.

Educational services to those in the Brentwood Forest neighborhood have been an ongoing ministry; tutoring, adult literacy, cultural programs, music lessons, sewing, trips and whatever is needed has, through the years, become a mainstay for both the school and the convent.

To this day, the outreach services have continued and expanded. Under the leadership of Sister Brenda Motte, O.S.P., and her benefactors, there is a very distinctive "Reaching Out Ministry" in the Brentwood Village community.

RALPH E. MOORE, JR.

And Still We Rise

S t. Frances Academy celebrated its 175th anniversary this year, making it the oldest African American educational institution in the nation. The community of women that leads it, among some of their other missions, is commemorating its 175th next year. For 133 of those years, the academy has occupied a huge four story building in what is now one of the most stressed neighborhoods in Baltimore City, Brentwood Village–Johnston Square.

The median household income in Brentwood Village is $10,100. Fifty percent of the housing sites are vacant lots or vacant buildings and unemployment is high, crime and grime threaten the quality of life for too many of the decent people who live and work in the community. Some days the view outside the windows of the school and its year-and-a-half old community center is grim, depressing and in a state of deterioration.

But the half-empty glass does not represent the true condition of the neighborhood. For in East Baltimore's Brentwood Village-Johnston Square stand the Academy, the oldest African American educational institution in the nation; a long-standing wholesale florist; and the Yellow Bowl Restaurant, a soul food center since Richard Nixon was first inaugurated president. There's also a new playground for tots as well as a small park, affectionately built and named by its occupants, "The Elders' Garden."

In other words, there are signs that the quality of life for residents, including the Oblate Sisters of Providence, students, staff and persons who work in the neighborhood, is still improving.

The new tot lot, built directly across from the academy, is brightly colored, filled with fun-invoking climbing devices, surrounded by rubberized ground cover and openly inviting to all of the community's littlest children. In the grand scheme of things, it is no big deal. And yet, it is a clean, safe, fun place for small children to play. Their lives are enhanced, admittedly in a small way, by the presence of the playground.

It took the love, care and concern of the neighborhood's adults (the Brentwood Village Neighborhood Initiative community association) to put it there.

On another scale, in 2002 the Oblate Sisters built and opened a 33,500 square-foot community center and gymnasium for the benefit of the school and community. The building contains a 750-seat state-of-the-art gym, six classrooms, a multipurpose room, a health suite, a state-of-the-art kitchen, a conference room and a couple of offices. All types of programs and events take place there: cooking classes for older folks and after school activities for the youngsters, a G.E.D. class, some employment counseling, some art work and lots of special events: an annual Halloween party, a job fair to honor Martin Luther King's birthday, a youth oriented political forum and lots of meetings.

The building, 60 years in the making, is a symbol of overcoming the odds.

My mother, the former Lorraine Vance, and my daughter, Zahra Moore, both attended St. Frances and waited for the same gym. And you're right, good things do come to those who wait. We just wouldn't mind waiting a little less time over here. But, the point is, persistence pays off; hanging in there while struggling for change has its ultimate rewards.

The Oblate Sisters' community has endured through much. It has seen the neighborhood surrounding St. Frances go through many changes. Amidst the most difficult of those times, they've educated, fed, clothed, babysat, reprimanded and cheered the children, comforted and buried the elderly.

They have been a lesson to many of us: keep going and keep rising through it all. It is truly the Christian thing to do.

St. Joseph Industrial School

In 1889, Father Jon DeRuyter, a Mill Hill Josephite known for his missionary work in foreign countries, was invited to accept a mission for African Americans in Wilmington, Del. In less than a year, Father DeRuyter had purchased property to build a church with a school. A convent for the nuns was also started. In 1891 a rectory was built and later turned into an orphanage.

By 1893, Father DeRuyter had lodging for over 200 boys staffed by 16 Sisters and he saw the need for larger facilities to house and train the boys. He convinced Mother Katharine Drexel, S.B.S., to donate a 200-acre tract of land in Clayton, Del.

Clayton was 36 miles south of Wilmington and west of Smyrna in Kent County. It was named in 1877 in honor of John M. Clayton, the first governor of Delaware (1793-1796), who was active in the U. S. government and a promoter of the Delaware Railroad. John M. Clayton died in 1798.

St. Joseph Industrial School for Colored Boys became known simply as "Clayton, Delaware."

Father DeRuyter, the director of the institution, had plans for the orphans. He wanted the youngsters to have more than an elementary education. In his plan for advancement of the youth, he felt that if the boys learned a trade, this would help them in their future life.

Father DeRuyter had another goal to accomplish. He hoped many of the boys would stay on when they came of age. They could select a partner for life and live on the farm. This objective never materialized for Father DeRuyter died suddenly.

Older boys of the ages 14-17 left the home in Wilmington for the Industrial School in Clayton. Baltimore Franciscan Sisters operated an orphanage with 39 homeless, of which seven were sent to Clayton. Immediately, some of them were sent to work on the farm. Other boys became apprentices to the carpenter and bricklayer.

The work at Clayton was brisk and lively. Several of the Josephite priests assigned to St. Francis in Baltimore were transferred to Clayton since they were familiar with working with colored people.

Some of the boys were blessed with a talent, and, being duly trained, worked in carving and painting statues. They repaired and painted the Stations of the Cross for Catholic churches. They also made rosaries.

The boys were also taught printing, which proved to be an asset for the Institution. They did most of the printing for the Josephites and for the general public, which turned a profit.

Between the farm and the print shop, these endeavors made the boys home self-sufficient. The farm produced food for the table. Carpentering and painting were also taught. Carpentry had the most boys enrolled because of the constant building and repairing at the school. The young men took pride in their work and their religious training.

Religious education was the order of the day. The boys attended Mass each morning and received religious instructions in the afternoon. During this time, they were taught Latin and how to be acolytes and respond to prayer in Latin. Father DeRuyter was a lover of religious music and he introduced his charges by teaching them to chant the litany in Latin and English.

One feels positive that some of the skills learned at Clayton were carried over and utilized in colored Catholic parishes. It was noted that at St. Francis Xavier in Baltimore some men in the congregation could recite all prayers in both Latin and English. It was apparent that they had Catholic backgrounds. The faith and love of the Almighty manifested itself in the Catholic Action lectures and the Catholic Evidence Guild.

Down & Up

When the black-eyed peas and greens were cooking in the pot as Blacks were awaiting the new year of emancipation and jubilation in 1863, the family went down in prayer.

Prayer is such a powerful force, a change agent, an inspiration, a transformational experience, and it is the center of the circle of life for many Black families. In tapping into the power of prayer (which changes things), Black families across the nation will "go down in prayer" to uplift the Black family on the national observance of the African American Family Feb. 4, 2001.

Across the nation family life as a whole has experienced challenges and changes. In spite of slavery, the agony of family separation, negative myths, mis-education, poverty, oppression and drugs, African Americans have survived because of the family. The African proverb, "I am because we are, we are because I am, and I am because God is" gives respect to the dignity of the family unit, appreciation to the extended family and credence to divine intervention in the composition of family. Designating a day of prayer for Black families on the first Sunday of Black History Month has purpose.

The National Day of Prayer for the African American Family was founded in 1989. During a United States gathering of Black Catholics in the Archdiocese of Atlanta, when those in Black leadership were sharing their problems, pains and dreams of the Black community, Father James E. Goode, O.F.M., addressed the assembly on the power of prayer and called the nation to go down in prayer on the first Sunday of Black History Month.

This National Day of Prayer was set aside to give special thanks to God for our families and to place our every care in the arms of Jesus. "We want every generation born of African descent to know that through it all we have been, and we are, a people of faith. We've come through trials, tribulations and persecution. Here we stand. Look how far we've come with the Lord," said Father Goode.

In particular, the National Day of Prayer for the uplift of African American families calls for all Black families to:

• Worship and pray as a family.

• Celebrate a meal together and tell your family story (Soul food).

• Make a family resolution, no matter how big or small, and strive to fulfill that resolution throughout the year.

Pope John Paul II says that "family prayer has for its own object family life itself, which in all varying circumstances is seen as a call from God and lived as a filial response to his call."

Let's organize right now within our families and within our parishes to "go down in prayer." There is inspiration and hope when we unite in this effort.

While we make a family resolution, why not use the opportunity to ask the church family to make a resolution to develop or strengthen a program that helps and assists families within your parish. After all, prayer is supposed to lead to action. The Office of African American Catholic Ministries' Effective Black Parenting Program continues to serve the community, upon request, and your request would be the best request.

For more information about this celebration and to obtain a copy of "A Prayer for African American Families" written by Father James Goode, O.F.M., call the Office of African American Catholic Ministries at 410-625-8472.

A Holy Advantage

Prayer is the key to our family. We were blessed from birth, both born into praying families. Devotion to Mary was paramount in our homes. Ann remembers the times in which her mother held hostage household visitors whom happened to be in their home at "prayer time" 7 pm. Catholics and non-Catholics were invited to participate in reciting the rosary. In those days, Father Peyton reminded his radio-listening audience that "the family that prays together stays together." With our families we attended novenas: "The Miraculous Medal, St. Therese of the Little Flower, Blessed now St. Martin de Porres and St Jude."

Prayer brought us together inspite of our 17-year age difference. Because of this age difference some of our own siblings voiced their skepticism in the stability and future of our marriage. Through prayer, this age difference was turned from a hindrance to a holy advantage. We have been married for 41 years.

We have 15 children, ten girls and five boys. Each birth was like Christmas. The babies kept us on our knees. When Claver was not teaching, he was selling real estate or Shackley products or working in the church as sacristan.

In spite of the work, God blessed us with enough money and ingenuity to take full family vacations each year. With our large, four apartment brick home fully paid for, we could travel during the summers. As the family grew, we grew from a smaller camp trailer to a larger one. During a trip to Tuskegee, our station wagon with trailer in tow, jackknifed in the middle of a four lane highway! With ten children and ourselves, prayer enveloped the situation. A white couple stopped and took us to a nearby hotel. Prayer changes things, and the Holiday Inn offered a family gesture of "kids eat free."

During Mass, we occupied two pews. Oftentimes our children served as acolytes. Today, we serve as eucharistic ministers and our children and grandchildren regularly accompany us as we visit the sick and shut-ins at hospitals and nursing homes.

Recently, our daughter, Maria received a $100,000 scholarship to continue her graduate studies in electrical engineering after inventing a specialized light to discover veins for medical procedures. Those who interviewed Maria for news-stories asked her what attributed to her success. Maria quickly answered that it was "the prayers she held onto and the fact that her parents attended Mass daily to pray."

Prayer and work resulted in our children completing high school and achieving higher education. We have been blessed with three children who are graduates of Coppin State University, two from Morgan State University, one from Cheyney University, one from Towson University and two from Baltimore City Community College. Benedict, now in financing/banking is about to purchase a franchise from a major fast food restaurant. Our other children have entered professional fields including: social work, nursing, education, church administration and acting. Some are poets, writers, and counselors. Some chose the honorable vocations of marriage and child rearing.

Prayer has taken us through family crisis and conflicts (we have buried three grandchildren; two died as infants, another in a fire in our home) as well as celebrations of graduations, reunions and marriages. We have been blessed with 33 grandchildren. Problems that arise, are settled through prayer. Births and birthdays are celebrated, too, through prayer.

It really does take a village to raise a child and our blood family, church family, school families and neighbors have become such a village. We are part of a large village of prayer and love – including relatives of the Neale, Brooks, Richardson and Wilson families. The Oblate Sisters of Providence, the Sisters of Charity, Father Donald A. Sterling and his family, Sister Ferdinand Tunis, RSM, and our parish of New All Saints are among those who provide prayer and support as the village.

Prayer is so essential and can be a holy advantage to any family.

JANICE CURTIS GREENE

Parenting

In Matthew 19:14 Jesus commands, "Let the children come to me, and do not prevent them; for the kingdom of heaven belongs to such as these." Children come into this world innocent of all but Original Sin, which only the waters of Baptism can cleanse. They need parents and mentors to protect, teach and set them on the right course.

For the past six years I have been a facilitator for the Effective Black Parenting, (EBP), Program for the Archdiocese of Baltimore and the Office of African American Catholic Ministries. This 14-week course was developed by Black educators, doctors and psychologists such as Dr. James Comer, suggesting guidelines specific to raising Black children in America. Scripture references and components of spirituality have been added.

After my training, I was a part of a team of facilitators that conducted courses at St. Francis Xavier, Cardinal Shehan School, St. Alphonsus-Basilica School and St. Cecelia. Other sites, which have sponsored EBP classes include: New All Saints, John Paul Regional School, Immaculate Conception Church.

The foundation of this course is "The Pyramid of Success for Black children." The path to the pyramid includes good health habits, good school habits, self-discipline, pride in Blackness and love and understanding. It is appropriate that a path represents the basis for this course because Proverbs 22:5-6 states, "Thorns and snares are on the path of the crooked; he who would safeguard his life will shun them. Train a boy in the way he should go; even when he is old, he will not swerve from it." We who minister to children provide that safeguard.

Another important theme of EBP is model and teach. The old adage, "Do as I say and not as I do," is unacceptable in the African American community. Children must know that role models are not on the stage, screen, sports area or corner. Parents and those who take on the task of parenting and mentoring are the true role models for our children. Our guide is Galatians 5:22, "The fruit of the spirit is love, joy, peace, kindness, generosity, faithfulness, gentleness and self-control." If these are characteristics we want for our children we must find a place for them in our own lives first.

After completing the course at the Cardinal Shehan School a parent wrote me a thank you note stating that her sons would always remember when she took a class especially for them. Being an EBP facilitator has blessed me in that I have learned as much as I have taught.

Not only mothers and fathers attend EBP training. Classes include aunts, grandmothers and teachers as well. The African proverb, "it takes a whole village to raise a child," must become a reality.

Raising African American children in a hostile society where they are constantly in physical and psychological danger is an overwhelming task for even the finest parents. African American children are labeled, feared, discarded, assaulted, and pitied by politicians, teachers, peers and sometimes even parents daily. Larger ratios of African American children live with drugs, poverty, crime, inadequate medical and mental services, exposure to lead paint and an inferior educational system than their white counterparts.

That is why African American parishes need to develop structured ministries to combat this crisis. For information about sponsoring Effective Black Parenting Programs in your parish contact the Office of African American Catholic Ministries at (410) 625-8472.

There are other ways to minister to our African American children. Some parishioners at New All Saints pay the tuition for students who wish to attend the Music Academy. We can adopt or become a foster parent, offer our services to Big Brothers and Sisters of Maryland, donate our skills as mentors or tutors or contact the nearest Department of Recreation to see if coaches, umpires or referees are needed. Time invested in the life of a child has guaranteed rewards. Remember Jesus' command and Samuel's exhortation in 1 Samuel 15:22, "Obedience is better than sacrifice."

Prayer
and
Spirituality

"Hush, Somebody's Callin' Mah Name

Hush, Hush! Somebody's callin mah name
Hush, Hush! Somebody's callin mah name
Hush, Hush! Somebody's callin mah name
Oh mah Lawd. Oh mah Lawd, what shall I do?

Throughout the centuries, African American Catholics have chanted this song of prayer. It was heard from the cotton fields of Mississippi to the tobacco plantations of Maryland, in basement chapels of Louisiana to the National Shrine in Washington, in the one room schoolhouse to the ever expanding Xavier University, and in house meetings, prayer meetings, parish meetings, diocesan meetings to national meetings.

This chapter presents messages and conversations of spirituality. Somebody's calling your name.

BISHOP GORDON D. BENNETT, S.J.

Responsibility to Inspire

During a summer which was replete with great sadness, I had the opportunity to attend two events which helped restore my hope in the overarching providence of God: World Youth Day in Toronto, and the Ninth Black Catholic Congress in Chicago.

Both of these events, because they focused on the person and the gospel of Jesus Christ, and because they called the entire church to a more faithful and heroic following of Jesus, lifted my heart and re-energized me in my service as bishop.

One of the aspects common to both events was the emphasis each placed on the evangelization and formation of our Catholic young people. Another was the great grace of the presence of young people themselves, both teenagers and young adults, in great numbers, along with the evident enthusiasm they exhibited for the faith and their commitment to it.

I came away from Toronto and Chicago entirely encouraged that the Holy Spirit, who calls each and every one of us to the holiness which is reflective of our own particular vocation, is being heard and generously responded to.

In both venues, the stereotypes of young people, particularly African American young people, with which we are daily assaulted by the media, are sensational and inaccurate.

Far from being selfish, violent and lacking self-control, I encountered hundreds of young people who were prayerful, faithful to the sacraments, and sincerely eager to spend their lives in service of the Gospel. In Toronto, the young people understood and took entirely to heart the exhortations of Pope John Paul II, whom they showered with unselfconscious appreciation for his pastoral concern for them, as the Holy Father encouraged them to live out their vocations to be "salt for the earth and light for the world."

In Chicago, at the Congress, young people participated in the discussions of the future of our church as equals, alongside their elders for whom they expressed great respect and appreciation. They presented themselves as talented and worthy, well prepared to assume the leadership roles which, even now, are opening to them.

These two events reminded me of how crucial the young are in the church and how sacred is our responsibility to nurture the faith in them. I was reminded of the words to parents, and by extension, to everyone in the church, when a baby is baptized: "On your part, you must make it your constant care to bring your child up in the practice of the faith. See that the divine life which God gives your child is kept safe from the poison of sin, to grow always stronger in his/her heart."

The question which then cannot help but confront each and every one of us, no matter what our age, is whether we are doing everything we can to bring up the young in the practice of the faith, whether we are doing what we can to keep them safe from the poison of sin.

As parents and significant others in the lives of young people, do we take seriously our responsibility to engender in them the habits which will support and sustain the life of an authentic Christian: a personal relationship with Jesus Christ, and a willingness to pursue a life in this world is marked principally by charity and by justice?

We need to commit ourselves to fostering in the young a life of prayer, of fidelity to the sacraments, especially the Eucharist and reconciliation, of familiarity with the Scriptures, and above all, with teaching them that their faith is not part of their life, it is their life. This is the responsibility of everyone in the church, and no one is exempt from it.

As it did for me this summer, I hope that believing so deeply in the goodness of our young people will inspire all of us to be better Christians and Catholics.

FATHER DONALD A. STERLING, D.MIN.

Fellowship with Mary

Does this not sound like 2002 life in the United States? A young teenage female is preparing for her marriage. She is engaged to a young man who is deeply in love with her. As they near their upcoming marriage, a very serious issue is revealed – "before they lived together, she was found with child ..." (Matthew 1:18).

According to local reports, this young girl claims that she has no relations with a man. She is thrust into a series of events over which she has no control.

She certainly has not considered an alternative to giving birth to this child. Because she has been raised in a God-conscious family, she decides to do what she believes God would have her do.

Let us look further. Let's suppose that this young pregnant woman went to visit her cousin and stayed with her for three months (Luke 1: 56).

In many instances (especially in earlier times) when a young woman was unwed and pregnant, her family sent her away from home until she gave birth. Normally in a stable African American family, a child – regardless of issues of conception – is raised as a sacred gift from God.

The introductory picture of Mary, the mother of Jesus reference above, captures in a superlative way the faith trust illustrated in the African faith journey.

There are some values that can be identified with a broad focus. In order to understand our Christian spiritually, it is essential that we have an adequate understanding of self.

Spirituality is our response to the grace of God wherein we become what we have been created by the Lord to be. The God of the African American is a personal God who is present in good times and bad.

This is a God at whom one marvels, and at the same time, a God who is the divine one who talks, laughs, cries and argues. This God is father, mother, brother and sister at the same time.

This is not an "either-or" God, but "this, that and more." This God rhythmically and harmoniously moves through one's heart, life, hopes, dreams and aspirations.

Mary, the mother of Jesus, is the model par excellence of this spiritually alive ideal.

In the typical African American household the most sacred person is "mom." Down through the ages, "You don't talk about my mother."

Within the traditional Black family, a pattern of mutual responsibility was fostered. This pattern recognizes the reality that in the Black experience there is the need to listen and respond to each member of the family if the family is to provide the nurturance and material needs necessary for growth and development.

Who is the primary leader in the development of healthy familial relationships, sensitivities and responsibilities? Mom! Mother!

We are not whole without mother. Mary, the mother of Jesus, was loved to the end, even at the cross. Equally, she was at the cross, never abandoning, never turning her back on the child whom she birthed.

A historical look at African Americans presents us with slaves and descendents of slaves. Their color, ranging from red to Black, marks them among the outcast, the least of the kingdom of God. Women bore too often for nine months the offspring of "masters," rapist, not just their husband.

Women loved these children, often not theirs by choice. Women continue to be remarkable towers of strength, faith and faithfulness, stability, compassion and love regardless of bodily height or social stature.

Why do Black people have such a great devotion to Mary? For reasons such as those presented above. Mary is a tower of strength. Mary is a model of untiring faith and faithfulness. Mary is a model of living compassion. Mary is a font of love and life.

KENNARD BROGDEN AND MARK THOMAS

Still Inspired

Young people still idolize Dr. Martin Luther King, Jr., because we agree with his message of peace, equality, civil rights and justice. Dr. King's message of peace is summarized in John 14:27, "Peace I leave with you; my peace I give you."

This means young people can be taught peace to settle any situation they are confronted with. This means young people must be taught not to take revenge for being mistreated but be taught to "Treat our enemies with kindness."

This task is very difficult but not insurmountable. Therefore, young people must think of peacemakers that they know and then ask themselves, "How can I be a peacemaker in my family, school and community?"

St. Katharine Middle School students have been taught to know that the source of our equality is Jesus Christ. Sister Dolorosa Bundy, O.S.P., our religion teacher, has highlighted for us the life and works of Dr. King and his commitment to equality and civil rights.

Young people sum it up this way: "everyone is equal!" This means that the church must regard all people as equal regardless of race, creed or national origin. This means that young people are "somebodies" and we should be allowed to have a voice.

Students at St. Katharine School begin and end each day with the Prayer of Peace by St. Francis of Assisi. Reciting this prayer twice daily gives young people a reference point to work from. Some of us come from communities and homes that do not promote peace, but given the opportunity to be in a peaceful atmosphere helps us to capture the peaceful spirit of Dr. Martin Luther King, Jr.

There are wrist bands, hats, shirts, socks, and bracelets that are titled WWJD (What would Jesus do?). We propose an additional one WWMD (What would Martin do?)

Catholic Schools must continue to be about the business of instilling peacemaking principles in our young people so that we can become proud examples to others.

With peace, equality and civil rights, young people can really see Dr. King's work for justice. The marches, sit-ins and protests for justice are examples of how followers of Jesus Christ lead with charity and compassion. The Sermon of the Mount is an example of how to infuse a conversation about justice with young people. God's justice demonstrates a total preference for the poor and the little people in our society.

Spike Lee's movie "Get on the Bus" is an example of working for justice. Young people can work for justice by understanding the Scripture passage, "I have come that they may have life and have it more abundantly," (John 18:10).

The principles of the Nguzo Saba (Kwanzaa) collectively allow young people to participate fully in issues and concerns of justice. For instance, there are two questions that must be asked of all young people.

First: In whom do we put our trust? The answer of course if Jesus/God, then we are compelled to live righteously and work for those who a less fortunate than ourselves.

Second: How does our lifestyle affect our brothers and sisters? Our life-styles must correspond to our conviction to work for justice, for the poor, homeless, those suffering from AIDS and those who are unable to help themselves.

Our spirit of justice can be summed up as the song goes: "If I can help somebody as I pass along, If I can cheer somebody with a work or song, If I can show somebody that he's traveling wrong, then my living shall not be in vain. If I can do my duty as a Christian ought, If I can bring back beauty to a world up-wrought, If I can spread love's message as the Master taught, Then my living will not be in vain."

SHARON H. WINCHESTER

Preparing a Place

One might think a year based on the life of Christ would begin with his birth. But our liturgical year begins with Advent, four weeks prior to the birth of Jesus.

It is the church's nurturing that directs our attention during the entire year to those events in the life of Jesus and the saints to remind us of our baptism and our commitment.

We begin with Advent and end with Christ the King. Throughout the year we are asked on these special days to think on the subjects selected by the church. But, on those other days, we are free to ponder Jesus, his life and ours in any way we choose.

Surprising, the church calls this "ordinary" time. I, however, consider it "special" time. Time for me to develop my personal relationship with Christ. And this, my friends, is the most special of times.

Do you have friends you don't see often throughout the year? Maybe they live on the other side of town, or they live out of town. No matter when you see them it's like you've been seeing them every day. It's as if there has been no time between you. There is much to plan when you and those friends are finally going to get together.

Well, if we don't use our "special" time wisely, that's how it is with Jesus. Preparing a place for Christ in your heart can make Advent just as special if we plan.

Week 1: Making the decision. Children should go to their parents to ask if Johnny can spend the night. Adults decide based on several reasons, but at some point decide to meet their friend or invite them to stay over.

Do you want to invite Christ into your heart? Can he occupy a little space, more space, how much space in your heart can be claimed by Christ?

Week 2: Reflection. What is it that is occupying the space in your heart now? Is your family taking up your heart room? What about your job and all those ministries, is that what occupies the room in your heart? Could it be forgiving an offense? Maybe it's sin.

Week 3: Cleaning up the space. The sacrament of reconciliation cleans up the space. A well-prepared penitent gains more empty space in the heart from this sacrament than anything else. Make notes, be open and honest. Before you perform your penance, pray, trust and expect freedom.

Week 4: Plan for the future. During this week add something to your diet or your life that can remain after Christmas has past. Drink more water, begin a daily exercise routine, attend daily Mass once a week, add an additional prayer period to your day. Christ is your friend.

There are times throughout the day when something may remind you of your friends. These things will remind you of Christ. They will also prevent the room you just emptied from being filled with something else. Eventually, you'll find more of your heart is filled with Christ than you ever thought possible.

Wow, when do we shop and cook if we're doing all of that? Most of that we can do while we shop and cook. We really don't need extra time to make Christ a part of our lives. We just need to use the time we have.

Hopefully, this Christmas season when we sing "Joy to the world, the Lord has come. Let earth receive her king. Let every heart prepare him room," we'll be able to sing proudly (maybe even better) because this Advent season we actually did prepare him room!

What's in Yours?

A short while ago a friend asked, "What do you want for Christmas?" I couldn't give him a quick answer because there are so many choices. After pondering my many choices, I said, "I want the Lord." His response was, "Is that all?"

I was really confused, I said I want the Lord and he says; is that all? I looked at him and slowly shook my head from side to side. The response kept ringing in my head, "Is that all?" "Is that all?" I felt sad for him and felt the need to pray.

As I knelt to pray, I felt an urgency to pray for this world of ours: a world that has reduced the value of a human life to a $10 bag of dope; a world that is blind to social injustice; a world in which "If it is not happening to me then it is not my concern;" a world that has built more storage buildings for earthly goods, than housing for the homeless; a world that builds stadiums and stadium-size churches while the hungry stand outside begging for food; a world that is intolerant to the cries of a baby, so they muffle the cries before they can cry; a world that worships people, money and acquiring material stuff and denies the gift of Christmas.

I don't know why I was confounded by his answer; one can see the love of Christmas is fading away. We are so much in love with material items and stuff. We spend our lives acquiring stuff and our worth, our self-esteem is measured by how much stuff we have.

We measure our worth by how much debt we can accumulate, "I am always going to owe somebody, let me live for today."

We live in a constant spiral of obtaining that we don't have time for church or the Lord. So we serve God electronically, while we balance our checkbooks. We have a morality that Dr. King describes as "survival of the slickest." Our major mode of operation is not to get caught. So we cheat, lie and steal to get more.

Our once proud love of God is decaying the trail of tears and toils, the legacy of the power of the Lord that our foreparents and ancestors laid out for us.

That phrase is still in my head and I can only ask, "Do you know the Lord?" The Lord I know is more than enough. My Lord is a good and gentle friend who has fought many battles for me. One who did not look the other way when I sinned, but smiled with forgiveness. A Lord who parted waters for us many, many times, so many we cannot count. A Lord that sits high but reaches low for all of us to let us know that "everything is gonna be alright." A Lord that is so big that one could never get enough.

I saw my friend the other day and asked him what did he want for Christmas? He started to list many of the things that he already has, but not as big, he wanted the world, but not peace.

As I prepare for Christmas, I pray during Advent that the crooked roads in my life will be made straight and bumps in the road will be made flat and that I will see the glory of the living God in the land of the living. We all will live in a world that is not in conflict, where the "Crips can live with Bloods" and the revival of the Lord will happen daily. I welcome the Lord in all that is good, because everything that God has made is good.

So my friend, the best gift that anyone can give me is his or her prayer that I continue to be in love with the Lord.

JANICE CURTIS GREENE

Christmas & Kwanzaa

I want to set the record straight; Kwanzaa is not a religious holiday. Kwanzaa is a cultural celebration highlighting the many accomplishments and achievements of people of African descent. Kwanzaa stresses family, community and culture.

In 1966, Dr. Maulana Karenga, professor and chair of the Department of Black Studies at California State University, Long Beach, saw the need to preserve and revitalize African American culture. He developed the celebration of Kwanzaa, which means "first fruit" in Swahili, the most widely spoken language in the continent of Africa and patterned Kwanzaa from fruit harvest celebrations, which began in ancient Egypt.

Kwanzaa is celebrated from December 26 through January 1 and therein lies the confusion over celebrating Kwanzaa and Christmas. This should pose no dilemma. As Catholic Christians we, of course, celebrate the birth of Our Lord and Savior Jesus Christ on December 25 and rejoice in that spirit of love and hope.

Since the festival of Kwanzaa is dedicated to uplifting African Americans and strengthening our families it is only logical to celebrate Kwanzaa at a time when relatives come together. During Christmas holiday schools are on winter break and many people take time off from their jobs thus offering a perfect opportunity for African American families to spend time together reflecting on their Christianity and their culture. Kwanzaa is also about love of family and hope for our communities.

The news and entertainment media paint such a negative picture of

African Americans portraying us as inmates, drug dealers, prostitutes, and thugs whose only successes are on stage or playing sports. This is a deliberate attempt to take away the hope of our young people. There are many obstacles facing African American communities like crime, poverty, HIV/AIDS and other health matters, which need to be addressed and I do not mean to diminish these issues in any way. However, the news of our neighborhoods is not entirely bad and that is why Kwanzaa is necessary, to erase myths and restore dreams.

During Kwanzaa Black families discuss the strides our people have made and how we can help our brothers and sisters. African Americans have survived the Middle Passage, slavery, racism and legislative and judicial systems determined to keep us down. We are nurses, doctors, educators, scientist, entrepreneurs, activist, scholars, inventors, students, bus drivers and homemakers who know how to feed our families on ham hocks and dried beans and much more.

Kwanzaa also offers seven principles, the Nguzo Saba, which if followed will revive and rebuild our communities. They are Umoja, Unity (Acts 2:1); Kujichagulia, Self–Determination (Mark 5:25-34); Ujima, Collective Works and Responsibility (Matthew 25:35-36, 40); Ujamaa, Cooperative Economics (Psalms 122:6-7); Nia, Purpose (Luke 4:18-19); Kuumba, Creativity (1Corinthians 12:4-6); and Imani, Faith (Hebrew 11:1-3, 40). There are also seven symbols of Kwanzaa: Kinara, Candle– Holder and Mishuma Saba, seven Candles (Matthew 5:14-15); Mkeka, Woven Mat (John 19:23); Kikombe Cha Umoja, Unity Cup (Luke 22:20); Mazao, Fruits and Vegetables (Matthew 13:18-23); Vibunzi, Corn (Genesis 41:5); Zawadi, Handmade or Cultural Gifts (James 1:17).

As I stated, Kwanzaa is not a religious holiday. Dr. Karenga deliberately separated the celebration from any religious affiliation thus making Kwanzaa available to African Americans of all faiths, or none, so that we can come together based on the rich and varied common ground of our African-ness. However, there is still the prevailing idea that Kwanzaa is some pagan ceremony created to replace Christmas. I have, therefore, included Scriptural references to dispel this fear and show that Kwanzaa indeed adheres to the Word of God and answers the question, "If God is for us who can be against us."

So go ahead celebrate Christmas and Kwanzaa. Put your manger and your Kinara side by side. Enjoy the richness of being genuinely Christian and authentically African, the best of both worlds.

FATHER RAYMOND L. HARRIS, JR.

Easter: Who is Risen?

When we consider the implications of the Resurrection of Jesus Christ, it does not mean that only his soul has gone to heaven or that his message continues in the hearts and minds of his followers. Christians believe that Jesus was raised body and soul from the dead.

This message is shared with us through the ministry of the church. Christians of the 21st century believe in the testimony of those first Christians: "We have seen the Lord." They recognized the Lord because they saw the wounds that he had suffered during his Crucifixion. They rejoiced because that which had sought to destroy Jesus did not defeat him.

We may wrestle with feelings of certitude and doubt in our journey of faith. Remember the story of Thomas the Apostle? His first response to this testimony was to refuse to believe it unless he was able to touch the wounds of Jesus. Some refer to him as "doubting" Thomas. At least he dealt with his doubts while remaining within the church. There was controversy and confusion within the church at its earliest stages as they dealt with the meaning of the Resurrection, but Thomas remained within the church. That is one of the reasons why he is called "St. Thomas" today.

We have chosen to believe in this testimony without being able to see the risen Lord. Jesus offers us a promise, "Blessed are those who have not seen and have believed (cf. John 20:29)." Let us consider the implications of the Resurrection of Jesus Christ for our lives, rejoicing that we are blessed beyond measure.

First, we are being redeemed. God shows his love for us by sharing in our humanity, living in solidarity with our joys and sorrows, even experiencing death. Jesus did not die so that we can excuse sin. Christ has risen so that we can be empowered to overcome sin by following what he teaches for our well-being and salvation.

The wounds of his crucifixion are still present in his glorified body. Jesus has overcome the wounds of rejection inflicted upon him. With his help, we can overcome not only our sins, but any source of suffering as well. God has never given up on us. Let us not give up on ourselves.

Second, we are being reconciled to God and to each other. Some question the necessity of the sacrament of reconciliation, but the witness of the early church is clear. Christ decided to forgive sins through the ministry of the church (cf. John 20:21-23).

God created us. He knows the psychological and spiritual value for us to be able to reveal our sins with a repentant spirit in a strictly confidential manner. Peace will flood our minds and souls as we receive the assurance that God has forgiven our sins, forgotten them, and has given us the chance to begin anew.

Some say that it is hard to celebrate this sacrament. Jesus looks at us with love, bearing the wounds that can heal the wounds of our sins, and invites us to trust that we can be healed in order to live holy lives.

Finally, we are being raised to new life. Holiness simply means to be conscious that we are living in communion with God and to govern our conduct accordingly. We are sharing a commitment of life and love with God. This impacts our relationships with others. We cannot separate what some call the "sacred" from the "secular." We are called to transform and sanctify our society by the power of the Gospel as it is practiced by us.

Our God has refused to abandon us to the power of sin and death because he is resolved to redeem us. Are we resolved to be redeemed, reconciled and raised to a new life in Christ?

Dr. Kirk P. Gaddy

When You Believe

The Easter story is one that confirms the faith story of victory over death. The Acts of the Apostles provides a major belief statement in that it reports "Not everyone saw him! He was only seen by us ... God told us to announce clearly to the people that Jesus is the one he has chosen to judge the living and the dead."

When we believe in the Easter story, our faith tells us that our loved ones who preceded us in death, are in the hands of God's providence. We believe that God is taking care of our loved ones; God wants the best for everyone and God can do for his people what nobody else can do.

Though this thought may be difficult to understand, I never thought that my brother, sister and I would be "normal" after the death of our parents, John and Beatrice Gaddy. My brothers, my sister and I kept praying that God's providence would allow for us to talk with him and ask him to be with us, to comfort us and help us to understand that our parents death was in the plan of our all-wise, all-loving and all-powerful, good and gracious God.

By continuing the legacy of our parents, my siblings and I invite all our relatives and friends to our parents' house for Good Friday. Here we pray, talk and laugh and we cry about those things that my parents cherished. We also provide a sumptuous meal for many people, those we know and for those whom we do not know. It is the spirit of our parents that helps us with the holy season of Easter. We partake in the life, death, and Resurrection of the Lord.

When we believe in the Easter story, our faith tells us that what God did yesterday, he does today. He watches over us like a loving Father. The Easter story opens our minds as believers as Psalm 26:1, tells us: "The Lord is the protector of my life; of whom shall I be afraid?" You and I know that God protected the three young men in the fiery furnace; that God saved Daniel from the lion's den; that God, especially in the life of Jesus, watches over his chosen people and provides for them who have faith in him.

This Easter, as we remember all our deceased brothers and sisters, in hours like these, we should think of the providence of God. We who believe must continue in the spirit of Proverbs 3:6, "In all thy ways think on him and he will direct our paths."

When we truly believe that God's providence has given us new life and a hope that lives on then we can conquer all things. As we remember our loved ones this Easter and remember the Easter story, recall that God wants everyone to be with him. Jesus' Resurrection from the dead is proof that death has no power over our lives with God. We, who believe, offer prayers to God that he continue to help us understand his providence; his care for us; and his love for us.

As families gather for their Easter brunches and dinners, remember, that all of our loved ones are in God's care. Let the stories of your deceased loved ones spice up your Easter brunches and dinners. It is good to know that when you believe in the Resurrection power of God, families can begin to heal and know that their deceased loved ones are at the banquet feast of the Lord. How wonderful it is to know that your loved ones are being cared for by God.

Power of the Lord

In the Old Testament it is written that "the Spirit of the Lord was upon them," but in the New Testament it is written that the "Spirit of the Lord was within them."

The Holy Spirit came on Pentecost Sunday, 50 days after Easter. It came in with a fiery blast, moving and stirring, pleased and anointed, sending forth frightened Christian disciples from their hiding place in Jerusalem to the four corners of the world.

It came suddenly with a mighty rushing wind with cloven tongues, like fire resting on each of them. It was fulfillment of not only John the Baptist's statement that Christ will baptize with the Holy Spirit and with fire but also of the constant abiding presence of the Holy Spirit within them.

The Holy Spirit, our comforter, was sent to live in us, work on us and walk beside us leading and guiding us in our daily living. Power is now in the house.

"Power in the house" refers to power in the housing that God has provided for each of us, known as our body. Ask the disciples. The power of the Holy Spirit moved them from attempting invisibility in the upper room to amazing visibility in the streets.

It moved them from inaction to action. The very nature of this power creates activity. It caused them to celebrate for they recognized a change had come not upon them, but within them – a change that meant a new walk, a new talk, a new vision. Power was now in the house!

The effects of this changing power were heard around the world. The power of the Holy Spirit revolutionized both the church world and the secular world.

At Pentecost, 3,000 persons were converted to faith in Christianity at one time. Some of these had assisted in the crucifixion of our savior. Black people were there, representing Egypt, Cyrene, Mesopotamia and Elam.

Within 32 years after Pentecost, the whole world had heard about Jesus the Christ. Realize the awesomeness of this power for there were no church buildings or printing presses. With the changing power of the Holy Spirit, actions and ambitions were recreated. Purposes were changed. The disciples became dedicated to a life of service. Practices changed. It was not business the same old way. That power brought about a deeper love of and for God and Jesus.

God has given us the Holy Spirit for a purpose – to advance the kingdom of God. Through the continuing power of the Holy Spirit, God has given us the power to witness and win others for his kingdom and to perceive the means of advancing his work here on earth. He has also given us the power to practice the seven fruits of the Spirit.

The Holy Spirit's power is necessary for the effective living of our new life in Christ. The power to make a difference is ours. With the power in the house, we need to face today's challenges – oppression, terrorism, social injustice/intolerance, lost children, addiction, poverty, the church.

As we walk with God on a daily basis, in the mundane duties of regular existence, the worship rituals, our daily devotions and our life of prayer will see us through.

Our African brothers and sisters say that on Pentecost Sunday, fires are lighted to remind Christ's followers to keep "the fire of faith burning" and that it takes "many to activate the mission." It is also a reminder that believers become the "fire" the second time.

Recognizing the power of the Holy Spirit within each of us, what are we going to do with it as we face Pentecost 2002? It is time to unleash the power of the Holy Spirit that is within us. Power is in the house. Now, what are we going to do with it in our house?

JANICE CURTIS GREENE

What Would Mary Do?

As a young girl growing up in a Catholic household and attending Catholic schools, I was always intrigued with the Catholic Church's devotion to the Virgin Mary, Mother of God. My Protestant friends found this affection rather odd and some thought it outright blasphemous. As a woman, wife and mother I do not know how I could have endured the most difficult time of my life without Mary as a model of courage and dignity.

When the angel told Mary that she was to bear the Son of God, she responded, "May it be done to me according to your word." When Jesus was 12 years old, he stayed behind in the temple in Jerusalem. Mary became anxious; however, Luke 2:51 states, "His mother kept all these things in her heart."

The fourth Station of the Cross depicts Jesus meeting his sorrowful mother on his way to Calvary and again Mary kept it all in her breaking heart and stood firm in her relationship with Jesus. The prediction of Simeon in Luke 2:35 that a sword would pierce her soul was now being fulfilled. Even at this awful moment we find this woman of extreme poise and faith not raving and wailing but as John 19:25 tells us Mary was standing strong at the foot of the cross of her dying Son, Jesus.

I always admired Mary; however, it was not until Oct. 4, 2002, that the respect became intimate. That was the day my oldest son died of diabetic complications at the age of 36 and a sword pierced my soul. I wondered how was I going to make it. Then I asked myself, "What would Mary do?"

The answer was quite clear; she stood firm in her unwavering bond with Jesus. She stood on the promise of Jesus to never leave or forsake us. She stood on his pledge that he would send another advocate to be with us always. In short, Mary stood on her faith that every word Jesus said was true. I knew that was what I had to do.

I have read all four Gospel accounts of Jesus' Resurrection. Mary, the mother of Jesus, was not with the other women that Easter morning. Was she too grief stricken to go to the tomb or was it that she knew that Jesus was no longer among the dead but had risen just as he predicted? I believe the latter. I believe that Mary was so in tuned that there was no need to visit Jesus' sepulcher because it would be empty.

Following Mary's lead is how I cope. I know my son, Calvin, is not with the dead, his soul has resurrected and he is at rest and peace with Jesus and his ancestors. That kind of personal kinship with Jesus, the way, the truth and life can only be maintained by prayer and reading his Word, the Bible.

Do I cry? Is it hard to stand? The answer to both questions is a resounding yes. But Psalm 30:5 tells me, "Weeping may endure for a night, but joy comes in the morning." In Matthew 5:4, Jesus assures me, "Blessed are those who mourn for they will be comforted." In John 15:11, Jesus tells me how much he loves me so that my joy might be complete. John 3:16 guarantees eternal life to all believers and Calvin believed in Christ.

The Word of God is the rock on which Mary stood and it will continue to be my firm foundation. I am blessed to have the Blessed Virgin Mary, Mother of God as my role model, friend, mother and intercessor. Together we stand.

Advent

Bring glad tidings to the poor. Proclaim liberty for the captives, recovery of sight for the blind and release to prisoners.

Sounds very optimistic when you think of it in secular terms. Even though we consider ourselves the Body of Christ, we deny his ability, through us, to perform any of these ministries routinely. And, even when we do, the anxiety of sustaining that level of righteousness scares us. We'd rather give our glad tidings through the United Way or the Cardinal's Lenten Appeal, than in person.

Yes, I know, the poor are in places that are dangerous. Most of us aren't doctors. So, we dismiss the healing. Do we know the difference between liberty for the captives and release to the prisoners? We would absolutely be outraged if the prisoners were actually set free. We've seen how quickly laws can be changed when a prisoner is set free.

So then, if we're not doing his will, how do we get his kingdom to come? Because, you know, we can always claim not to be Christ and dismiss our ability to do any of that.

Christ gave us a hint recently when we celebrated Christ the King. He said his kingdom was not of this world. I think what he meant was that we can't judge how well we're performing our ministry from a secular sense. We have to measure our ability to perform the tasks on a spiritual basis. All we have to do is be just.

Sounds better than optimistic when you think about it in spiritual terms. But, now there is a problem. Why? Well, it's not because we feel we can't do those things. It's because we can, but we don't. Justice requires us to do spiritually that which, if looked at from the secular sense, might seem a little crazy.

The just understand, first and foremost, that we can go to a dangerous place, but that's not always necessary. We can volunteer at a shelter, a place where the poor are fed or any agency that allows us to assist.

Glad tidings. Just the words make you feel like they have to be given in person. When slavery existed in this country, it was clear that there needed to be liberty for the captives. But even after their freedom, African Americans were captive by the laws of the land.

In my opinion, liberty for the captives requires us to do some not so tremendous deeds. We've got to stay well informed, register and vote, voice our opinions when those whom God has in positions of authority are not performing as justly as they should.

Recovery of sight, lets us know there was sight at some point. Could this sight have been an ability to see Christ somewhere in the world? And maybe because of all that's going on in the world, a person can't seem to find Christ anywhere.

Well, let's be Christ. Do something that appears crazy! Be there for an enemy; call someone you wrote off a few years ago because they did something to you or said something about you; mend the wounds that divide your family.

When human beings don't understand that all we ever need is Christ, they are prisoners. Some of us are prisoners. On occasion, something else has our heart more than Christ does. We can tell others they are loved and show them through our actions. We can teach them of God's love by our behavior, but we must love ourselves first.

During Advent, let's remind ourselves of the just acts we've performed. We've done many things individually and as the Body of Christ to bring about his kingdom. There is much that remains. As we welcome him again into our hearts, let us commit to doing those things we can to continue the ministry of justice that Christ began.

Social Justice Streets

We will walk this week with Jesus as he climbs the hill to Calvary and lay his body on the cross – suffering for the redemption of all humankind.

Howard Thurman, noted theologian, minister and professor, tells a story (in his book, *"Deep River"*) about a group of African Americans who visited Mahatma Ghandi in India. Ghandi asked the visitors to sing one song in his presence, "Were you there when they crucified my Lord?"

This request intrigued Thurman and contemplated on its significance. Thurman gained a profound insight – identification in suffering makes the cross universal and that the mystery of the cross is found deep within the heart of the experience itself.

We have to experience the walk to Calvary, the weight of the cross, the people encountered, the suffering endured. This is why we repeatedly say the Stations of the Cross throughout Lent. This is why we walk to Calvary through the streets of Baltimore.

We know what Christ went through because we have met him in high places of pain, and we claim Jesus as our brother!

Can we not pray through action – social justice action:

• Jesus is condemned. O Lord, how many times in life have we been guilty of unjustly condemning each other and blaming those who are poor for being poor. Forgive us, O Lord!

• Jesus takes his cross. O Lord, there are so many people who are carrying crosses. Help us to share your name through action with those who feel abandoned.

• Jesus falls the first time. O Lord, whenever we fall down in service to you, help us to look up to the many acts of charity and mercy your Son did. If we look up, we can get up!

• Jesus meets his mother. Jesus, we know what you are telling us. To watch the pain of those we love is harder than to bear our own. Help us to reach out and comfort those we meet through the actions we provide.

• Simon helps Jesus. O Lord, help us to remember that we are here to help each other and to carry each other when necessary.

• Veronica wipes the face of Jesus. O Lord, we marvel at Veronica's willingness to reach out to the wretched and the suffering. Fill us, Lord, with the courage to reach out to those considered "wretched of this generation" – the substance abuser, the mentally ill and homeless families.

• Jesus falls the second time. Lord, when the road to justice becomes littered with obstacles, help us to be determined to stay on course. O Lord, forgive our apathy!

• Jesus speaks to the women and children. Lord God, even in your suffering you acknowledged the women and the children. O Lord, when we become "caught up in living" help us to remember others. Lord, forgive us of our self–centeredness.

• Jesus falls a third time. Lord God, on the road to Calvary you fell down, but you got back up. O Lord, when the arm of injustice knocks us down, help us to get back up and stand for justice! O Lord forgive us our self-pity.

• Jesus is stripped. O Lord, release us from the material trappings of this world and make us poor in spirit so that we may be rich in you.

• Jesus is crucified. Lord God, we pray that the sin of racism, and all "isms," are nailed to the cross this Good Friday.

• Jesus dies on the cross. Lord God, "in dying you restored our life." O Lord, we pray that we live a life committed to justice and not "just us."

• Jesus is taken from the cross. Love, tenderly, took you from the cross. O Lord, we pray that love will move us to remove others from the crosses they bear.

• Jesus is laid in the tomb. Acknowledging your human dignity, your friends gave you a proper burial. Lord God, forgive us our disrespect for life. Resurrection awaits every time we act justly and strongly in the Lord!

DEACON PAUL D. SHELTON

Abuse Crisis

Anger, hurt, shame, disappointment, frustration, disillusionment, confusion, embarrassment fail to adequately describe the current experience of many in our church. The terrible actions of a small number of priests and the bad judgment of an even smaller number of bishops have caused immeasurable harm. Some people have told me that they are experiencing a crisis of faith and may leave the Catholic Church. Many people have also told me that they would not encourage young men to enter the priesthood because of the current events.

We should not be surprised or shocked that there are some sinful priests and bishops in our church. We certainly would not deny or be shocked that there are some sinful people in the pews of our churches. We readily accept that all of us in the pews sin at times and make mistakes. We also acknowledge without experiencing a faith crisis, that there is a serious problem in the vocation of marriage and that some sinful parents abuse their children.

Certainly it is understandable that as a result of the current events, many of us are experiencing a crisis but not in a crisis of faith. We were reminded by Christ in the Gospel reading for the fourth Sunday of Easter that "thieves and robbers" would get into the sheepfold (John 10: 1-10). We were also told by Christ that he is the one true shepherd. This is a time to deepen our faith in Jesus Christ as our true shepherd.

This is not a faith crisis but a time to affirm and focus our faith in Christ. Some of us have put too much trust in the priesthood of father and the bishop and too little trust in our share of Christ's priesthood. Through baptism and confirmation, all of us were given a share in the priesthood of Jesus Christ. This share in Christ's priesthood does not come through or from a priest or the bishop; it comes to us from Jesus Christ.

For too long we have depended on those ordained into the priesthood to do what those of us baptized and confirmed into a share of Christ's priesthood could and should do for one another as the church. We have become too dependent and passive. Now is a wonderful opportunity for our church leaders to acknowledge the grace and calling of all of our people and to trust in the gifts of the Holy Spirit.

Too few of us really live as if we are the mystical body of Christ. We are different parts with different gifts and blessings that are available to support and serve the body.

When Christ needed to share his message and demonstrate his saving power that the Father had given him, he looked beyond the small number of Apostles and called on 72 disciples to go forth and work great miracles and signs in his name. The 72 came back rejoicing and amazed at what they could do in the name of Jesus.

We will also be amazed at what we can do if we come out of the pews and place our trust in our share of Christ's priesthood. Accept our rule as members of the mystical body and accept responsibilities of our baptized and confirmed disciples.

The challenge is not the few sinful priests but the priests who do not see their role to empower discipleship. While ordained priesthood will always be of great importance to our church, it does not encompass all of priesthood. For too long too many of us in the pews and the pulpit have thought that the totality of priesthood was in ordained priesthood. All of us are called to holiness, to grow closer to Christ. Priests, sisters, deacons, brothers and bishops are not called to be holier than everyone else. All of us are called to become holy through the vocations that Jesus has given us.

This moment in history is a unique opportunity for ordained priests to begin to empower disciples, for those in the pews to claim their share in Christ's priesthood and to take greater responsibility for the ministry of the church. The truth is that with a large number of active disciples, we only need a few apostles. Perhaps, just perhaps, the shortage of priests is an opportunity for many of us to live as disciples and participants in the priesthood of Jesus Christ.

What I Am Told

Recently, I received an e-mail titled, "No More Excuses." It contained a list of Old and New Testaments people whom God called and all their excuses why they did not feel they could answer the call.

This e-mail had an impact on me because I had a bushel of excuses to avoid answering God's call. I used excuse after excuse until I ran out of excuses. The first excuse I used was that I was too old, but I was reminded how old Abraham was when he started his journey. I next used that I was too short, but that's why we climb trees to get a better view. I told God that I was too busy and he reminded me that I should build up my treasures in heaven instead of on Earth. Many materially wealthy people tried to take their treasures with them, but their wealth was still in the tomb after their bones had turned to ashes.

After many failed excuses, I finally had the ultimate excuse, I was so proud of it. I knew this was a winner. I used the "I am just not good enough excuse." That distinction is for the chosen few and I know that I wasn't one. And the ultimate excuse was that being African American I just wasn't good enough to be an officer in the American Catholic army.

I quickly found out that excuse was as lame as the others and maybe the worst yet. As St. Paul informs us through his letters, God's gift is for all of us if we acknowledge that Jesus Christ is our savior. We are to share in the wealth of the Kingdom of God, to be priests, prophets, kings and queens and to manifest the glory of God with what we do with our lives.

With that information I felt trapped, there were no more excuses that

I could use, I had to surrender. For many years I have eaten the fruit of God's love and in turn I refused to hear his call. I know that many of us are like that; we will take, take, take and not give back. I can honestly say that God has been good to my family and me, through good and bad times.

I surrendered to the message of God and started the diaconate program. There were times when the waters were rough and others when there were no storm clouds. The biggest problem I encountered was worthiness and my ability to be what God wanted me to be. I continued to use other excuses, while I was going through the classes, but the grace of God and prayers from many sources kept my boat afloat.

Today, I wonder how many more African American Catholics are reaping the benefits of the church and not working in the vineyards? We are called to be a part of God's church on Earth, to serve our brothers and sisters. God did not just call me. If we allow God's word to penetrate our worldly shield, we will know our place in the kingdom.

Ordination is not for everyone, but there are many other positions that are vacant and have been for a long time. Brothers where are you? Real men love God and are not afraid to demonstrate their love by their service. There is still room at the table for priests, deacons, Brothers, Sisters and lay leaders. The harvest is ready; so don't let the fruit rot on the tree.

Our ancestors labored long and hard to carve a legacy within the American Catholic Church. Are we to let this legacy fade because we are not taking up our crosses? There are many vineyards that we as African Americans can express our answer to the call of God. We have gone too long sitting on the sidelines. It's time to suit up, step up and do what you are told.

JOANN T. LOGAN

Going Deeper

"Going Deeper With God To Rethink Our Possibilities" was the theme of the first retreat held by this current board of African American Catholic Ministries at the Oblate Sisters of Providence motherhouse.

The retreat was a time of reflection, renewal and recommitment by board members Franklin Collins, Roberta Epps, Nina Harper, Father Raymond Harris, Ella Johnson, Brenda Rigby, Marie Washington, Darron Woodus and me as we re-examined our role as an advisory body to the Office of African American Catholic Ministries in its mission to promote evangelization and leadership with and among African American Catholics.

Joining the board was the office's Executive Director Therese Wilson Favors, Harambee Coordinator Howard Roberts and Clare Collins, wife of Franklin Collins.

We were truly blessed to have as our retreat leaders Bishop Gordon D. Bennett, S.J., and Father Raymond Harris, Jr., who, through Scripture, prayer and song, reminded the board that we are called to holiness by virtue of our baptism and challenged us to start afresh with Jesus Christ, looking at him as our model, and to examine obstacles which prevent us from moving toward that end.

The weekend began with a libation ceremony to remember those who struggled for our liberation, our development of faith and for our well being as a people. All libation ceremonies involve remembering the past, celebrating the present and looking forward to the future. Libation was poured for our African ancestors of faith who came before us; for those among us who continue to walk by faith and not by sight; and for those who will come to us this year, next year and in future years.

In our first session, titled *Obstacles To Holiness And Working Your Way Into Holiness*, Bishop Bennett extolled Jesus as healer, teacher, worker of wonders and consoler. Through Scripture, Bishop Bennett advised the board on how we can get to that place of wanting holiness enough to conquer all obstacles in our way.

Father Harris in session two, *God's Pulling Always Takes Us Into Another Zone*, taught that answering the call to holiness and walking with the Lord always take us to higher ground, to places where we have not been before, into new possibilities.

In session three, *Anxious to Please God Is a Good Thing*, Bishop Bennett cautioned the board that the world calls us to materialism and provides distractions. Reiterating the seven capital social sins – wealth without work, politics without principles, pleasure without conscience, knowledge without character, science without humanity, commerce without morality and religion without sacrifice – Bishop Bennett reminded us that our culture is content living on the surface, with each sin having a cost. Each is a real resistance to going deeper with God.

In the final session, *Where You Lead Us Lord, We Shall Follow*, Father Harris reminded us that as disciples of Jesus, we choose to follow Him. Where is Jesus leading the Board of African American Catholic Ministries?

The outcome of that session was the establishment of three board subcommittees – evangelization, leadership, and youth and young adults – which will assist the Office of African American Catholic Ministries in implementing and increasing awareness in the archdiocese of recommendations from the National Black Catholic Congress held last summer.

The board's inaugural retreat was truly a Spirit-filled, reviving experience that was a momentous occasion for all in attendance.

Soul Sisters Untapped

O n a beautiful July morning I joined Black women from many different parishes throughout the Archdiocese of Baltimore on a bus bound for Charlotte, N.C., and the first national gathering for Black Catholic women sponsored by the National Black Sisters' Conference.

The conference theme was, "Black Catholic Women … Untapped Treasures … Magnify the Lord."

We were the "soul sisters" from Baltimore going to get our blessings. We left behind families and households as varied as we were, but God had called and made a way for us to be together on this journey of faith.

We began with a poem written for the occasion by Jacqueline Johnson from St. Edward church. Along the way we prayed, sang and fellowshipped. When we arrived in Charlotte we were joined by additional lay and religious delegates from Baltimore bringing our total attendance to 83, perhaps the largest conference representation.

I had always been a part of a Black Catholic community. I attended Black Catholic schools taught by the Oblate Sisters of Providence. So I did not understand until I became part of the larger universe that a Black Catholic was an oddity to the rest of the population.

With that realization came a certain feeling of isolation, but when I entered the main ballroom of the Adams Mark Hotel and saw the ocean of more than 800 Black Catholic women, my separation disappeared.

The opening prayer and praise began with a group of spiritual dancers from Kentucky who moved like angels. The assembly poured libation, called on our ancestors, sang and clapped. We worshipped the

Lord with the reverence of our Catholic background and the spirit of our African heritage.

Sister Antona Ebo, F.S.M., set the tone for the conference. She reminded the audience that we're God's treasures, earthen vessels fit for the master's use, even if it meant breaking tradition.

Dr. Diana Hayes provided the keynote address for Saturday morning, giving conference attendees a historical perspective on racism in the Catholic Church. She spoke of a woman's responsibility to educate our children to keep them from leaving their Catholic faith.

The afternoon's speaker was Sister Jamie Phelps, O.P., who presented the listeners with the stumbling blocks on the path of our spiritual journey. They consisted of yielding to doubt and insecurity; approaching life as if it were warfare; not relying on the power of God; functional atheism; fearing chaos and denying death.

Sister Anita Baird, D.H.M., who invited all within the sound of her powerful voice to magnify the Lord, rendered the closing. She recalled other women of faith like Mother Mary Elizabeth Lange, Henriette Delille, Harriet Tubman, Hagar and Mary of God who stepped out of convention to serve mankind and serve the Lord.

The workshops consisted of spirituality and how to communicate with God; solidarity and how to treat one another; health and how to care for God's temple; social and political empowerment and how to make our presence known; economic development and how to spend and invest wisely; and vocations and how to answer God's call.

The gathering ended with a liturgy celebrated by Bishop William G. Curline of Charlotte. Also presiding were African American clergy Bishop John H. Ricard of the Diocese of Pensacola-Tallahassee, Fla., and Monsignor Mauricio W. West, who offered a stirring homily honoring women.

The weekend went by all too fast, and the return to the almost forgotten outside world was upon us. However, our approach to external forces would be different because we had been forever changed. "When the time for Pentecost was fulfilled, they were all in one place together. And suddenly there came from the sky a noise like a strong wind, and it filled the entire house in which they were" (Acts 2:1-2).

Together the women who attended the national gathering had experienced Pentecost and an infusion of the Holy Spirit.

Congress IX

Y ou should have been there when more than 3,000 Black people gathered in Chicago for the National Black Catholic Congress IX. The theme was "Black Catholic Leadership in the 21st Century: Solidarity in Action." Your soul would have leapt with joy, as Elizabeth's infant in her womb jumped with joy at the greeting of the Virgin Mary. This was an enormous family reunion of Black Catholics oriented for action.

We were no longer sojourners in a strange land. Members from the Archdiocese of Baltimore were especially proud of Bishop Gordon Bennett as a homilist; Therese Wilson Favors as congress facilitator; and Howard Roberts as all-around worker.

If you were there, your heart had to be filled with gratitude and praise to see family members of every hue and shade come to the mountaintop to get their blessing and then leave to serve.

Spirituality is one of the eight concerns that presently challenge and call Black Catholics as the whole American Catholic church to action. "Insomuch as all people are called to a life of holiness, we as Black people faithful to the grace of the Holy Spirit must seek to pray and work in the spirit of our ancestors in the Faith."

Father Cyprian Davis said in his seminar that Black spirituality is profoundly rooted in African history, embedded in Scripture, Christ-centered and socially conscious, and marked by the cross and Resurrection.

The Spirituality Pastoral Plan of Action reached by consensus of all in attendance at the small group discussions sets forth one-year, three-year, and five-year action plans. Now is the time for us to step up to the plate. We can't wait. We appear to be peculiar or UFOs not only to the wider Catholic Church but also to the rest of the Black community. We are indeed a peculiar people because we are God's people. God calls us now to bring our spirituality into the parishes and the larger Catholic Church to which we belong.

We are his creations and made in his own image. Our culture is representative of who we are and we need to bring it as treasure into our households of faith. Our children need to see positive images of them and recognize that they are valued. They need to hear our stories. We are needed in the church and have priceless, worthwhile gifts and talents. Faith without action is no faith at all. We need to be on one accord in taking these action steps.

Let us not assemble at Congress X in 2007 to discover that we have not completed our action tasks agreed upon by group solidarity in sentiment and belief at Congress IX.

Within a year, we are to plant the spirituality seed by identifying and incorporating cultural symbols, language and experiences in parish liturgies; initiating parish-based Scripture study programs from an Africentric perspective for all age groups; and promoting and supporting the interest and response of Black women and men desiring to dedicate their lives to various aspects of church ministry.

Within three years we are to nurture growth by developing parish and archdiocesan lecture series or seminars that teach about the contributions and history of Black Catholics in the church.

Within five years, we will establish roots by creating a National Black Research Institute (in partnership with the National Black Catholic Congress and other national organizations of Black Catholic leadership) to identify resources and maintain a current national database of resource speakers, facilitators, teachers, and other experts who can be called upon to assist parishes and dioceses in ministerial development and program implementation for peoples of African descent; by commissioning the publication of a well-researched and inspirational manual on the lives of Black saints, and by collecting and disseminating information on Black Catholic interests and concerns (spirituality, canonizations, social and cultural demographics, poverty, etc.).

You should have been there, but the work is just beginning! All of us present or not in Chicago, now need to ensure that we complete our mission.

JANICE CURTIS GREENE

On Retreat

In 2002 the National Sister's Conference held the first National Gathering of Black Catholic Women in Charlotte, N.C. It was a spiritually and emotionally uplifting experience. The women from the Archdiocese of Baltimore who attended returned filled with the fire of the Holy Spirit and ready for the next gathering to refuel; however, the next gathering was not scheduled until August, 2004, in Houston, Texas, a two-year wait.

The women of St. Gregory the Great and the Office of African American Catholic Ministries decided to organize a retreat for Black Catholic Women in 2003 to continue the spirit of solidarity that had begun in Charlotte. The retreat was held Oct. 10-12 at the Sea Trail Resort and Conference Center in North Carolina.

This retreat was the vision of sister Roberta Epps, of St. Gregory the Great church. I call her sister not because she has taken any formal religious vows, but because she is my sister in culture and Catholicism. The vow she has made is to serve the Lord and to preach his word, which she did in outstanding fashion during the retreat. But I am getting ahead of myself.

The bus ride to the conference center was long but the distance helped to separate us from the problems we left at home. We arrived tired and hungry. Sea Trail provided dinner to feed our bodies.

Therese Wilson Favors led the initial session, which nourished our souls. Inspired by Revelations 7:9-17, she reminded us that we were Soul Sisters of Survival. She spoke about the five "Cs" that women of color must remove from our lives. They were: Conflict of spirit:

Remember we are worthy to be saved. Crisis of identity: Why are we dissatisfied with God's creation? Confusion about our purpose: Are we trying to serve two masters? Competition with one another: How can we collaborate? Contradictions: How do we overcome the contradictions in our lives as we seek to follow Jesus?

The session on Saturday morning was centered on finding joy in the midst of the storm because "In God's presence there is fullness of joy" (Psalm 16:11). The Sister-to-Sister group from St. Gregory the Great performed a skit about the baggage women carry through their lives: addiction, abuse, teen pregnancy, debt, disappointments and shattered dreams. The skit ended with the proclamation of the best news in the universe, "God makes all things new. God makes all people new."

Then Roberta announced that the lesson she so painstakingly prepared and saved on a disk could not be read. She announced that the Holy Spirit had given her a new plan at 5:30 in the morning.

Through Roberta, God revealed that joy was as necessary as food, water and sleep. Having joy does not mean not having trials, but joy is the absence of depression during life's adversities. Roberta advised the retreat participants that joy keeps our difficulties from sticking to us; joy makes us Teflon sisters. We danced, sang, laughed and cried. We prayed the rosary, witnessed and testified.

The plan was for the assembly to attend Saturday evening Mass at St. Brendan the Navigator church; however, the time we had been given for Mass was incorrect and we arrived late. We were all a little upset about the error until we realized that our plan was not God's plan.

So, we ended the retreat with a beautiful Sunday morning Mass. The sun shone brightly and the distractions of fatigue and hunger, which would have been present Saturday, were eliminated. God wanted our full attention for the celebration of His Eucharist.

"Count it all joy, my sisters, when you encounter various trials, for you know that the testing of your faith provides perseverance. And let perseverance be perfect, so that you may be perfect and complete, lacking in nothing." (James 1:1-4).

Now, we are ready for Houston.

Going Forward

To move forward in 2002, much creativity and faith will be needed. Housing, health, education, public works operations and projects will function as they have in their most recent past.

However, programs that indirectly affect the quality of life in the city will be funded more with grants or partnering with other larger companies or nonprofits. More with less will be the watchword, but it is important that less won't cripple needed programs or make effective programs ineffective.

In any tight money situation, jobs are always an issue. As the recession unfolds and technologies increase, the unskilled and underskilled job market will diminish. The majority of people affected live in the city.

Those with limited education, chemically dependent and the mentally challenged will be the first to feel these effects. Unfortunately, the majority of the affected are African Americans.

Job retaining programs funded privately and with federal dollars should increase. Skill standards, if not already being introduced, should be so that future industry downsizing would not necessarily displace a worker from a job but allow that worker to quickly and efficiently move skills into another industry "job" since skills are "standardized." Just as factories need to be retooled, so do people.

It is people who make up our churches. While God remains a constant in our lives, the way our churches function and spread the Gospel changes.

Some of Baltimore's larger non-Catholic churches have expanded their ministries to include catering, child and adult day care, senior living, both assisted and non-assisted, as well as low cost housing and various counseling programs.

In each instance where possible, members of the church are involved in program development and operations. More and more deacons are utilized in these churches. Aside from their spiritual grounding, these deacons have secular expertise, which the church utilizes in its growth.

I anticipate that local parishes will begin to expand their ministries by utilizing a stronger diaconate program, utilizing both the spiritual fullness of the individual coupled with their management and technical skills. Deacons and lay leadership are more important going forward as we will see more shared ministries due to the shortage of parish priests.

The events of 9-11 forced people to take a deeper look at their lives. People woke up to discover again that God is the only constant while everything around them changes. God remains a part of them, never changing and ready to hear and answer prayer.

I anticipate an increase in church attendance as more and more people begin to exercise their spirituality and go to the gym (church) to get stronger. You can see it in TV evangelization, which is growing due to increased followers and financial support.

You can even see it in the political leadership of the president, who supports and spearheads the effort to have faith-based organizations provide services to the poor and disenfranchised.

Attention at the federal-funding level for faith-based organizations has been diverted because of the war in Afghanistan. However, eventually, I anticipate monies being allocated to faith-based organizations – all the way down to the parish level – to provide needed services to their respective communities.

I see more hope than I see despair. Churches will play a much greater role in the delivery of services to the poor. They have done it longer and do it better. It was for this reason that I did not and will not support the taxing of nonprofits. I do not see any attempts in the future to tax the efforts of those nonprofits that not only save souls but heal bodies as well.

Our churches, while diverse, share one belief and one mission, salvation through Jesus Christ. It is this belief and the spirit it instills in each one of us that will make for an enduring church on every corner of Baltimore City.

Conclusion

To develop and publish this book a wide circle of imani (faith) and kujichagulia (self-determination) was drawn with African American Catholics who serve as Guest Columnists for *The Catholic Review*. Together we, created the content of this book; a compendium of articles. It is a step into the future, an opportunity for us to speak our special truth of God's revelation in our midst. It has become a moment of history and an act of theologizing for. "every group of people, every race, thinks about God out of its own state of being, its own understanding of itself and out of its own condition of life" (Gayraud S. Wilmore, *Black Theology*) We acknowledge that our task to evangelize and educate through the publication of this book was of God and without God all of our efforts would turn to ashes.

In celebrating the thought of this book, we gathered together. In our assembly we began in prayer. Father Donald A. Sterling led us in a unique and powerful prayer. The prayer called us to be attentive to the lies of society and challenged us to our Christian responsibility to dispel lies and myths. "A lie can't live forever, thus O Lord we seek your blessings on the publication of this book."

Bishop Gordon D. Bennett, S.J., sent a letter of congratulations read by Ms. Joann Logan, president of the archdiocesan board of African American Catholic Ministries, "I am absolutely delighted to extend both congratulations and appreciation to you for the wonderful contributions you have made towards educating our people and evangelizing them by your contributions to *The Catholic Review*. As we celebrate two important anniversaries in the march towards greater racial justice in

327

America, the Supreme Court's decision in the case of Brown versus the Board of Education, and the United States Conference of Catholic Bishops' Pastoral Letter, *Brothers and Sisters To Us*, your efforts to publish these stirring and relevant articles are an enormous help in breaking down the walls of prejudice and ignorance and building bridges of healing and understanding".

To date 55 African American Catholics, including Bishop Bennett, S.J., have contributed to the Africentric Page, formerly called *What We Have Seen and Heard*. We pray that the articles have been stirring and relevant, discussing issues of the heart, mind and soul.

Writers

Deacon Wardell Paul Barksdale serves St. Bernardine parish.

Sister M. Annette Beecham, O.S.P., is Superior General of the Oblate Sisters of Providence.

Bishop Gordon D. Bennett, S.J., is bishop of Mandeville, Jamaica and former urban vicar of the Archdiocese of Baltimore.

Kennard Brogden is an eighth-grader at St. Katharine Catholic School.

Agnes Kane Callum is a noted historian and parishioner at St. Francis Xavier Church.

Dr. Beverly A. Carroll is Executive Director of the Secretariat for African American Catholics, National Conference of Catholic Bishops and a parishioner of St. Peter Claver.

Kathy Coleman is a family support services coordinator in the Circuit Court for Baltimore City and a parishioner of St. Matthew.

Nicholas M. Creary is an assistant professor of History at Marquette University in Milwaukee, Wis., and was a visiting assistant professor at Georgetown University in Washington, D.C.

Dr. Kenneth M. Dean, Jr., is director of New All Saints' music ministry and artistic director at the Baltimore Metropolitan Center for the Performing Arts.

Danise Jones Dorsey is an anti-poverty activist. She is a parishioner of St. Gregory the Great.

Toni Moore Duggan MS, CRNP, works at Elder Health Care, Inc., and is vice president of the national board for the canonization of Mother Mary Lange.

Ellen T. Dutton is an active parishioner of St. Peter Claver and former member of the archdiocesan board of African American Catholic Ministries.

Roberta L. Epps is a parishioner of St. Gregory the Great.

Therese Wilson Favors is the Director of the Office of African American Catholic Ministries and parishioner of St. Cecilia.

Kirk P. Gaddy is principal of St. Katharine School, part of the Queen of Peace Cluster.

Patricia A. Pinkney-Gaither is a parishioner of St. Veronica.

Sister M. Reginald Gerdes, O.S.P., is archivist for the Oblate Sisters of Providence.

Sister Magdala Marie Gilbert, O.S.P., is the director of vocation/formation for the Oblate Sisters of Providence and a graduate of the Institute for Black Catholic Studies.

Janice Curtis Greene is a facilitator for the Effective Black Parenting Program and a parishioner of New All Saints.

Nina R. Harper is the area deputy for KPC Ladies in Baltimore and Washington and a parishioner of St. Francis Xavier.

Myra A. Harris is the past vice president of the Pastoral Council, a former Sunday school teacher and an active parishioner of St. Pius V. She is also the retired principal of Madison Square Elementary School.

Father Raymond L. Harris, who has served in all three vicariates of the archdiocese, is the chaplain and director of campus ministry of Mount St. Mary's College and Seminary in Emmitsburg.

Glendora C. Hughes is general counsel for the Maryland Commission on Human Relations and a parishioner of historic St. Francis Xavier.

Sister Fredericka Jacobs, S.N.D., worked in Africa for 30 years.

Clinton E. Jiggetts is the director of the Cottage Avenue Community Program in Park Heights and a parishioner of St. Ambrose.

Jacqueline B. Johnson is a parishioner of St. Bernardine.

Gwendolyn A. Lindsay is a parishioner of New All Saints.

Joann T. Logan is president of the board of African American Catholic Ministries and a parishioner of New All Saints.

Dr. Antoinette Gabriel Lyles is the principal of St. Bernardine's Catholic School and a parishioner of St. Bernardine. Dr. Lyles received her Ed.D in administration policy and urban education from Fordham University, New York.

Irene Mallory is a parishioner of St. Cecilia.

Michelly B. Merrick is director of Human Resource Services for the Archdiocese of Baltimore and a parishioner of historic St. Francis Xavier.

Ralph E. Moore Jr. is director of the Community Center, St. Frances Academy.

Ismael Muvingi is the former Africa campaign coordinator for Catholic Relief Services.

Sister Gwynette Proctor, S.N.D., is the director of Christopher Place Employment Academy, foundress of the Harambee Youth Organization and former director of Our Daily Bread.

Melvllle W. Pugh, Jr., is a parishioner of St. Mary of the Assumption.

Melanie A. Reese is a parishioner of St. Cecilia.

Joseph Claver and Ann Richardson are parishioners of New All Saints.

V. Esther Sanders is a national board member of the Mother Lange Guild, an O.S.P. lay associate, and parishioner of St. Bernardine.

Deacon Paul Shelton is an attorney and permanent deacon.

Tully Keith Sullivan is an active parishioner of Immaculate Conception.

Dr. Hilbert T. Stanley is executive director of the National Black Catholic Congress and a parishioner of St. Bernardine.

Father Donald A. Sterling, D. Min., is the pastor of New All Saints Parish.

Deborah Johnson Sterrett is a parishioner at New All Saints.

Carl F. Stokes is vice president of business development at Mid-Atlantic Health Care, Inc.; former Baltimore City councilperson; former president of the board of African American Catholic Ministries; and parishioner of historic St. Francis Xavier.

Mark Thomas is an eighth-grader at St. Katharine Catholic School.

Charles G. Tildon, Jr., is a parishioner of St. Gregory the Great.

Councilwoman G. Agnes Welch is a parishioner of St. Edward and a member of the Baltimore City Council.

Beverly C. White is a parishioner of St. Bernardine and serves as the director of religious education.

Barry F. Williams is president of the Pastoral Council at St. Pius V Parish.

Sharon H. Winchester is a parishioner of St. Bernardine. She is also a member of the Na'imah Outreach group, which assists others with teaching from an Africentric perspective.

Darron C. Woodus serves as a security analyst in the mortgage bank industry and is an active parishioner of St. Cecilia.

Acknowledgments

The Office of African American Catholic Ministries extends Thanks and Appreciation to all who contributed to this publication

His Eminence Cardinal William H. Keeler, Archbishop of Baltimore
Most Rev. Gordon D. Bennett, S.J., Bishop of Mandeville, Jamaica
Most Rev. John H. Ricard, S.S.J., Bishop of Pensacola-Tallahassee
All The Writers Who Submitted Articles
The Cathedral Foundation
Daniel Medinger – Editor of "The Catholic Review"
Catholic Printing Services
Rev. Cyprian Davis, OSB and his legendary book *"The History of Black Catholics In The United States"*
Staff at the Archives who gave assistance to writers in researching historical data
Rev. Paul K. Thomas – Archivist Emeritus – Archdiocese of Baltimore

Special thanks to those who edited sections of this book:

Dr. Beverly A. Carroll
Roberta L. Epps
Dr. Kirk P. Gaddy
Sr. M. Reginald Gerdes, O.S.P.
Sr. M. Magdala Marie Gilbert, O.S.P.
Joann T. Logan
Melville W. Pugh, Jr.

And we are grateful to those who proofread the text:

Sister M. Alice Chineworth, O.S.P.
Sister M. Elaine Frederick, O.S.P.

We remember the contributions of those who have gone to Glory:

Rev. Peter Hogan, S.S.J., noted Historian and Archivist of the Josephite
    Archives;
Janet E. Jones, former secretary for the Office of African American
    Catholic Ministries

We ought to thank God always for you ... because your faith flourishes.
(2 Th. 1–3)